Africa's
Gift to America

AFRICA'S GIFT TO AMERICA

The Afro-American in the
Making and Saving of the United States

With New Supplement
AFRICA AND ITS POTENTIALITIES

HELGA M. ROGERS
1270 FIFTH AVENUE · NEW YORK, N. Y. 10029

HELGA M. ROGERS,
1270 Fifth Avenue
New York, New York 10029

Revised and enlarged

CIVIL WAR CENTENNIAL EDITION

© Copyright 1961

HELGA M. ROGERS

ISBN 0-960-22946-9

Printed in the United States

CONTENTS

FOREWORD

The history of man on this planet from prehistoric times until now is a continuous whole. There is no fact, however remote, that does not have a bearing of greater or less importance on the destiny of the whole human race. Much has been buried, lost, forgotten but within man's consciousness is a burning desire to know as much of it as possible. Within the past four centuries this desire has increased until today there is no civilized land without a museum. In these museums are momentoes of the past which, though they might seem valueless to some, are precious to the scientist, scholar, thinker. On excavations in Upper Egypt I noticed that every spadeful of earth was carefully sifted lest some article of the ancient past be lost, even though but a bead.

All of this helps man to understand himself the more. It awakens possibilities of continued progress. I recall the world-wide interest in the discovery of the tomb of Tut-Ankh-Amen of 1350 B.C.; or of dinosaur eggs a million or more years old in the Gobi Desert. More than ever today the search for lost civilizations is being pursued. The floor of the ocean and the moon are alike objects of increasing curiosity. Every new discovery widens our concept of things in general and gives us that thrill which discovery of the truth gives to those who seek it.

But there have ever been those who oppose any new historical or archaeological discovery disturbing to the old order. Certain geographers and map-makers of Columbus' day called him a liar when he told of the discovery of the New World. It had put their maps and books out of date. Persecution and even torture were used to prevent any change in accepted beliefs, in short, anything that gave a new and disturbing vision of life on this planet. Galileo was forced by the Church to deny his astronomical discoveries. His proof that the earth revolved around the sun which made day and night was denounced as heresy. Vesalius was attacked for dissecting the human body. But without that modern surgery would have been impossible. Giordano Bruno was burnt alive in 1600 because his views on the universe differed with theological dogma. Andrew D. White in his "Warfare Between Science and Theology in Christendom" has told the story. The sewing-machine was bitterly fought; and the first railroads in the

United States ridiculed and opposed. In short, those who benefit from the status quo have always opposed progress and have had abundant support from those with fixed minds. But in spite of all persecution, all censorship, truth eventually wins and bitterly opposed ideas of today become the truisms of tomorrow.

Take slavery in the United States. For three centuries most Americans believed it was right, even God-ordained. But the belief that it was wrong grew until for four years they slaughtered one another in the dispute over it. Today it is only the rare exremist who argues it is right.

The spirit of suppressing uncomfortable facts is very much alive. Voltaire said history was a lie. Napoleon called it a fable agreed on. John Quincy Adams, who made history himself, wrote in 1822, "The public history of all countries and all ages is but a sort of a mask, richly colored; thus the interior working of the machinery must be foul." These strictures are to a large extent still true. American history has been prettified until it now looks like a Christmas shop-window.

Edward Larocque Tinker, noted authority on Louisiana life and history, aptly illustrates this in an article entitled "Whitewashing." He tells how eager to see the letters of Lafcadio Hearn, another famous Louisianian, he went to a wealthy and famed private library in New York City, which he heard had them. There he learnt, to his horror, they had been destroyed by a relative. The Hearn letters were "smutty" said the librarian. But, says Tinker, he was in for a still greater shock. The librarian went on to boast how she had destroyed letters of George Washington. Tinker tells the story thus:

"But that's nothing," she continued with perfect sang-froid, "I've destroyed right in this very room letters written by George Washington." I became rudely indignant; I wanted to ask rude questions as to her qualification for the post of expurgator to the Father of her Country. I sat on the safety valve, however, as a cool voice continued, 'Oh yes, they were smutty, too, so I did not ever want them to become public and destroy the ideal of Washington that had flourished so long. It was only a question of money. (A large sum had been paid for the letters). Could we afford to pay the price and then destroy our investment? We could and did."

"But," I sputtered, the strain becoming too great, "do you think it's right to aid this suppression, nay, destruction of evidence to the manufacture of a purely apocryphal historic character?"

"Yes," was the calm retort, "even if it only served to keep alive in our schools the story of the cherry-tree." (This story, by the way, was a pure concoction of Parson Weems).

Tinker adds that the above gained immediate support of his wife who declared that suppression of this sort "was useful to the maintaining of proper allegiance." But, concludes Tinker, "the suppression of historical data can only spell the prostitution of history." (The Bookman (American).

Vol. 60, pp. 719-20, Feb. 1925). By the way, letters of Alexander Hamilton met the same fate.

Now this is precisely the sort of thing that has been done to the popular history of the white people of the United States to the detriment of the Negro. The popular conception is still that expressed by Lord Bryce in his "American Commonwealth" in 1880 where he pictures the Africans who came to America as "a body of savages" and the whites "three or four thousand years in advance of them in mental capacity and moral force." This falsehood was revived on a national scale in January 1959, and made to appear as if it were true of the moral and intellectual status of the Aframerican today.

Striking examples of how the accomplishments of the Negro in America have been ignored and the credit for them given to the whites can be seen in the National Museum in the Smithsonian Institution, Washington, D. C. One in particular deals with the Civil War. As will be seen later in this book, Lincoln positively said that the Negro provided the balance of power that won the war for the Union. In one battle thirteen Negroes won the Congressional Medal of Honor; yet in this extensive exhibit I saw after a long and careful search the picture of only one Negro. He was loading a musket for a white man. And that white man was a Confederate!

Why This Book Was Written

This book comes in answer to the revival of anti-Negro literature that followed the ruling of the United States Supreme Court against segregation in the public school system in 1954. Research by the American Jewish Committee revealed that this literature reached a new high in 1958 (*New York Times,* January 21, 1959). In addition there have been the bombing of homes, churches, integrated schools, restrictive legislation in several states, and vengeance against private individuals. There has been since 1955, 532 cases of racial violence. New Orleans increased the number with its riots in December, 1960, Athens, Georgia, with riots in January, 1961, and Alabama riots in May, 1961.

The Bible, particularly, has been used to promote this hate literature. An example was a widely-issued pamphlet, "The Racial Issue," by the Florida Baptist Institute declaring that "God Is A God of Segregation," with abundant Bible quotations. Full-page ads paid for by racists appeared in Northern dailies, the chief of which was that of the first week of January 1959 in over 30 Northern dailies as the *New York Times* (January 5), the *Wall Street Journal,* and the Pittsburgh *Post-Gazette* in an open letter to the President. The writer, Carleton Putnam, is "a distinguished New Englander . . . member of the famous New England Putnam family," graduate of Princeton and Columbia, author of a "widely-praised" biography of Theodore Roosevelt, and the founder and president of the Chicago and Southern Air-Lines. The ad "was paid for by individual donations from hundreds of citizens throughout the South."

Mr. Putnam's chief support for the inferior position he would assign to the Negro is based on what Lord Bryce, British statesman and once ambassador to the United States, said on Negro "barbarism" in "The Present and Future of the Negro" in his "The American Commonwealth" published in 1880. Bryce's work was considered a classic, the finest then produced on the American government. He was also considered a great friend of the United States.

Mr. Putnam quotes Bryce:

"History is a record of the progress towards civilization of races originally barbarous. But that progress has in all cases been slow and gradual. . . . Utterly dissimilar is the case of the African Negro, caught up in and whirled along with the swift movement of the American democracy. In it we have a singular juxtaposition of the most primitive and the most recent, the most rudimentary and the most highly developed types of culture. . . . A body of savages is violently carried across the ocean and set to work as slaves on the plantations of masters who are three or four thousand years in advance in mental capacity and moral force. Suddenly, even more suddenly than they were torn from Africa, they find themselves, not only free, but made full citizens and active members of the most popular government the world has seen, treated as fit to bear an equal part in ruling not only themselves, but also their recent masters."

When Bryce wrote that the Negro had already been in the United States 368 years—since 1512 with the Spaniards and 1619 with the English. The great majority of these Africans had come before 1808, or 72 years before Bryce wrote. Thus very, very little had been left psychologically of the original African. Uprooted from their native land and ways and scattered among the white population there was nothing left for the Negroes but to adopt the language, customs, religion and general teaching of the whites. They adopted these so much that it is a matter of record that the descendants of Africans born among the whites generally looked down on the newly-arrived African. In short, though black without, they were white within. In addition, a vast amount of white strain had entered into the American-born Negro and very much, too, of Negro strain into the whites. Bryce, then it is clear, ignored all of this and wrote from the prevailing misconception that the whites represented the summit of civilization and that the Africans and their descendants here the depth of primitive savagery. Bryce in mentioning the "moral force" of the whites, ignored the fact that a vast number of early white Americans were convicts and other most objectionable persons, while the only black convicts that came were those living among whites in Europe. Africa, at least the part from which the slaves came, had no jails, bolts, locks, bars, or any need for them. Again, the Irish immigrants, generally, were much more degraded than the Africans.

Bryce, in short, wrote with little or no research on his subject, that is, ignorantly. Putnam gives him hearty approval, however. He says, "One does not telescope three or four thousand years into the 78 years since Bryce wrote." The inference is that the Negro is still what Bryce erroneously believed him to be.

To justify his position on Bryce's theory, Mr. Putnam quotes from Lincoln in the Lincoln-Douglas debates of 1858 as follows:

"I am not, nor ever have been, in favor of bringing about in any way the social and political equality of the white and black races; I am not nor ever have been in favor of making voters or jurors of Negroes, nor qualifying them to hold office . . . I will say in addition to this that there is a physical difference between the white and black races which I believe will forever forbid the two races living together on terms of social and political equality. And in as much as they cannot so live, while they do remain together, there must be the position of superior and inferior, and I as much as any other man am in favor of having the superior position assigned to the white race."

Now Mr. Putnam gushes with love and sympathy for the Negro. 'Personally I feel only affection for the Negro," he says. But it happens that this Lincoln quotation has been a favorite with the great Negro-haters for the past eighty years — from Tillman of the Reconstruction to Bilbo of our time. All such felt that was sure-fire argument. Was it not Lincoln, great "friend" and "liberator" of the Negroes saying that? Putnam, who loves them so, runs true to their form. "The Negro," he says, "owe more to Lincoln than to any other man."

Mr. Putnam's ad is effective because of the general ignorance not only of white friends but of most of the Negroes on the true history of what has happened since the arrival of the Africans here 446 years ago. The facts have been presented here. It is left to the reader to judge.

5

Fossils Trace Man Back 600,000 Years In Gorge in Africa

LEOPOLDVILLE, Belgian Congo, Aug. 23 (Reuters)—Human fossils about 600,000 years old—possibly the earliest known trace of man—have been found in Tanganyika.

Dr. Louis S. B. Leakey, a prominent anthropologist, said that his wife, also an anthropologist, had found the fossils among animal remains in the Oldoway Gorge in Tanganyika, July 17.

Dr. Leakey, 56 years old, a British expert on East African anthropology, has searched for many years to prove his belief that man originated in Africa. He is curator of the Corydon Museum of Natural History in Nairobi, Kenya.

Dr. Leakey reported his wife's find to the Pan-African Congress of Prehistory here yesterday. Sixty delegates from fifteen countries, including the United States, are at the congress.

Crude tools were found with the fossils, suggesting some form of human culture, Dr. Leakey said. He said a reconstruction of the bones showed a skull that was estimated to date from the second half of the Pleistocene geological era 600,000 years ago.

N.Y.Times,Aug.24,1959.

National Geographic Magazine, Sept. 1960, has a picture of one skull, and quotes Prof. Leakey as saying that it was that of the first tool-making human ; and that the discoveries "strongly support Charles Darwin's prophecy that Africa would prove to have been the birthplace of mankind."

Prof. Leakey has since discovered a still older skull "considerably more than 600,000 years old." With it were other human relics, one of them a child. (New York Times, Feb. 25, 1961).
N. Y. Times, Aug. 24, 1959.

* * *

The age of the skulls is now set at 1,750,000 years. (*New York Times,* July 23, 1961.)

6

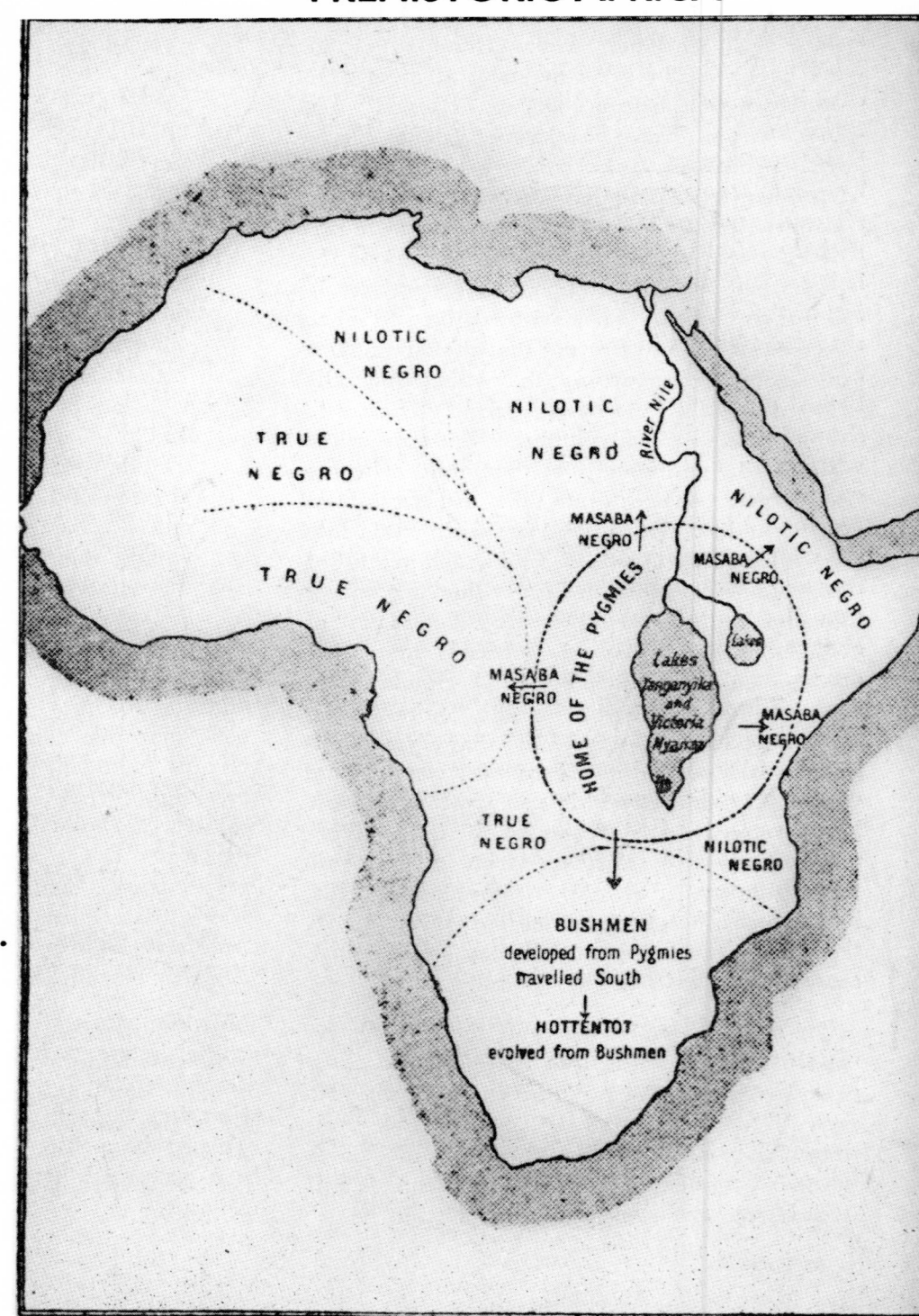

Map prepared by Albert Churchward, M.D. renowned British archaeologist and authority on the origin of races, showing where world civilization originated. It is the area marked "Home of the Pygmies." Dr. Churchward asserts that Freemasonry originated among the Nilotic Negroes (upper right) and found its grand climax in the Great Pyramid. The map is from his "Origin and Evolution of Freemasonry." (See especially Chaps. 4 & 5.) He gives the earliest known freemason signs. Other books by him on the subject are: Arcana of Freemasonry, 1915; and Origin and Evolution of the Human Race. 1921.

Part One

THE AFRICAN BACKGROUND

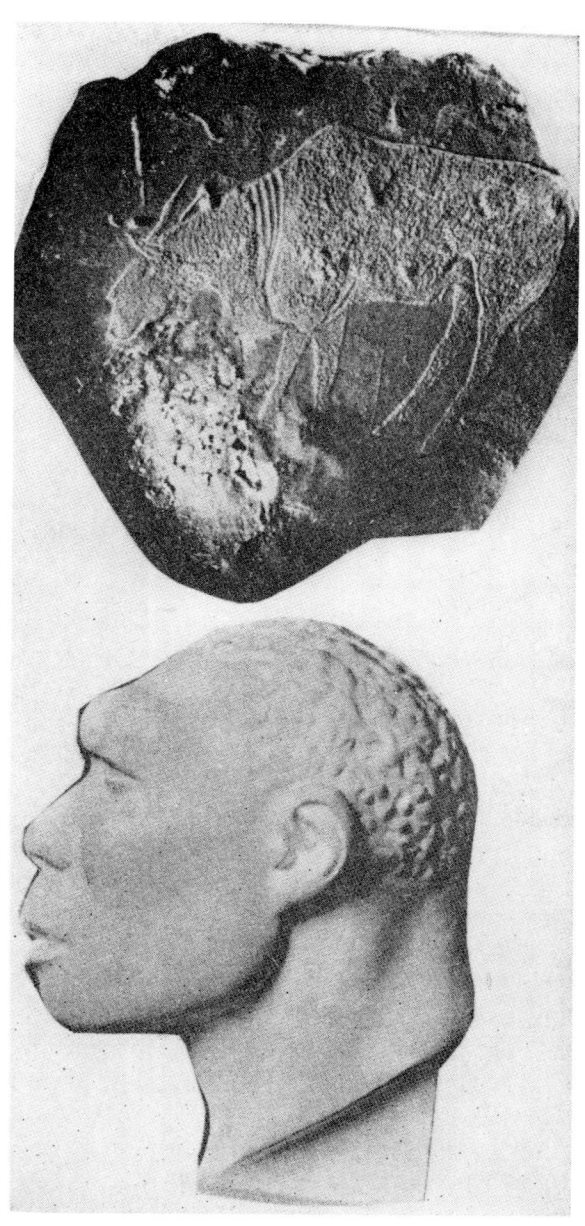

Upper: A masterpiece of pre-historic African art found in South Africa and now in the Pretoria Museum. Done about 30,000 years ago and by flint instruments on rock.

Lower: Reconstruction of the skull of an African who lived in the same region about the same period and very likely the type of artist that made this drawing. Modern art critics marvel at the skill and accuracy of these Stone Age artists and declare that nothing finer has been done since. (See Sex and Race, Vol. I, pages 26, 35. 1942.

AFRICA'S GIFT TO THE WORLD

"Ex Africa semper aliquid novi." (Out of Africa comes something always new) — Ancient Greek saying quoted by Pliny, Roman historian, 23-79 A.D.

"He who has drunk of the waters of Africa will drink again." — Ancient Arab saying.

"I speak of Africa and golden joys." — Shakespeare, II Henry IV, v. iii.

"There is Africa and all her prodigies in us." — Sir Thomas Browne, English physician and author, 1605-1682.

"It is one of the paradoxes of history that Africa, the Mother of Civilization, remained for over two thousand years the Dark Continent. To the moderns Africa was the region where ivory was sought for Europe and slaves for America. In the time of Jonathan Swift (1667-1745), as the satirist informs us, geographers in drawing African maps would fill in the gaps with savage pictures. Where towns should have been they placed elephants." — Dr. Victor Robinson, Ciba Symposia, 1940.

"The African continent is no recent discovery; it is not a new world like America or Australia. . . . While yet Europe was the home of wandering barbarians one of the most wonderful civilizations on record had begun to work out its destiny on the banks of the Nile. . . ." (History of Nations, Vol. 18, p. 1, 1906)

To ancient Europe Africa was for fully two thousand years the civilized world. "How low the savage European must have looked to the Nile Valley African looking north from his Pyramid of Cheops," says Professor Dorsey. When this Wonder of the Ancient World was some two thousand years old, Greece, first part of the European continent to be touched by civilization, was a wilderness. Athens, later to become the leader in world culture, was as late as 1500 B.C., totally unknown. Civilization came to Greece from Egypt by way of the island of Crete, as Sir Arthur Evans, has shown.

And this civilization was Negroid. For this we have the word of Herodotus (484-425 B.C.), who travelled in Egypt and saw the Egyptians of his day. In Book Two, Chapter 57, he says they were "black" and in Book Two, Chapter 104, they were "black and wooly-haired." The hair of the Ethiopian he said was "very wooly." He adds that in other parts of the Near East he visited he saw other nations with the same racial characteristics as the Egyptians. "Several nations are so, too," he said.

Two thousand years later another famous traveller, Count Volney, said on his visit to Egypt in 1787, that what Herodotus said had solved for him the problem of why the people were so Negroid in appearance and especially the Great Sphinx of Ghizeh, supreme symbol

Upper: The Sphinx as it looked in 1798. (From a drawing by Baron Denon).
Lower: As it looks today. Note the pronounced Negroid features.

of worship and power. Reflecting on the then state of the Egyptians compared with what they had been, he said, "To think that to a race of black men who are today our slaves and the object of our contempt is the same one to whom we owe our arts, sciences and even the very use of speech." Of the blacks he saw in Upper Egypt among the ruins of the colossal monuments there, he said, "There a people now forgotten discovered while others were yet barbarians, the elements of the arts and sciences. A race of men now rejected from society for their sable skin and wooly hair, founded on the study of the laws of nature those civil and religious systems which still govern the universe." (Oeuvres, Vol. 2, pp. 65-68. 1825; Ruins of Empires, pp. 16-17. 1890).

Two other famous European scholars of that time who saw the Sphinx, Baron Denon and Gustav Flaubert, were of the same opinion. Denon, who made a sketch of it in 1798 said, "The character is African . . . the lips are thick. Art must have been at a high pitch when this monument was executed." (Travels in Upper and Lower Egypt, vol. 1, p. 140. 1803). Flaubert said (1849), "It is certainly Ethiopian. The lips are thick." (Notes de Voyage, p. 115. 1910).

With the rise of white racism, whose real aim was to justify the enslavement of the blacks, certain noted scholars denied that the Egyptians were black. They were pure white, such assert. But Herodotus saw them. They did not. Moreover what of the Negroid appearance of certain Egyptian rulers such as I have reproduced in Chapter Three of my Sex and Race, Vol. One? Other leading white scholars, however, are of the same opinion as Volney.

Volney wondered why Europe of his time with Africa so near knew so little about it. The answer is that with the rise of European power chiefly after the earlier Caesars, Africa lessened in importance until it became a land of fable and legend. The blacks and mixed bloods of the north-west part of the continent had a resurgence in the eighth century when the Moors invaded Europe but the rest remained unknown and almost forgotten.

This was true even of Egypt, which had the only remaining one of the Seven Wonders of the World. For instance, the Temple of Amen, most colossal structure of its kind ever built, Together with the adjoining buildings it surpassed in grandeur the Acropolis of Athens and the Foro Romano but was so buried by centuries of wind-blown sand that villagers lived in huts on the top of it entirely oblivious of the architectural marvels beneath their feet. As for the Sphinx all that was seen of its 194 feet length and its 66 feet height was the head and that was being cut off by the action of the sand.

Interest in Egypt was not revived until its invasion by Napoleon in 1798. As for the other buried and decayed civilizations further south as Meroe, Axum, Gida, Zymbabwe, Dhlo-Dhlo in Rhodesia, they were forgotten until our own times. More are being unearthed even now.

As late as Stanley's time, what was said of Africa was mostly wild imagination. It sounded very much like what the most ancient travellers said of parts of Europe and Asia they visited. Thomas Jefferson actually believed that in Africa the ourang-outang preferred the black woman to his own species. Long after Columbus the legend of Prester John of Ethiopia, "mightiest monarch on earth" persisted. His realm was said to extend to India as well as the Middle East. He "surpassed in riches all other potentates and no less than sixty kings were his vassals." Maps of Columbus' time and much later showed Ethiopia extending as far south as the Dominion of South Africa. The South Atlantic, the unknown sea over which Columbus sailed to reach the new world, was known as the Ethiopian Ocean. The Persian Gulf was first known as the Ethiopian Sea. Arabia was then a part of Ethiopia.

As for West Africa, Songhay with its capital, Timbuctoo, which flourished in 1500 A.D., and was more advanced than most countries of Western Europe, was known only to rare scholars. Other civilizations as the Mandingo Empire, Yoruba, and Ife were totally forgotten. Ghana, one of the greatest, had its name cor-

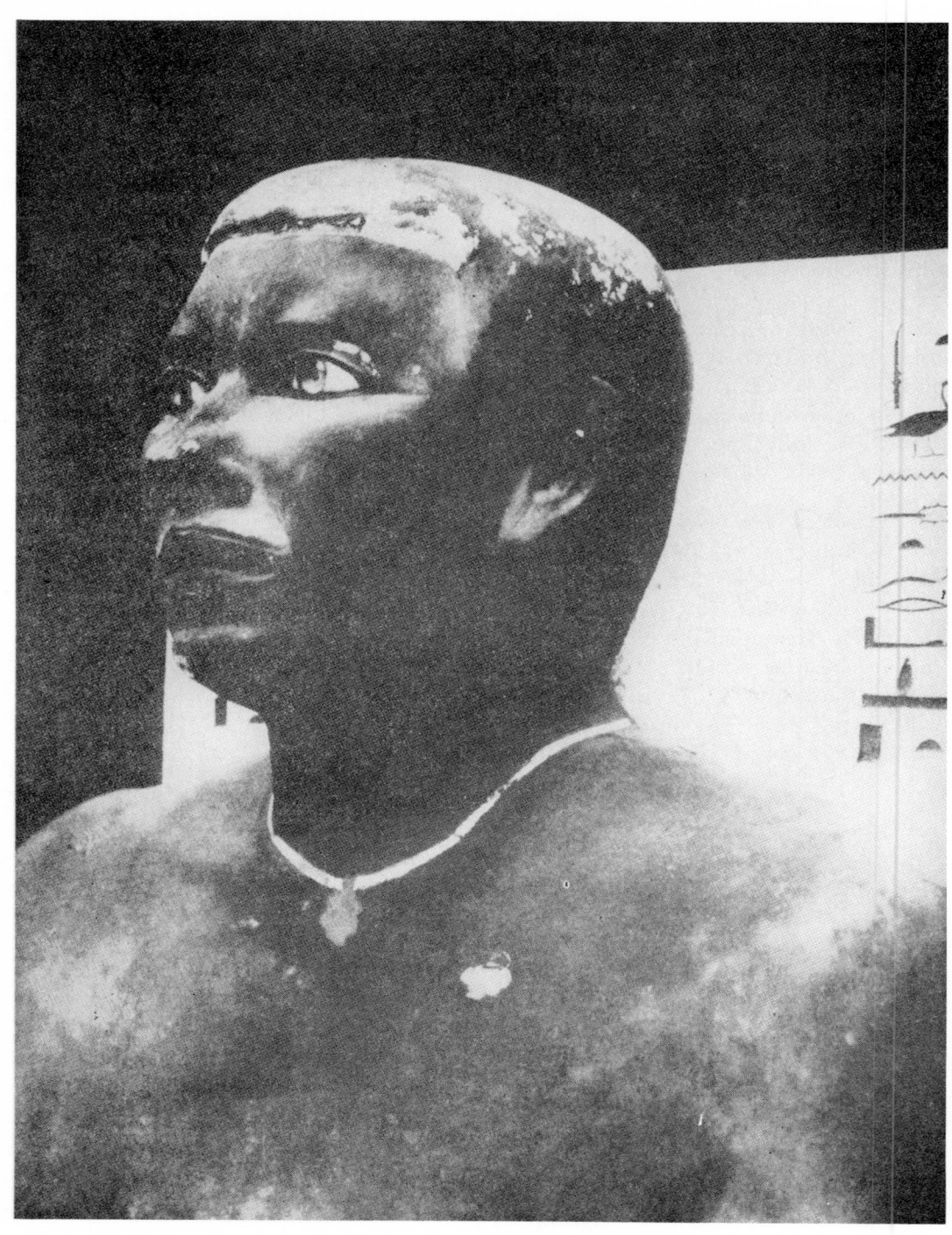

Prince Rahotep, about 3000 B.C., of Egypt.

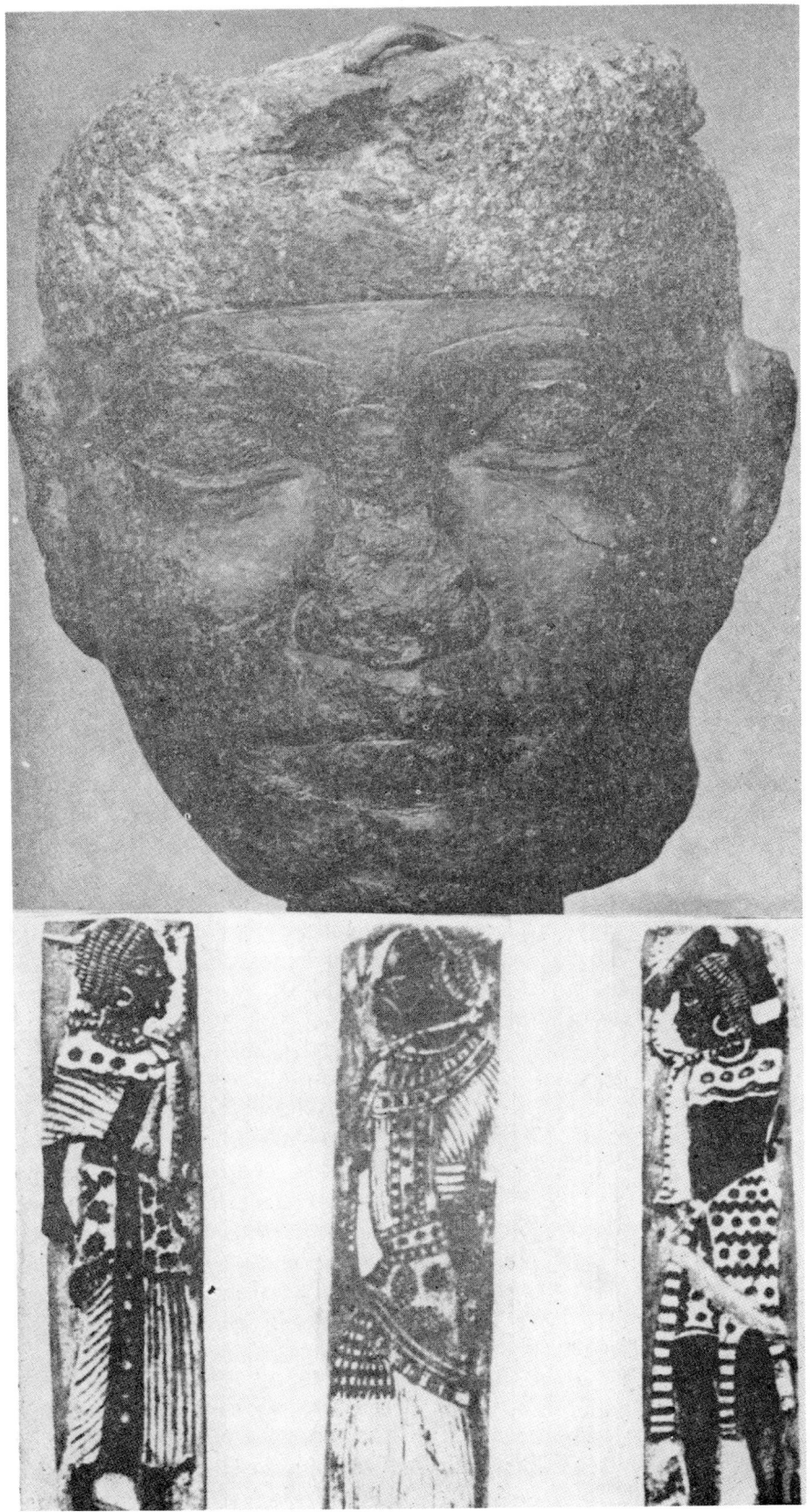

Upper Tirhaqua (Taharka) Ethiopian ruler of Egypt and conqueror of Palestine, 525 B.C. (Carlsberg Glyptotek, Copenhagen). Lower: Egyptians of 1180 B.C. and their dress.

rupted to Guinea. Then the world's richest producer of gold, its name was given to England's largest gold coin — the guinea. All that part of Africa came to be known as the Slave Coast.

Interest in Africa was not really revived until the nineteenth century when warships of the so-called Barbary States dominated in the Mediterranean and the Atlantic off the coasts of Spain and Portugal, and forced the United States to pay tribute to them to sail those waters; also the seizure of Algeria by France in 1830. But it wasn't until the 1870's that the interest of the West, and principally of the United States, was really captured. What did this was Stanley's search for Livingstone. Stanley's sensational dispatches to the New York Herald and the English press aroused the European powers to the immense potentialities of this undeveloped continent and a race for Africa began that reminds one of that for America in the sixteenth and seventeenth centuries. But Stanley's tales and use of the term "Darkest Africa," made it appear a land of wildest savagery. It was not until the 1910's that a German scholar and explorer, Leo Frobenius, by his researches, restored humanity to the people of Africa, and changed the popular concept for those minds susceptible to change. In his principal work "Und Afrika sprach," translated into English as "The Voice of Africa," Frobenius urged:

"Let there be light!

"Light in Africa. In that portion of the globe to which the stalwart Anglo-Saxon Stanley gave the name of 'dark' and 'darkest'. Light upon the people of that continent whose children we are accustomed to regard as types of natural servility with no recorded history." But "The spell has ben broken. The buried treasures of antiquity again revisit the sun." He gives abundant proof of rich archaeologic and other finds, which since have been supplemented by the Mond expedition in the Sudan; the researches of Professor L. S. Leakey in East Africa; and Professors Broom and Dart in South Africa. Leakey discovered remains of the Boskop Man,

a Bushman type of some 30,000 years ago; and Broom and Dart types that go still farther back. Their researches appear to bear out what an earlier anthropologist, Prichard, said in his "Physical History of Man," namely, "The primitive stock of men were probably Negroes and I know of no argument to be set on the other side." Europe, itself, when it was still joined to Africa, was tropical and was inhabited by Negroes. Abundant evidence of them have been found as far north as Russia. I have given in my other books, principally the first volume of Sex and Race, what leading archaeologists have said on this together with pictures of their finds.

As regards the title, "Africa's Gift to America," it is fitting to recall, also, that Africa played a role, perhaps the chief role in the earliest development of America — a period that antedates Columbus by many centuries, namely Aztec, Maya and Inca civilizations. About 500 A.D. or earlier, Africans sailed over to America and continued to do so until the time of Columbus. This does not call for any particular stretch of the imagination. Africa is only 1600 miles distant from South America with islands in between among them St. Paul and Fernando Noronha. This also wasn't as great a feat as that of the Polynesians (also a Negroid people) who crossed the Pacific to Easter Island, off the coast of Chile.

Most United States archaeologists will deny that Negroes could possibly have been here before Columbus even though figures with pronounced Negro features appear on the most ancient American monuments. They say that the American Indian is of Mongolian stock, having come by way of the Bering Strait. This might be true of the North American Indians but it certainly is not of those that lived below the Rio Grande.

If we say that the Negro wasn't here before Columbus, why the typically Negro faces on the monuments? Deny that they were here and the only explanation left is that the American artist before Columbus dreamed up those features. Yes, one must either deny it or be forced

Mameluke and his children from a drawing by Baron Denon. The Mamelukes were the rulers of Egypt at Napoleon's invasion in 1798. Note Negroid features of the children.

to make an explanation as ridiculous as that made by Ignatius Donnelly in his book, "Atlantis," published in 1882. Donnelly's theory was that the New World was peopled from the western part of the Old, and in proof gives pictures of Negroes on the ancient monuments. He calls these "idols." But to square with the doctrine of "Negro inferiority," he says that these blacks were "slaves" brought from Africa since "Negroes are not a sea-going race." If the blacks were "idols" the only conclusion left is that ancient Americans worshipped their slaves!

However, most South and Central American archaelogists do agree the Negroes were here before Columbus. I have given in two of my earlier books quotations from these Latin-American scholars and will repeat some of them:

C. C. Marquez says, "The Negro type is seen in the most ancient Mexican sculpture . . . Negroes figure frequently in the most remote traditions." Riva-Palacio, Mexican historian, says, "It is indisputable that in very ancient times the Negro race occupied our territory (Mexico) when the two continents were joined. The Mexicans recall a Negro god, Ixtilton, which means 'black-face'."

Colonel Braghine says in "The Shadow of Atlantis" that he saw in Ecuador a statuette of a Negro that is at least "20,000 years old . . . Hitherto the ethnologists imagined that Negroes appeared in the New World only during our own epoch as slaves. Some statues of the Indian gods in Central America possess typical Negro features . . ."

N. Leon says, "The almost extinction of the

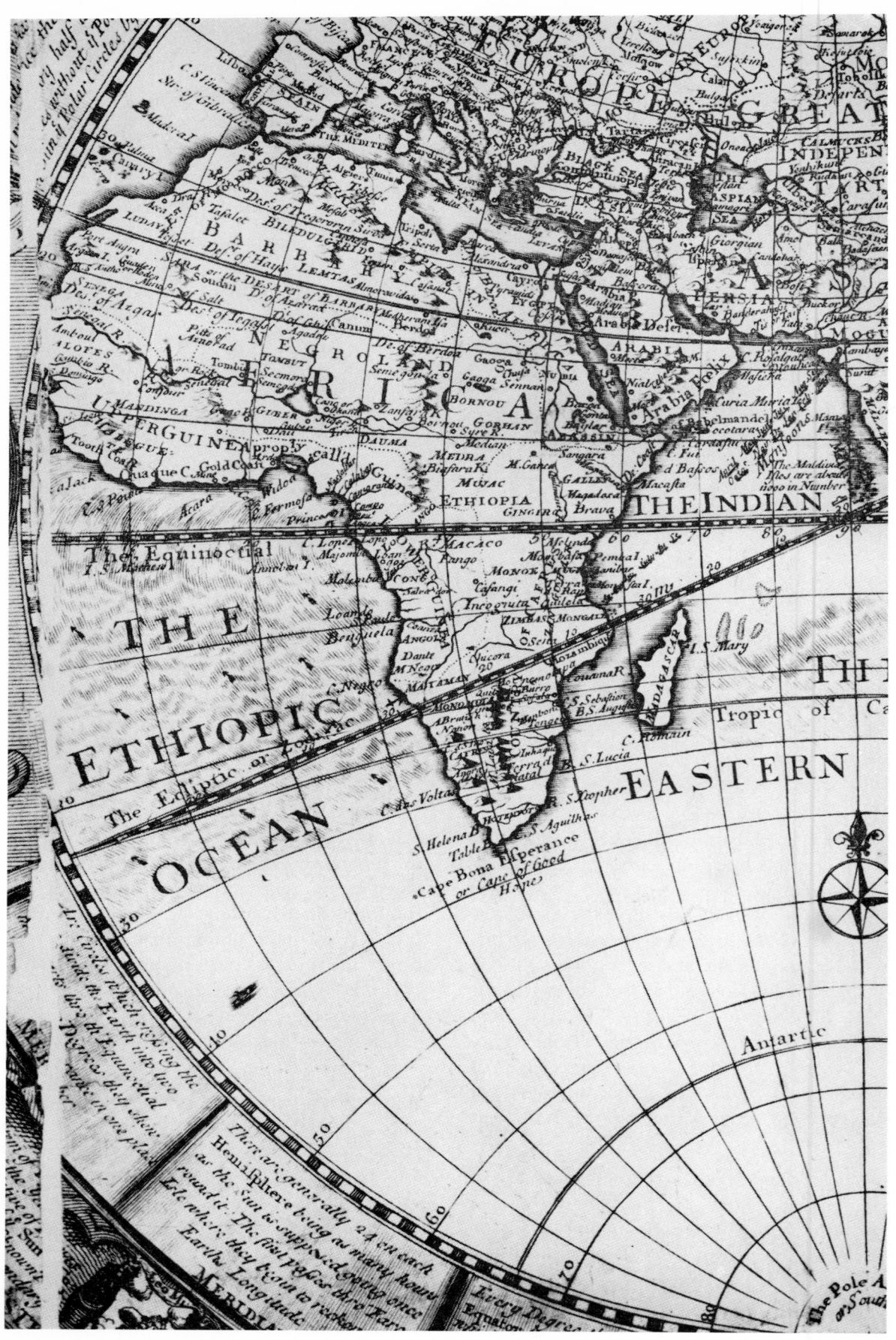

As late as 1650 the South Atlantic was called the Ethiopic, or Ethiopian Ocean, and most of Africa as far as South Africa was called Ethiopia.

original Negroes during the time of the Spanish conquest and the memories of them in the most ancient traditions induce us to believe that the Negroes were the first inhabitants of Mexico."

Columbus in his "third Voyage" tells of seeing Negroes and when Balboa discovered the Pacific Ocean in 1513, he found Negroes in Panama. Peter Martyr, historian of the expedition, says "These were the first Negroes seen in the Indies." Balboa found them at war with the Indians and thought they had sailed over from "Ethiopia." A notable exception to the United States' archaeologists and their denial that Negroes were here before Columbus was the late Leo Wiener, professor of philology at Harvard University. In his three-volume work "Africa and the Discovery of America," he gives abundant proof that they were. He says, "The presence of Negroes before Columbus is proved by the representation of Negroes in American sculpture and design; by the occurence of a black nation at Darien early in the 16th Century and more specifically by Columbus' emphatic reference to Negro traders from Guinea (Ghana), who trafficked in gold alloy of precisely the same composition and bearing the same name (Guanin), is frequently referred to by early writers on Africa."

Professor Wiener, found that these Negro traders travelled as far north as New England. Their relics have been found in graves there, most notably a pipe with a Negro face.

It is even possible that Columbus had heard of the New World from Africans who had been brought to Spain and Portugal in his time. Furthermore, Columbus spent some time in West Africa just before he left Spain for America. The south-south-west direction he took might be a proof of this.

In the fifteenth century we find other of those periodic influxes of Africans into Europe which began under the Pharaohs. They came this time not as conquerors, like the Moors, but as slaves, principally in Portugal and Spain and as far north as England. The year is 1440 or 1442, fifty years before the discovery of the New World. Having proved so useful, it was inevitable that the Spaniards would bring them to the New World. In 1502 they are in the Caribbean. Their exportation continued until 1865 or later. In those three hundred and sixty-three years an estimated fifty millions were brought. Even a half of that would constitute a very substantial contribution. They were first brought to what is now the United States in 1512, and continued to arrive until 1861. In those three hundred and forty-nine years an estimated fifteen millions came. According to the testimony we shall present from many of the most prominent whites over those centuries the United States could not possibly have been the nation it became without them.

Elizabeth Lawson in her "Study Outline" of some of the early accomplishments of the African peoples names the following

Rock painting (still preserved) ; rhythmic music; imaginative and poetic folklore. By the Bushmen of South Africa.

Domestication of animals by the Hottentots of South Africa.

Agriculture, and a system of exchange using cattle, sheep, or goats as the medium of circulation. By the Bantu of South Africa.

Gold and silver mining; trade in precious stones; building construction (houses and fortifications) ; pottery; metal work. By the peoples in the region of the Great Lakes.

Agricultural system, law, literature, music, natural sciences, medicine, and schooling system. In the kingdom of Songhay.

Cotton weaving in the Sudan (as early as the eleventh century).

Leaving consideration of separate portions of the continent and considering Africa as a whole, we may say that the Africans were at one time the greatest metal workers of the world they were the first to smelt iron and use the forge. They were masters of the art of basketry, pottery, and cutlery. They made many contributions to dancing, music, and sculpture. According to some authorities, the stimulus to Greek art came from Africa.

The Negroes brought art and sculpture to prehistoric Europe. They invented many musical instruments, and created sculpture in brass, bronze, ivory, quartz, and granite. They also had a glass factory.

Writing was known in Egypt and Ethiopia and to some extent elsewhere in Africa Over one hundred manuscripts of Ethiopian and Ethiopian-Arabic literature now exist. The

First known picture of Timbuctoo, capital of the mighty Songhay Empire of Africa founded 1490 A.D. Southern portion of the City. (Drawn by Rene Caille, French explorer in 1828).

Epic of the Sudan is considered by scholars as one of the world's greatest classics. The Africans also had a rich folklore and store of proverbs, and such tales as the Uncle Remus stories have grown out of this folklore..

Probably the most lasting and most important of the discoveries of ancient Africa was the smelting of iron, which Africa taught the rest of the world. Franz Boas says:

"It seems likely that at a time when the European was still satisfied with rude stone tools, the African had invented and adopted the art of smelting iron. Consider for a moment what this has meant for the advance of the human race. As long as the hammer, knife, the saw, drill, spade, and hoe had to be chipped out of stone or had to be made of shell or hard wood, effective industry and work was not impossible, but difficult. A great progress was made when copper found in large nuggets was hammered out into tools and later on shaped by smelting, and when bronze was introduced; but the true advancement of industrial life did not begin until the hard iron was discovered. It seems not unlikely that the people who made the marvelous discovery of reducing iron ore by smelting were the African Negroes. Neither ancient Europe nor western Asia nor ancient China knew iron, and everything points to its introduction from Africa."

The great Mosque of Timbuctoo as it appeared in 1828.

eft: Southern part of the Great Wall of Zymbabwe, Rhodesia, South Africa. Built about 2000 B.C. Right: passage to the temple.

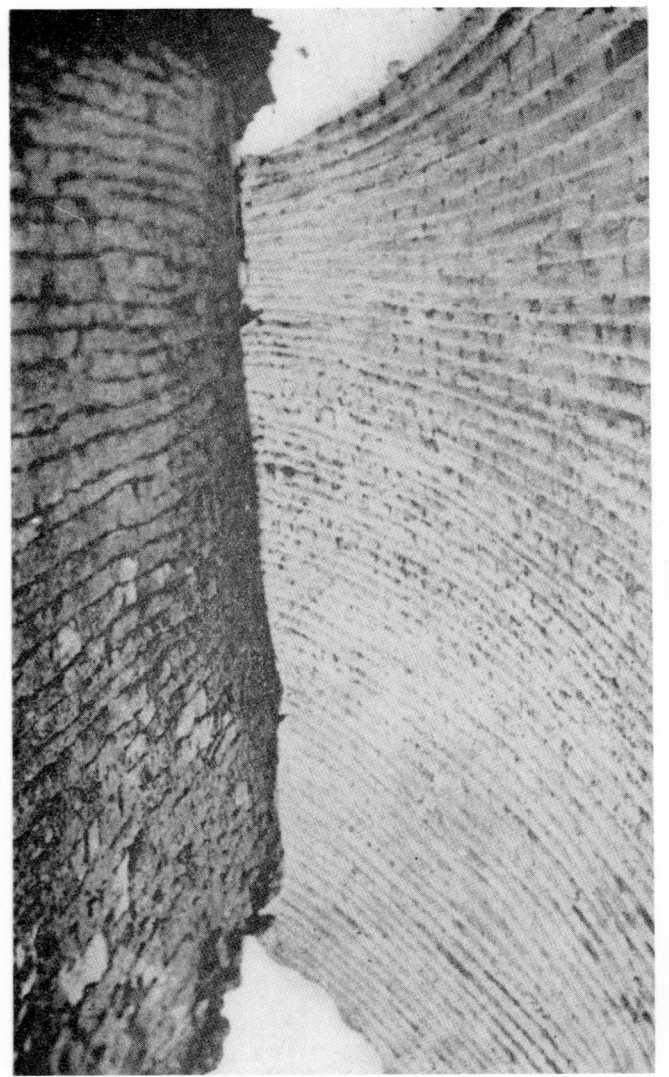

Upper parallel passage of Temple, Zymbabwe.

A chamber of the mighty Sun Temple of Amon at Meroe, ancient Ethiopia.

Pyramids of Meroe, Ethiopian civilization of about 3000 B.C. They are the tombs of kings. This region is now Sudan.

Centuries Shroud Ruins of Zimbabwe Ancient Gold-Mining Center in Africa

FORT VICTORIA, Southern Rhodesia, (AP) — The archaeologists are brooding again about the Zimbabwe ruins.

Despite a new round of digging, sifting and scholarly contemplation, they are still unable to explain the baffling mystery of the ancient and still impressive granite structures that stand not far from here.

The ruins were discovered in 1868 and archaeologists have been at work on them for about fifty years.

Dr. Karl Mauch, German geologist and explorer, visited the site in 1872. He decided the conical tower must certainly be the local treasury and burrowed into the base. He found nothing.

Gold undoubtedly played an important part in the establishment of the mysterious settlement. This part of Rhodesia is dotted with old gold mines, some of which are still being operated. The nearest to Zimbabwe is about twenty miles away.

One cake of gold was found at Zimbabwe in 1902.

It is considered likely that Zimbabwe was a center for gold smelting at some point in its history since one ingot mold was found in the ruins. It was reported to be similar to ingots used by the Phoenicians in their trading days.

One of the most enlightening discoveries was made by S. D. Sandes, curator at the ruins for the last ten years. He found two pieces of wood in one of the temple walls. No other wood has been found in the structure.

The wood was subjected to radiocarbon tests and it was found that the tree from which it had been cut had died about 1,200 or 1,300 years ago.

ANCIENT OBJECTS DUG UP IN NIGERIA

Figures Indicate Civilization Dating to 12th Century— Some Artifacts Found

Special to The New York Times.

LAGOS, Nigeria, March 5— An advanced Negro civilization that existed centuries before the first white man set foot in Africa is slowly coming to light here as a result of archaeological discoveries in this area.

For the last two months experts have been digging and sifting a site at Ife, Western Nigeria, where a workman found a group of metal and clay figures that revived interest in the little-known civilization of the ancient Yorubas.

The figures are thought to be of the twelfth century, when the Yoruba civilization was in full flower. The first Portuguese arrived in the area late in the fifteenth century.

1939 Discovery Recalled

The discovery at Ife is the most important of its kind since the world-famous bronze heads were found at Wunmonije in 1939.

No Shrines in Neighborhood

No shrines or other holy places are known to be in the vicinity, but the area is named after Yemoo, the wife of Orishanla, a former Oni (chief) of Ife.

A total of seven pieces was found. The most impressive is a complete standing figure of an Oni in the full regalia still used at coronation ceremonies. The present Oni of Ife, Sir Adesoji Aderemi, confirms that he has regalia that are the same as those on the Ita Yemoo figure and that the regalia were used at his own coronation in September 1930.

Lower left: Ruins of Dhlo Dhlo, one of 150 ancient buried cities of South Africa. Built about 500 B.C.

Loanga, capital of the Kingdom of Loanga, in the region of the Congo, West Africa, fro

awing made about 1650. This City was built before the coming of the white man.

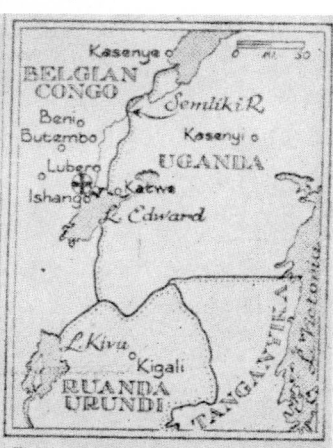

Ruins of Southern Sudan (From Architeichtur der Stadte des Sudan, Tafel 98).
(About 400 years old.)

ANCIENT AFRICANS KNEW ARITHMETIC

8,000-Year Old Ishango Finds Include an Acabus-Type of Calculating Device

By JOHN HILLABY
Special to The New York Times.

ISHANGO, Belgian Congo, May 23—The remains of a sophisticated prehistoric civilization called the Ishango people have been unearthed here. They lie on the northern shore of Lake Edward.

Although the Ishango people probably flourished here in Central Africa about eight or nine

The New York Times June 6, 1957

ANCIENT TOWN FOUND: Ishango (cross), in the Belgian Congo, dates back about 3,000 or 9,000 years.

Translation of the above in part: "The Great King, Monomotapa. Very powerful and rich in gold. Several kings are tributary to him. His territory comprises lower Ethiopia. . . . His empire is very large and has a circuit of 2,400 miles. His court is at Zimboae (Zymbabwe). There are women in his guard . . . . He has a great number of them in his army which give great help to the men. He also has a great number of elephants. His subjects are black, brave and swift runners, and he has very fast horses. Idolaters, sorcerers, adulterers, and thieves are severely punished."

Massive head of Negro god from Mexico. Carved about 500 A.D.

Another of the five gigantic heads of Olmec deities. Weight about five tons. From full-size reproduction in the American Museum of Natural History, New York.

Negroes in America before Columbus: Upper left: Head of god from Tenochtitlan, Mexico. Right: Figure found in ancient Indian grave in Connecticut.
Lower left: Massive head from Yucatan (National gallery, Washington). Right: California Native before Columbus.

THE AFRICANS IN THE MAKING OF AMERICA
THE FIRST EUROPEANS

"What would have been the fate of the New World had there been no Africa?" — *Jose Antonio Saco, Spanish-American historian.*[1]

"What would have been the fate of the Southern portion of the British American possessions had the African not come?" — *J. W. DuBose.*[1a]

At the founding of Santo Domingo its first town in 1496, the New World, from Canada to Argentina (excepting small areas in Mexico, Guatemala, and Peru), was but one vast wilderness. Its most urgent need was labor — hard manual labor to fell forests, build roads, towns, and homes, grow crops, and work in the mines. Would the Spaniard have done these, asks Saco. He replied that they were adventurers in search of loot — gold, silver, precious stones — and were thus by nature unfitted for manual work. Besides, there seemed little reward then for industry of that kind. Robert Beverly of Virginia, writing as late as 1705, said, "The discouragements were enough to terrify any man."[2] Life was tough. Forty-four of the Pilgrim Fathers died in their first winter in America and Governor Bradford said of the survivors, "scarce fifty remained and of these were only six or seven sound persons." George Thorpe, a highly educated colonist thought, however, that despondency was the real cause. He said in 1621, "More do die here of the disease of the mind than of their body."

But even if the Spanish newcomers were diligent, Spain, of herself, could have done little. What with her continuous wars, she hadn't the immigrants to spare. The only labor available was that of the Indians, whose enslavement began at once. And there were millions of them. Could they have been counted on? The blunt truth is that the first colonists, Spaniards and English, were able to do little with them. First, they were unfitted by their mode of life for the hard work needed of them. The male Indian was a hunter not a laborer. Hard work was left to the women. As Duke de la Rochefoucald-Liancourt wrote as late as the 1790's, "Among the Indians the husband does not work at all; all the laborious services are performed exclusively by the wife."[2a] There hadn't been any need among them for such labor as the whites demanded. What Beverly said of the Virginia Indians was generally true of all Indians. "They had escaped," he said, "the first curse, of getting their bread by the sweat of their brows; for, by their pleasure, alone, they supplied all the necessities; namely by fishing, fowling, and hunting; skins being their only clothing . . . living without labor and only gathering the fruits of the earth." This would be even more true of those in the warmer regions, settled by Spain. Thomas Jefferson didn't think very highly of them either. He said they were "useless, expensive, ungovernable allies."[3]

The Spaniards considered Indians just one step above the beast. They called them *gente sin razon.* Finding them unwilling and useless laborers, they massacred them and fed their flesh to dogs. Las Casas' account of this is one of the most horrifying of all documents on man's inhumanity to man. They even sent Indians to be sold in Europe. Columbus, himself, took 400 for sale there in 1498.[4]

The early American whites were almost as cruel. Connecticut whites massacred the Pequot Indians. Infants were torn from their mother's breast and hacked to pieces. The heads of the parents were chopped off and kicked about in the streets. Governor Bradford wrote, "It was a fearful sight to see them frying in the fire and the streams of blood quenching the same and terrible was the stink and stench thereof. But the victory seemed a sweet sacrifice and they (the whites) gave praise thereof to God."

Less than a century and a half after Columbus, the Indians were virtually extinct in such older colonies as Santo Domingo, Cuba, and Jamaica. Saco thinks that had their exclusive use continued they would all have perished everywhere.

The failure of the Indian to fit into white civilization comes right down to our day. In 1958, when leaders, representing sixty-five tribes, met in a National Congress of American Indians in New York, one spokesman called his people "the sickest, poorest, least educated people in the United States today."[5] And at that, Indians are further advanced in the United States than anywhere else in the New World.

The Navajos of Arizona live in filthy log huts with dirt floors, smoke holes, and old kerosene drums for stoves. Those of Great Falls, Montana, live in awful squalor. The Indians in Nevada lived below the level of the poorest I saw in any part of North Africa. Of course, thanks chiefly to oil, there are wealthy Indians in Oklahoma. In Montana are well-to-do cattlemen. But the general standard of the Indian, as I saw it, even now in New York State, is no higher than that of the average northern Negro a century ago. Besides, of the millions of Indians who were in the United States at the arrival of Ponce de Leon in 1512, there were in 1950 only 343,910, of which a very small percentage is of original stock.

In all fairness, it must be said that it was largely the white man's fault why the Indian didn't get along with him or adopt his ways. The Indian to whom hospitality was a creed, welcomed the whites at first but soon found they had but one idea — loot. One of the first acts of the Pilgrim Fathers on touching American soil was to steal corn from them. Nathaniel Morton, their historian, tells how when the Pilgrims stopped at Provincetown and the Indians ran away, the Pilgrims, seeing "divers fair Indian baskets filled with corn" took them back to the ship as the Hebrew spies of the Bible did the grapes of Eschol.[6] This was typical of all that followed. Mark Twain rightly said that the Pilgrims on landing "fell on their knees and then fell on the aborigines." These "salvages," as they called them, had no rights that a Christian European was bound to respect. Had the Pilgrims touched some European shore and seen there baskets of corn, wouldn't they have considered that theft? Later they were to capture Indians and sell them as slaves in the West Indies.

As a result Indians all over the New World developed an apartheid psychology. Patrick Henry tried to overcome that in Virginia by proposing intermarriage, but nothing came of it. Over all the two Americas, Indians still live to themselves. The Indian reservations in America foster this apartness even thought most of the dwellers there are only traditionally Indian. For instance, the Shinnecock Indians of Long Island, among whom I have been, are indistinguishable from Harlem Negroes. According to Virginia law, an Indian is only so on the reservation. The real cause of the Indian's backwardness is his pride of race — the feeling that he is the first American. One finds a parallel between him and the poor whites of the Tennessee mountains (the hill-billies) and the poor barefooted whites of some British West India islands. The wretched poor-whites of Barbados—the Red-Legs—are extremely proud of their descent from the Irish slaves sent there by Cromwell and keep off to themselves.

In short, events have proved Saco was right when he said that had Indian labor been depended on, the New World wouldn't have been what it is.

THE NORTH EUROPEAN

Saco spoke chiefly of the South European and what he hadn't done. What of the North European?

He, too, lived in a greater or less degree of comfort at home. Thus it was only the most adventurous and desperate who would tear themselves away to go to a wild land. The discouragements, to quote Beverly again, were "enough to terrify any man that could live easy in England from going to provoke his fortune in a strange land."[7]

Gondomer, writing in 1612, said, "This colony (Virginia) is held in such bad repute that not a human can be found to go there in any way whatever." He cites the case of two Negroes of London, brought before the Mayor for theft. The Mayor told them they could be hanged, but he would pardon them on condition that "they should go and serve the King and Queen in Virginia, they replied that they would much rather die on the gallows here and quickly than to die slowly so many deaths in Virginia."[8]

The first Englishmen who went to Virginia had positively no intention of settling there. Such a land was no place of abode for them.[8a] They had fancied America was like India with plenty of gold, diamonds, and silk, and expected to return laden with loot. Which they didn't. They called themselves "gentlemen adventurers" and would have scorned the kind of labor that settlement demanded.

MOST EARLY SETTLERS WERE CONVICTS

If then the colony was to be peopled, how could it be? Stockholders in the Virginia venture found the answer. Use it as a place of punishment. Ship the convicts and others of England's unwanted there. Why hang a strong man for stealing a shilling or breaking into a shop when you could use his labor? In 1611, Governor Dale urged James I to banish all condemned persons to Virginia. Before that they were shipped to India. But the voyage round the Cape was long and costly. America was so much nearer. Those from Oxford Gaol were sent and young people with previous criminal records.

And so as slavery lessened cannibalism, transportation to America made less work for the English hangman. One can imagine the rage of sadistic Chief Justice Jeffries, who used to send offenders to the gallows in droves, at this arrangement.

Later, the Committee of Trade of New York petitioned the authorities to send to New York all prisoners to be transported from Newgate Prison.[9] It is doubtful, says Alexander Brown, if any other class of white labor could have been secured to open up Tide-water Virginia at that time than such as were sent." And these were unsatisfactory.[10] "It is a fact," said the American Historical Review, "that the transportation of convicts was a regular and systematic pursuit through the seventeenth and eighteenth centuries."[11] An estimated 20,000 of these felons came to Maryland alone between 1737 and 1767, among them 115 on the *York* from Newgate Prison, March 22, 1739. Their names are given.[12]

Of course, all sent were not actual criminals. Some were debtors, others political dissidents, prisoners of war, labor agitators and the like. Some might have stolen only a loaf of bread or whitened farthings to make them look like sixpences. But a good many were murderers, robbers, forgers, counterfeiters, house-burners, highwaymen and the like. Most of these convicts came from Newgate Prison. A reading of Rayner and Crooks' five - volume "Newgate Calendar" will give the type of usual criminal there at the time.

It cannot be denied either that deportation

to America was England's favorite way of getting rid of her loose women. The first ones sent were undoubtedly this kind. Narcissus Luttrell, writing in his diary, Thursday, November 17, 1692, tells of eighty such women being sent to Virginia. He mentions a ship "going for Virginia in which the magistrates had ordered 50 lewd women out of the houses of correction and 30 others who walked the streets after 10 at night."[13] Chambers mentioned another shipment of Scotch prostitutes in 1695.[14]

England didn't care whether such women were given to whites or Negroes. In 1787, when 351 ex-slaves were being sent from England to Sierra Leone, West Africa, the authorities picked up all the loose women they could find on the streets of Portsmouth, some sixty of them, herded them aboard, and had them married to the blacks. An Englishwoman, Mrs. A. M. Falconbridge, who saw these women in Sierra Leone four years later, tells of them.[15]

Leading Englishmen and Americans protested vigorously. "It is a shameful and unblessed thing," said Bacon, "to take the scum of people and wicked and condemned men to be the people with whom ye plant." [16]

The American Mercury, February 14, 1720, says of the arrival of "above 180" of these "malefactors" from the prisons of Newgate and Marshalsea, "These ways of transporting villains amongst such a flourishing people is to lessen our improvements and industries by filling the vacancies of honest men with tricking, thieving, and designing rogues who will hardly be brought to get their livelihood by such laborious and settled means." The Mercury, October 29, 1720, lamented that the plantations "cannot be ordered to be better populated than by such absolute villains and loose women, as these proved to be by their wretched lives and criminal actions, and if they settled anywhere in these parts can only by natural consequence leave bad seeds amongst us."

The Virginia Gazette, May 24, 1751, says "When we see our papers filled continually with accounts of the most audacious Robberies, the most cruel Murders and other infinite villainies perpetrated by the Convicts transported from Europe, what melancholy and what terrible Reflections must it occasion. . . . These are some of thy Favours, Britain. Thou are called the Mother Country; but what good Mother ever sent thieves and villains to accompany her children; to corrupt them with infectious vices and to murder the rest."

In 1753, Benjamin Franklin complained that English and German jails were being emptied in America. He wrote the London Chronicle in 1769, "Their emptying their jails in our settlements is an insult and a contempt, the cruelest that ever one people offered to another." He threatened to send King George a cargo of rattlesnakes in return.

Chief Justice Stokes of the Colony of Georgia wrote, "The Southern colonies are overrun with a swarm of men from the eastern parts of Virginia and North Carolina, distinguished by the name of Crackers. Many of these people are descended from convicts that were transported from Great Britain to Virginia at different times and inherited so much profligacy from their ancestors that they are the most abandoned set of men on earth."[17]

So many desperadoes and others were sent that the American colonies came to be regarded as Australia was to be after 1787 or Devil's Island in our time. The celebrated Dr. Samuel Johnson said in 1769, "They (the Americans) are a race of convicts and ought to be thankful for anything we allow them short of hanging."[18]

Johnson was undoubtedly prejudiced against America. He hated slavery. In his "Taxation No Slavery," he asked, "How is it we hear the loudest yelps for liberty among the drivers of Negroes?" But James D. Butler, who went into the subject thoroughly, says Johnson wasn't altogether wrong. "His research," says Butler, "has filled him with surprise that our colonial convict element was so large. He is inclined to confess that English views on this matter have been more correct than those prevalent in America. He cannot wonder that Johnson, who was employed in editing the Gentleman's Magazine, had hundreds of times chronicled the reprieve of gallows-birds that they might be made American colonists, should hold in low esteem the regions they pervaded and peopled. It seems more natural that he should speak as he did and declare that he could love everybody but an American."[19]

In its May issue, 1747, this magazine reported that 887 convicts had been shipped to America to date that year.

Views as that of Dr. Johnson, naturally deterred the more respectable type of colonists. But many of the latter began to arrive, these mostly indentured servants, semi-slaves, who sold themselves for a number of years. The Germans and Pennsylvania Dutch, made especially good immigrants.

Another forced type of immigrant were the kidnapped, chiefly children, husbands and wives who were in the way, and heirs to fortunes and titles. One of the latter, James Annesley, tells how he was held as a slave in his "Memoirs of An Unfortunate Nobleman Returned from A Thirteen Years' Slavery in America, 1743." These latter were slaves for life.

France also sent her unwanted to the New World. Fleurian, an official, complained of the quantity of criminals being sent to Louisiana and on May 9, 1720, the French Council of State ordered that no more "vagabonds, criminals and cheats" be sent there. Instead they were to go "to the other colonies." (Louisiana Hist. Quar. Vol. 1-3, p. 124. 1917-18).

It is clear from the foregoing that the earliest immigrants to the United States, English predominating, made up chiefly of a few aristocrats, "gentlemen," debtors, kidnapped, political prisoners, prostitutes and the outright vicious, added up to a source of manual labor that left much to be desired.

PILGRIMS AS DRUNKS AND SODOMITES

Even the early pilgrims of New England though very pious, or were forced to appear so, weren't all the hardworking, very desirable characters we've been led to believe. Governor Bradford, writing in 1642 of the severity of punishments in his colony, said, "And yet all this could not suppress the breaking out of sundry notorious sin, especially drunkenness and uncleanliness, not only incontinence between persons unmarried, for which many both men and women have been punished sharply but some married persons, but that which is even worse, sodomy. . . ."[20] Nevertheless Mayflower ancestry is still considered the highest in the United States.

The Saturday Evening Post, November 29, 1958, in an article, "Let's Have Less Nonsense About the Pilgrims," quotes Professor Morison of Harvard on the great amount of "bunk" written about them.

The very presence of Indians, badly armed, who could be forced to do the rough work, had a tendency to make even some of the most industrious colonists shiftless. The presence later of the Negroes made great numbers positively indolent. What Colonel William Byrd of Virginia said of this in 1736 will be given later.

England continued to empty her jails in America until 1783. That, however, was the year of America's independence and when two shiploads of convicts arrived, she refused to let them land. As a result London's Newgate Prison overflowed. Knapp and Baldwin say in *Newgate Calendar*, "The year 1783 which gave independence to America crowded the prisons to a degree never before known." (Vol. 3, p. 124, 1824-28.)

Finally in this matter of colonization there was a factor more important than the type of immigrant, good or bad, which came. It is that Europe hadn't the population to spare. The Thirty Years' War (1618-1648) had left most of the nations, including England and France, weaker. The War of the Spanish Succession that followed depeopled Europe still more. One nearby continent had millions available, whose people could be dragged off with impunity, and who, though called heathen, were free from vice and crime, and needed neither bolt nor bar to protect their posessions from one another: *Africa.*

NOTES

1. Esclavitud de la raza africana, t. 1, pp. 77-78, 1879.

1a. Life and Times of Yancey, p. 176. 1892.

2. Hist. and Present State of Virginia, para. 3.

2a. Travels in America, etc., Vol. 1, p. 156. 1799.

3. Ford II, 88. 1776.

4. Bolton and Marshall. Coloni. of N. America, p. 23, 1921.

5. N. Y. Times, March 3, 1958.

6. New England Memorial, pp. 40-41. 1926 ed.

7. Hist. and Present State of Virginia, para. 65.

8. Brown, Alex. First Republic in America, p. 219. 1898.

8a. Colonial Civilization of N. America, pp. 31, 33, 1949.

9. White Servitude in New Jersey. Americana, Vol. 15, p. 26, 1921.

10. Brown, Alex., p. 249.

11. Transportation of Convicts to the American Colonies, Vol. 23, p. 232. 1933-34.

12. Maryland Maga. of History. A List of Convicts Transported to America. Vol. 43, pp. 55-60. 1948.

13. Brief Hist. Relations (1678-1714), Vol 2. 1857.

15. Voyages to Sierra Leone, 1791-2-3, pp. 64-66. Utting, F. A. Sierra Leone, p. 81, 1931.

16. D'Auvergne, E. B. Human Livestock, p. 160. 1933.

17. Documentary Hist. of American Indus. Society, Vol. 2, p. 165, 1910.

18. Boswell's Life of Johnson, Vol. 3 p. 36. 1824.

19. British Convicts shipped to America, p. 33. 1896.

20. Hist. of the Plymouth Plantation, p. 459. 1898 ed.

AFRICA AS THE ECONOMIC FOUNDATION OF THE UNITED STATES

"The discovery of African labor was an American enterprise. It was the introduction of a hitherto unknown muscular force, proving on trial to be the most perfect agent of production then known to commerce . . . African labor fixed with eagerness the marvellous power in the varied and exhaustless wealth of the South." — J. W. DuBose.

The United States, both as a colony and a young nation, wasn't highly thought of in Europe. When Thomas Jefferson was president he offered to give a site in Washington to any European nation that would build a legation on it; none accepted. Many leading writers even considered the new nation hopeless, among them Count Gobineau, Sydney Smith, and James McSparran. Gobineau was expressing a sentiment long popular in Europe when he said "Americans represent the most varied specimens of the races of Old Europe of whom the least possible can be expected. They are the refuse of all the ages—Irish; Germans, often mixed-blood; some French; and Italians, who outnumber all the others. The mixture of all these degenerate types, gives, and will continue to give birth to new ethnic confusions. These mixtures have in them nothing good. Italian, Frenchman, Anglo-Saxon will amalgamate in the Southern States with the Indian, Negro, Spaniard and Portuguese already there. From such a mixture one can imagine nothing but horrible racial results—nothing but an incoherent juxtaposition of the most degraded beings."[1] Still another writer called America, "the graveyard of the white race," and

American-born Bayard Taylor said an American is "an Anglo-Saxon relapsed into barbarism."

In the Bible it was asked what good could come out of Nazareth. In a similar vein, Sydney Smith, celebrated writer and wit, asked in 1820, "In the four quarters of the globe who reads an American book? Or goes to an American play? Or looks at an American picture or statue? What does the world yet owe to American physicians or surgeons? What new substances have their chemists discovered or what old ones have they analyzed? What new constellations have been discovered by the telescopes of Americans? What have they done in mathematics? Who drinks out of American glasses? Or eats from American plates? Or sleep in American blankets?"[2]

But less than a century after that, America was not only doing all it was said she couldn't do, but had taken the lead of all the nations on earth. Indeed, the rise of America from a wilderness over which roamed Indians and buffaloes to world power; and from a people once so pressed by hunger that some were driven to cannibalism[3] to a nation with enormous surpluses of food is nothing short of the miraculous. Britain took 1920 years to become the world's foremost power—1643 years from Julius Caesar's invasion, 55 B.C., to the defeat of the Spanish Armada in 1588; and another 277 years to Waterloo, 1815. The United States took only 353 years, that is, from the founding of St. Augustine, Florida, to the end of World War I.

Coming centuries later, America had, of course, the advantages of man's knowledge accumulated since but she had also some terrific disadvantages, not the least of which was the long struggle with the Indians, which sometimes ended in massacre of the colonists as in Virginia in 1622. In spite of hardships greater than those met by colonists south of the Rio Grande, the British North American colonies, a little over a century after the founding of St. Augustine, took the lead in the New World. Cuba, Hispaniola, Mexico, Puerto Rico, were colonized before the United States. They, too, had the advantage of man's accumulated knowledge. Why did they drop behind?

Those who attribute human advancement to "race" will say, America was a "white man's land," that her racial origin was North European. It is true that the Spaniards and Portuguese, pioneers in the lands to the south, were mixed with Africans from very early times and very much so after the Moorish invasion of 711 A.D., but why were the South Europeans at the top in 1492 and the Nordics so far below them? Also, why did the United States outstrip Canada, which has been and still is, more racially Nordic?

THE REASON FOR AMERICA'S ADVANCE

Why did America take the lead so early in the New World? The answer is Trade.

Trade in what? The reply to that sounds so utterly preposterous now that one must be bold to state it. However, there were those living then who did not hesitate to say it as well, as certain candid writers of our time. *It was trade in Molasses.* A pro-American bulletin of 1731 said, "The molasses trade is the most (if not the only valuable one) of New England."[4] And John Adams, second president of the United States, said, "I know not why we should blush to confess that molasses was an essential ingredient in American Independence."[5] He added that Washington also thought highly of molasses. Which Washington certainly did. In 1776, he sent one of his slaves, Tom, by a ship-captain to be exchanged for molasses. (Washington, Writings of, Vol. 2, p. 211. 1889)

THE MOLASSES TRADE

Why molasses? Molasses meant rum. Why rum? Rum was for exchange of Africans on the African West Coast. In short, it was the sale of Africans in the New World—the Slave Trade—that laid the financial foundation of the United States. It was Africa's great gift to America.

More will be said of this in the proper place.

THE COMING OF THE AFRICANS

Africa as a source of labor was discovered by the Portuguese in 1440, that is, for the period of which we are speaking. The first batch of Africans brought to Lagos, Portugal, sold readily, as Azurara, an eyewitness, tells us. They proved so useful and were brought in such numbers, that before long Southern Portugal was peopled largely by them and their mulatto offspring. Spain, Italy, France, and even England, were soon importing them, too. A century of almost continuous wars had depleted their populations.

When Columbus and the first Spaniards came, it was inevitable that Africans should be with them. But since there was no intention then of using them on a vast scale, only a few were brought in 1502. Since there were plenty of Indians, why bring in other labor? But as was said, Indian labor soon proved unsatisfactory.

The use of Negroes came about thus: Good Bishop Las Casas (1474-1566) seeing the Indians dying under the tasks imposed on them, suggested the Africans instead—a step that has made Las Casas go down in history as the father of the African slave trade. He lived to regret it bitterly. He said in his old age that had he known its consequences, "he wouldn't have done it for the world."[6]

Orders came to use Negroes instead. Herrera de Tordesillas (1559-1625) says "they were more useful. The work of one Negro was equal to that of four Indians."[7] That order was issued again ten years later. Africans became such a necessity that in 1540, when Charles V ordered their liberation, the command was ignored. Herrera tells of their great vitality as compared with the Indian. "They flourished in the Spanish Isles so well," he says, "that they were thought to be nearly immortal as for some time no one had seen one die except by hanging. Like oranges they seemed to have found their natural soil."[8]

The labor of the Africans now became the most important single factor in the development of the New World. On them fell the crude work. And more than a little of the skilled one. Some had brought with them their ancient skills in metals, weaving, carving and agriculture. And as a colony grew, so grew the call for them. Nations fought one another on the high seas to seize their cargo of Africans. The Dutch counted heavily on such captures for their colony of New Netherland (New York).

Louisiana Historical Quarterly quotes Dixon, an official of 1722," It is absolutely necessary to send a great many Negroes here . . . Just as the islands of American were established by Negro slaves Louisiana will never be established until a sufficient number of them is sent." (Vol. 1-3, p. 101. 1917-18)

Planters would say, "Negroes are the lifeblood of the plantations. Without them we could not exist." Southern planters, quoting the Bible, called Africans "the one thing needful." Others said, "They are the sinews and strength of the Western world; the lack of them, the great obstruction." Peter Stuyvesant, Dutch governor of New York, said, "Everything is by God's blessing in good condition and in consequence of the employment of Negro slaves." Cotton Mather, New England divine, when presented with a Negro slave, said in his diary, December 13, 1706, that it was "a mighty smile from Heaven upon my family." In 1724, Virginia petitioned the King to let them have more Negroes, they being especially needed for the settlement of two new counties.[9] Patrick Henry declared that while he would not and could not justify slavery, he found Negroes a necessity. "I am drawn along," he said, "by the general inconvenience of living without them."[10] In his address to the Virginia Convention, June 24, 1788, he deplored "the necessity of holding his fellow-men in bondage" but that "their manumission is incompatible with the felicity of the country.[11] Thomas Jefferson and other humane slaveholders said much the same. James Parton, writing of the Negroes in the 1770's, said, they were indispensable. "What a debt we owe to the jolly, amiable, indispensable Negro,"[12] he said.

Georgia is a striking example of a colony that couldn't get along without the African. Named for George II, it was founded in 1732 as a refuge for persecuted Protestants, the poor, and the unfortunate, among them some who had run afoul of the law. The first colonists, some 2,000 in number were pricipally English, German Lutherans, Italians, Swiss, Portuguese and Jews. Two of the principal conditions were no African slaves and no rum. One of its leaders, John Wesley, father of Methodism, and a great opponent of slavery, had said, "The slave trade is the execrable sum of all villainies."

Another reason for barring Negroes is the following, by the Earl of Egmont, who said in his Journal (1738-39), "where there are Negroes, a white man despises work, saying, what, will you have me slave and work like a Negro?"

Due de la Rochefoucauld-Liancourt, a visitor in America, observed as late as 1795, or twelve years after the Revolution, "In a country abounding in slaves the white do not apply much to labour. Their ambition consists in buying Negroes; they buy them with the first sum of money they get and when they have two of them leave off working themselves."[13a]

The sturdier whites of Georgia — Scotch Highlanders, and the Salzburgers as well as the clergy, opposed slavery and petitioned the trustees not to allow it. White servants were brought in but as Johnson says they were "a shiftless, saucy group, some filthy and infected with itch, they often deserted their masters to hang around the town to be fed from the common store. . . . The plague of idle, roguish servants increased daily. Their worthless character strengthened the demand for slaves. . . ."[13b]

Without Negroes, Georgia rapidly declined. Its 2,000 souls dwindled to six or seven hundred. The Earl of Egmont wrote, "The industrious went away because they found that without Negroes they could not subsist. . . . Numbers who have left the colony would return if Negroes were allowed and many from Carolina would do so, too. . . . If Negroes were allowed, the colony would people apace. . . ."[13c]

Twenty-nine years after its founding, Edmund Burke, celebrated English statesman, found the Georgians in "a famished condition." He said, "They neglected their agriculture to hunt for gold and provoking the Indians by their unguarded behavior." They found the climate too warm, he said, "the consequence of which was that the great part of their time, all the heat of the day, was spent in idleness."[13d]

Another writer of that time said, "In spite of all endeavor to disguise this point it is as clear as light itself, that Negroes are as necessary to the cultivation of Georgia as axes, hoes, or any other utensil of agriculture."

Matters got to a state where the colony either had to be abandoned or the African brought in. It had had three previous failures. Bringing in whites each time simply did not help. Even the staunchest opponents of slavery now gave in. In 1748, one of them, the Rev. Brozius, wrote the trustees, "Things are now in such a melancholy state I must humbly beseech Your Honours not to regard any more our, or our friends' petition against slavery."[14]

George Whitfield, most dynamic preacher of his time, a close associate of Wesley, and once a bitter opponent of slavery, also came out in favor of it. He saw how the neighboring colony of South Carolina was prospering thanks to the Africans. Proving from the Bible that slavery was approved by God, he said in a letter, March 22, 1751, "Hot countries cannot be cultivated without Negroes. What a flourishing country Georgia might have been had the use of them been permitted years ago! How many white people have been destroyed for want of them and how many thousands of pounds spent to no purpose at all." (Reproduced in Tyerman, Life and Times of John Wesley. Vol. 2, p. 132. 1878). Whitfield, who had left the colony for England, returned to it, bought slaves, and even left them to his heirs in his will.

The Negroes, brought in, saved the once "drooping colony" so much so that twenty-five years later it was able to play a role of more than a little importance in the Revolution.

Another great advantage to Southern economy was that the slaves were not only capital and labor combined but they were a form of capital that could look to its own welfare. A strong healthy, intelligent slave was the finest currency. One such might fetch $2,000, or about five times that now. In 1785, Virginia valued her slaves at 6,370,400 pounds sterling, or $31,-292,000.[15] According to Thomas Jefferson, she had 270,762 of them. The free population, of whom some were Negroes, was 296,852.

General Pinckney of South Carolina said at the National Convention in 1787 that "South Carolina has in one year exported to the amount of 600,000 pounds sterling, all of which was the fruit of the labor of the blacks." And whenever the price of cotton, tobacco, and rice, rose so did the price of slaves. Slave-grown tobacco was once Virginia currency. At the first Constitutional Convention in 1787, the Southern slave states declared their wealth in Negroes made them equal of the free New England ones. Butler of South Carolina said, "The labor of a slave in South Carolina was as productive and as valuable as that of a free man in Massachusetts. Wealth ought to be considered equal to the number of free men in New England;

States ought to have weight in the Government in proportion to their wealth." **Lowndes of** South Carolina said that the North with its few slaves "want to exclude us from this advantage." that is, the South's real wealth.[16]

The Negro was, in short, the backbone of the South. To quote J. W. DuBose, eminent authority on Confederate history, again, "**What would** have been the fate of the Southern portion of the British American possessions had the African not come? Whence would have come the immigrants of the seventeenth and eighteenth centuries to America; and where would they have settled had not African labor been available? African labor . . . was the introduction of a hitherto unknown muscular force, proving on trial to be the most perfect agent of production then known to commerce." (Life and Times of Yancey, pp. 159, 170. 1892)

THE MOLASSES TRADE

The events leading up to the trade in rum and molasses are these: England, with **Sir John** Hawkins (1532-1595), had taken the lead in the slave trade. The Royal African Company had the monopoly but it was unable to supply the demand and Parliament ordered the trade opened to all British ships "for the well supplying of the plantations and colonies with sufficient numbers of Negroes at reasonable prices."

New England Yankees who had inherited the maritime spirit of their motherland now entered this trade with such zest that they soon became rivals of the English merchants. The Yankees had discovered that molasses, the best article for making rum, was either being fed to the hogs or thrown away in the French sugar islands of the Caribbean, and therefore could be had very cheaply. The molasses trade, in turn, gave impetus to other New England industries as distilling, fishing, shipbuilding, lumber and horse— and cattle-rearing. In 1708, Governor Cranston of Rhode Island reported that his colony had built 103 ships since 1698. In 1749, Boston had 469 ships tied to the slave trade. G. F. Dow has a special chapter on American ships engaged in the trade.[17] The New England merchants, says Louis B. Wright, had discovered "two commodities which enriched them and their ports, rum and slaves."[18]

Thanks to rum and the slave-trade, New England became commercially dominant in the New World. She not only dominated the Caribbean trade but that of Virginia, the Carolinas, and the rest of the South. She had very few slaves herself. Her climate and agriculture did not make them profitable. In 1776, the six New England colonies had only 16,034 slaves as compared with nearly 300,000 in Virginia alone. Her type of industry made white servants, who were semi-slaves, more profitable. In 1652, Rhode Island abolished Negro slavery, not from humane reasons but because what she gained from it locally was trifling in comparison with what she made from the trade. In abolishing her own slavery, she had specially provided that "nothing in the Act shall extend or be deemed to extend to any Negro or mulatto slave brought from the coast of Africa into the West on board any vessel belonging to this colony."[19]

This was the procedure. New England ships with their cargo of rum would sail to West Africa, where they would exchange it for slaves and such articles they could pick up as gold dust and ivory, thence to the West Indies where they disposed of them at high profit, then return with molasses for more rum, then again to Africa. This was known as the Triangular (or Three-Cornered) Trade. Molasses, be it noted, was slave-produced, too.

Distilling became the chief home industry of New England, especially of Massachusetts and Rhode Island. There were hundreds of distillers. Boston with her then small population alone had sixty-three. But they could not keep pace with the demand.

"The trade in Negroes from West Africa," says Weeden, "absorbed immense quantities of spirit. The African demand was very importunate." Letters of ship-captains of the period prove it. In 1752, when Captain Isaac Freeman wrote

for a cargo of rum, he was told that he wouldn't be able to get that quantity even in three months. "There are so many vessels loading for Guinea we can't get one hogshead of rum for the cash." Captains were advised to water their rum. One satire ran "Water ye rum as much as possible and sell as much by the short measure as ye can. An overwhelming Providence has been pleased to bring to this land of freedom another cargo of benighted heathen to enjoy the blessings of a gospel dispensation."

Dow says, "Molasses was the all-important feature of the slaving trade, which required rum as a means of barter for slaves for without molasses there could be no New England rum." He reproduces letters from ship-captains of the time telling how great a necessity they found rum. There are also letters from distillers. "In whatever branch of trade we now find ourselves," said W. B. Weeden, "we are impressed by the immense prevalence and moving power of rum, lumber, Negroes . . . all feel the initiative and moving impulse of rum. . . . Rum distilling and Negro importation gave more than direct profits to Newport (Rhode Island), great as they were. They gave a tremendous impulse to more than legitimate industry and commerce and compelled the exchange to follow in the wake of the 'rum' vessel and slaver." Molasses, says James Parton, in his "Life of Franklin," was the basis on which a great part of the commerce of America rested. . . . The single article of molasses did actually par, and was therefore the equivalent of the bulk of the numberless articles which Yankee traders took to the French West Indies." (Vol. 2, p. 298. 1865). Pitman says likewise, "In the great slave communities to the southward, Americans found the only great and permanent market for all their staples. It was the wealth accumulated from West India trade which more than anything else underlay the prosperity of New England and the Middle Colonies."[20a]

New England made better rum, sold it cheaper, and pushed it so energetically that it began to displace English rum and even French brandy.

"He had no wool on the top of his head.
Where the wool ought to grow—ought to grow."—OLD SONG.

The war of the American Revolution really began in rivalry over the African slave-trade. The American colonies, principally New England ones, were taking it away from the mother-country principally by using rum as barter for slaves, ivory, gold and o products. This later cartoon from Punch of London illustrates the English viewpoint. America is shown getting all the benefits f Africa; England who started the exploitation is getting nothing. John Bull is asking why.

Yankee success galled not only the slave-trading moguls of Bristol and Liverpool but the British government, itself. Under the Assiento of 1713, England had the monopoly of supplying slaves to the Spanish colonies of the New World. Slave-trading, the profits from slave products, and African trade in general, were very important in the British economy. Karl Marx did not exaggerate when he said, "The population and wealth of England after slumbering for seven hundred years began to develop itself under the influence of slave-acquired capital." How dared Americans, colonials, to become their rivals, demanded the English. Were not colonies founded for the benefit of the mother-country? To make it still worse the Americans with their trade were helping to develop the colonies of their great rival, France. The British West India planters were especially angry. They joined with the mother country in demanding that Americans either be prohibited from using foreign molasses or from making rum. They presented a petition to Parliament urging an "Act for the better securing and encouraging the trade of His Majesty's Sugar Colonies in America."[21]

American interests in London replied, "The trade between the Northern colonies and French islands is absolutely necessary for the continuance and being of the Northern colonies and is so far from being a trade detrimental to Great Britain, that in its natural consequence, it brings great riches to this Kingdom. . . .

"The British Northern colonies, a laborious, industrious people that furnish a great strength to this nation must grow poor, their trade in general be so greatly reduced that they will be utterly disabled from making returns to England for one-half of the manufactures of this kingdom they now consume. . . . The Molasses trade is the most (if not the only) valuable one New England hath."[22]

The Americans, in short, wanted free trade. But they protested in vain. Two years later (1733), Parliament passed the Molasses Act (6 George II. Chap. 13), placing a duty of sixpence (about thirty cents) on each gallon of imported molasses, or about half as much as the purchase price. But that was not all. The molasses of the British West Indies was already twenty cents a gallon dearer than the French one. And as if to make it worse there was an export duty on the British molasses. That is, the cost of molasses to the Americans would be double what they had been paying. To make it still worse, the British islands were poorer and could buy much less of New England goods than the French ones. Moreover, the British islands did not produce enough to supply the American demand. F. W. Pitman in "The Development of the British West Indies" gives figures of the times in proof.

The Americans saw ruin ahead. They called it atrocious discrimination. John Adams gave an idea of what the law meant to New England industry: On the seven million gallons of molasses imported annually, Britain would collect about $875,000 a year, a sum worth about ten times that now, he said.

The Rhode Island Assembly sent a strong "Remonstrance" to George II. The colony, it said, had one hundred and fifty vessels engaged in the West India trade and imported "14,000 hogsheads of molasses whereof a quantity not exceeding 2,500 hogsheads" came from the British islands.

Governor Hopkins protested, "Upwards of thirty distil-houses, erected at vast expense for want of molasses must be shut up to the ruin of many families and of our trade in general. Two-thirds of our vessels will become useless and perish upon our hands. Our mechanics and those dependent upon the merchant for employment must seek subsistence elsewhere." It would affect the mother country, too. He added, "An end will be put to our commerce; the merchants cannot import any more British manufactures, nor will the people be able to pay for those they have already received.",[23]

Massachusetts was equally indignant. Most of her distilleries would have to be closed; seven hundred ships, including fishing ones, would be tied up and some five thousand sailors thrown out of work. Most of New England industry, including fishing, was tied to the slave trade. "The Act," says Woodrow Wilson, "cut at the very heart of New England trade. . . . For the vast majority of the merchants, the Act meant financial ruin."[24] Governors of other states, including Colden of New York and Franklin of New Jersey joined in the protest. Talk of severance from Britain began. The American Revolution really started at this time. As Pitman rightly says, "The West India planting interest had laid substantial foundations in the realm of economic life for that great discontent which culminated in the American Revolution."

Samuel G. Arnold makes it even more emphatic. Of the protest of Partridge, Rhode Island representative in England, he says, *"The war-cry of Revolution, which was ere long to rally the American colonies in the struggle for independence was here first sounded by the Quaker agent of Rhode Island to cease only with the dismemberment of the British Empire."*[25]

In the face of American defiance, England did little to enforce the act. Smuggling continued almost openly for the next thirty-one years. "If," says Schlesinger "any serious attempt had been made to enforce the statute, the prosperity of the commercial provinces would have been laid prostrate. It was the West India Trade, more than anything else which had enabled them to utilize their fisheries, forests and fertile soil to build up their towns, cities, and to supply cargoes for their merchant marine and to liquidate their indebtedness to British merchants and manufacturers. The entire molasses output of the British islands did not equal two-thirds of the quantity imported into Rhode Island alone. Moreover the prices of the British planters were 25 to 40 per cent higher than the foreign islands."[26] This in addition to the heavy export duty, as was said.

"The terms of the Molasses Act were so drastic," says Albert Bushnell Hart, "that evasion seemed justifiable."

Another objection of the Americans was that the Europeans tried to cut in on their trade. Dr. Belknap, writing then, said, "I do not find that European adventurers had any other business here than to procure cargoes of our rum to assist them in carrying on the slave trade."

The smugglers operated in areas less frequented by the English patrols. And, of course, there was much collusion with the English revenue agents. But the Act, says James Truslow Adams "constituted a perpetual grievance against England. Moreover, as it lowered the moral tone of the community, it decreased the respect for law."[27]

So it went on until 1764. The Peace of Paris had just ended Britain's long war with France and Spain and she was badly in need of revenue to pay her huge national debt. America, at peace, had been growing more and more prosperous. Visitors to America took back to Europe glowing tales of the wealth of its upper-class, "the rich plate, fine mansions, furniture, carriages-and-four, costly wines, silks and satin of the ladies" and generally sumptuous living with troops of slaves to wait on their slightest whim. The English press and Parliament demanded that America be made to help bear the burden. The Molasses Act, now called the Sugar Act, was revived. Britain sent out twenty-seven warships to patrol the New England coasts and soldiers and revenue agents to enforce the act.

American shipping and general commerce at once felt the effect. Providence and Medford, chief slave-ports, suffered heavily. So did other cities as far south as Charleston. One merchant wrote, "What are the people of England going to do with us? Nothing but Ruine seems to hang over our Heads."

American defiance grew. The Boston Evening Post, July 8, 1765, declared the Act was being enforced so that West Indian Creoles "could roll in gilded equipages through the streets of London at the expense of two million Americans." James Otis, openly defied Britain. John Adams quoted him with approval. "If the King of Great Britain in person were encamped on Boston Common at the head of 20,000 men, with all his navy on our coasts, he would not be able to enforce it."[28] "The Act of April 5, 1764 can be set down as a landmark in the development of the forces that led to the Revolution," says Hart.[29] And Weeden, "The new enforcement of the Sugar Act was the most powerful cause in exciting the discontent of the colonies."

Thus the wealth gained from the sale of Africans and their labor not only laid the foundations of America's commerce, but the attempt to deprive her of the benefits of the slave trade was the most direct cause of the Revolution. The Encyclopedia Britannica says that the Molasses Act "contributed to the beginnings of revolutionary activities in the colonies," but whoever reads the heated discussion over it will realize that this appraisal is much too low. Note how close all of this happened towards the Revolution.

Rum and slave-trading are not glamorous and patriotic items therefore most popular historians and text-books omit them. Instead, stress is laid on the Stamp Act, which came into being to make up for the loss of revenue on the reduction of the taxes on sugar and molasses. The Stamp Act, long used in England, forced Americans to use stamped paper on all legal documents. It also taxed newspapers, pamphlets, magazines, advertisements, almanacs, playing cards and dice. The Molasses and the Sugar Acts had struck directly at the slave merchants and at the general population only indirectly. But the Stamp Act and the tax on tea affected all, especially the masses, and were thus much more effective issues for capturing general discontent. The real, the underlying irritant, however, was still the rivalry between the slave moguls of New England and those of Bristol and Liverpool. Proof is that the cry for independence continued even after the repeal of the Stamp Act. That and the tax on tea didn't bring in enough to pay the cost of collection and were abandoned in consequence. Note, also, that John Adams' statement that "molasses was an essential ingredient in American independence." was written thirty-five years after that event. In his letter to John Tudor, August 11, 1818, he shows how far more the economic, than the purely patriotic, stirred Americans of his day. Later, we shall see how the importations of Africans and the products they grew were to cause bitterest rivalry and armed conflict among Americans themselves. It is impossible to overestimate the impact of the African and the Afro-American on the United States from 1512 to 1865.

Certain present-day writers of whom one hears little, as Taussig, Weeden, Schlesinger, and Wiener, do tell of the part that slave-trading played in the demand for independence. "Commerce and politics," says Wiener,[30] "were so mixed that rum and liberty were but liquors from the same still." That "rum was the spirit of '76" is more than a pun.

The falsifying of this period for patriotism's sake was amply illustrated in 1925 at the ceremonies commemorating the hundred and fiftieth anniversary of the battle of Lexington and the ride of Paul Revere and his companion, William Dawes. Vice-President Dawes (descendant of Dawes), General Pershing, ex-Mayor Fitzgerald of Boston and others made patriotic speeches. New York City celebrated with a great gathering at the Church of St. John the Divine at which were a score or more of patriotic organizations as the Daughters of the American Revolution, Sons of the Revolutions, and the Society of Colonial Dames. Of course, not a word was uttered about rum, slavery, and Africa. However, some newspapermen dug into what had really happened and gave something of another story. The New York Times, April 21, 1925, said, "Few, if any of the speeches as yet delivered at Boston or elsewhere, in the course of celebrating the hundred and fiftieth anniversary of the Battle of Lexington have contained any American history except of the kind that used to be in all of our school textbooks and still fills most of them. One or two of the orators indeed have hinted that the men of those early days were a human lot with the ordinary human failings but that is as far as they have gone and for the rest they have proclaimed the standardized theories and the accepted myths and let it go at that."

Of the ride of Paul Revere and William Dawes, the Times said, "History seems to leave no doubt about one thing; Paul Revere and William Dawes were dispatched on their history-making rides on different routes from Boston to Lexington and Concord. There was nothing in the plan of the patriots who sent them calculated to call out the Minute Men, cause immediate resistance to the British forces and precipitate war. They were sent out quietly to warn Hancock to flee and escape military arrest and also to tell the patriots of those towns to hide their military stores."

One item the Americans wished particularly to keep out of the hands of the British was rum. The British were seizing all they could of it not only to hurt America's slave trade but because rum was then an important item in the British soldier's ration. Now it is significant that Revere's first stop was at the home of one of the biggest distillers, Isaac Hall, who was also captain of the Medford Minute Men. Frank W. Blair (New York Times, May 2, 1925) thinks that Hall gave Revere a shot of rum that really sped him on his way. Justin Winsor, foremost American historian of his time, says that the popular version of Revere's ride "paid little attention to the exactness of fact." Hall was what we would call a bootlegger.

In plain language, therefore, it was the profit from the sale of Africans and the wealth they produced that was the underlying cause of the Revolution. In short, had there been no Africa, the United States might still be attached to Britain as Canada which is older than New England. Or if America did win independence might it not have been delayed like Mexico and Brazil?

Of course, this will sound preposterous to most. But suppose the Americans hadn't discovered Africa and the Africans as a source of wealth and had remained a poor colony would Britain have singled them out for such crushing taxation? And even if she did would America have been financially strong enough to beat England? The wealth of most of the New England families was founded on the slave trade. John Hancock, great patriot, made his fortune as a slave smuggler. F. W. Taussig in "Rum, Romance and Rebellion," names several of these families. Colonel Isaac Royall, who gave two thousand acres of land to Harvard made his money that way, too. (Journal of Commerce, Oct. 6, 1865).

ONE ENGLISH VIEW
WHY AMERICANS REBELLED

One popular English view was that the Americans did not rebel principally because of taxes but from the arrogance and conceit bred into them from slavery of the blacks. They compensated this way for their own lowly, despised origin, it was said, and had grown so overbearing, so quick to anger and violence, they could no longer submit to authority. Edmund Burke, a great friend of America, himself, gave this as one cause. In his speech "Conciliation with with America" he said that "the vast multitude of slaves" had made "the spirit of liberty still more high and haughty. Freedom is to them (the Americans) not only an enjoyment but a kind of rank."[31]

This pride was sharpened by the contempt that aristocratic English officials had for native-born Americans and their frequent reference to "convict" origin. Beverly mentions some, Governor Nichols of Virginia, in particular. Nichols called Virginians "Dogs and their wives, Bitches."[32]

Some Americans as Colonel William Byrd of Virginia, Thomas Jefferson and Alexander Hamilton did think that the presence of Negroes had made Americans arrogant. Byrd, in a letter to Lord Egmont, July 12, 1736, said the presence of "these Aethiopians amongst us . . . blow up the pride and ruin the industry of our White People who seeing a rank of poor Creature below them detest work for fear it should make them look like slaves. It disposes them to pilfer, who account it more like Gentlemen to steal than to dirty their hands with Labour of any kind."[33]

Thomas Jefferson, who once had to rebuke his grandson, Jefferson Randolph, for conduct of this sort, wrote, "The whole commerce between master and slave is a perpetual exercise of the most boisterous passions; the most unremitting despotism. Our children see this and learn to imitate it; and thus nursed, educated, and daily exercised in tyranny can not but be stamped by it. . . ."[34]

Hamilton said, "The contempt we have been taught to entertain fo rthe blacks makes us fancy many things that are founded neither on reason nor experience."

One English visitor, Andrew Burnaby in 1759, made much the same observation. He said of the Virginia whites, "Their authority over their slaves renders them vain and imperious and entire strangers to that elegance of sentiment which is so peculiarly characteristic of refined, polished nations. Their ignorance of mankind and of learning exposes them to many errors and prejudices, especially in regard to Indians and Negroes."[35]

44

NOTES

1. l'Inegalite des Races Humaines, Vol. 4 p. 313, 1853.

2. Edinburgh Rev. Vol. 33, Jan. to May 1820, in his review of Seybert's book on America. McSparran wrote, "America Dissected," in 1753. Gustavus Myers discussed these detractions in "America Strikes Back."

3. Captain John Smith (1580-1631) wrote, "So great was our famine that a savage we slew and buried, the poorer sort took him up again and ate him; and so did divers ones another boiled and stewed with herbs. And one amongst the rest did kill his wife, powdered her and had eaten part of her." The General Historie of Virginia. The Fourth Booke, p. 294 (1606-1625). Neill E. D., quotes the Virginia Assembly of 1623 in its complaint against Governor Thomas Smythe, "One man killed his wife to eat for which he was burned. Many fed on corpses. "Terre Mariae (Maryland), p. 30. 1867. Other instances of eating corpses and killing Indians and eating them occurred as late as 1846. The Donner party, lost in the Sierras in the dead of winter, was driven to this. State of California Bulletin. The Donner Party Tragedy, pp. 10, 11; Croy, Homer. Wheels West. Stewart G. R. Ordeal by Hunger: Story of the Donner Party, pp. 132-35. 1960. This is significant because one great charge against Negroes was that their ancestors were cannibals.

4. Case of the Northern Colonies, p. 3, 1731.

5. Works of John Adams, Vol. 10, p. 345 ed. by C. F. Adams.

6. Helps, Sir A. Life of Las Casas, p. 67. 1868. Also Encyc. Brit.

7. Hist. Gen. de los Hechos de los Castillanos. Dec. 1, lib. 2, c. 5; Dec. 2, lib. 2, c. 8.

8. Dec. 2, lib. 3. c. 14.

9. Virginia Calendar of State Papers, Vol. 1, p. 206.

10. Quoted by Bancroft, G. Hist. of the U. S., Vol. 4, p. 233, 1882.

11. Correspondence of Patrick Henry, V. 1, 3, 1881. Ed. by W. W. Henry.

12. Biography of Benj. Franklin, Vol. 1, p. 2151. 1887.

13a. Travels in North America, etc. Vol. 2, p. 290. 1799.

13b. Johnson, A., Georgia As Colony and State, p. 71. 1938.

13c. Colonial Records of Georgia, Vol. 5, 1738-44, pp. 452, 476, 605.

13d. European Settlements in North America, p. 212. 1762.

14. Quoted by Coulter, Short History of Georgia, p. 64, 1933.

15. Va. Maga. of Hist., Vol. 23, p. 410.

16. U. S. Constit. Convention, 1787, July 11, Vol. 1, pp. 580, 592.

17. Slave Ships and slaving, pp. 255-265, 1927.

18. Colon. Civiliz. of N. America, p. 105, 1949.

19. Rhode Is. Col. Records, VIII, 251-2.

20. Economic and Social History of New Eng., 1745-50, Vol. 2, pp. 584, 641, 753. 1890: Williams, E., Golden Age of the Slave System in England, Jour. of Negro Hist. Vol. 25, pp. 60-106. 1940.

20a. Development of the British West Indies, p. vii. 1917.

21. Case of the Northern Colonies. 1731.

22. Case of the Northern Colonies. Brochure, pp. 2, 3. 1731.

23. Rhode Is. Colonial Records, VI, 381. Field E., State of Rhode Is. and The Providence Plantations, Vol. 1, p. 215.

24. Hist. of the American People, Vol. 4, p. 35. 1918.

25. Hist. of Rhode Island. Vol. 1, p. 124. 1874.

26. The Colonial Merchants and the American Revolution, 1773-76, pp. 43-4. 1918.

27. Revolutionary New England, 1691-1776, p. 153. 1923.

28. Works of John Adams, Vol. 10, p. 349.

29. Hart, A. B., Commonwealth Hist. of Mass., Vol. 2, p. 473. 1928.

30. The Rhode Island Merchants and the Sugar Act. New Eng. Quar., Vol. 3, pp. 464-500, 1930. See also: Taussig: Rum, Romance and Rebellion.

31. Works of Ed. Burke, Vol. 1, p. 467. 1864.

32. Hist. and Present State of Virginia, para. 150.

33. American Hist. Review, Vol. 1, p. 89.

34. Notes on Virginia, p. 200.

35. Travels, etc., p. 54.

WERE AFRICANS THE ONLY SLAVES?

Since a great many Americans of African ancestry are sensitive about slavery and an equally great or greater number of Americans of European ancestry are proud that their ancestors once held the ancestors of the former as slaves it might do well at this point to look into that.

Whenever Africans are mentioned, they are usually associated with slavery—natural servitude, as Frobenius says. But what people can be mentioned that were not slaves at some period in their history? Jose Antonio Saco, foremost authority on slavery, names about all of them in his six-volume work, "Historia de la esclavitud desde los tiempos mas remotos hasta nuestros dias," (History of Slavery from the Remotest Time to Our Day).

The laboring element of Greece and Rome and even many of the scholars, doctors, and overseers, were slaves. Later the Christian Church, itself, kept slaves as Paul Allard shows in his "Les Esclaves Chretiens." St. Paul advised one slave, Onesimus, to return to his master and counselled slaves to be obedient to their owners. There is undoubted proof that as early as the fifth century A.D. white people were sold as slaves in Africa. St. Jerome (340-420) wrote, "Who would have believed that the daughters of that mighty city (Rome) would one day be wandering as servants and slaves on the shores of Egypt and Africa."

In fact, slave," itself, was first used for white people. It comes from "Slav," a blond, blue-eyed people, captured by the Germans and reduced to servitude. Slav originally meant "people of glory." As Gibbon says in his "Decline and Fall of the Roman Empire," "From the Luxine to the Adriatic, in the state of captives or subjects" the Slavs overspread the land and their name was degraded "from the signification of glory to that of servitude." When one encounters "slave" in the French language today it means "a female Slav." The earlier name for those held in bondage was "serf" from the Latin "servus." (Some trace it to Greek). In Russia that was the name used. In 1861, 40,000,-000 of her serfs or slaves were freed, that is, only four years before the American Negroes. By all accounts they were more debased and treated more barbarously than the American slaves.

It happens, too, that while Europeans and white Americans were raiding Africa for slaves, Africans were raiding the coasts of Europe as far north as Sweden and Finland for slaves and had been doing so for centuries. The evidence on this is abundant and indisputable. For 400 years (1400-1800) collections were taken up in the churches of Europe for ransom of these slaves. The "Ordre Franc de Trintaires" was founded especially for this purpose. Sallee, in Morocco, was the great slave-market for these white captives.

J. G. Jackson, writing in 1809, said, "They (the Moors) carry the Christian captives about the Desert to the different markets to sell them for they soon discover that their habits of life render them unserviceable, or very inferior to the black slaves from Timbuctoo. After travelling three days to one market, five to another,

ole peoples with their household goods and cattle were carried away into slavery in ancient times. This scene is from the Monuments of Nineveh.

nay, sometimes fourteen, they at length become objects of commercial speculation and the itinerant Jew traders, who wander about Wedinoon to sell their wares find means to barter them for tobacco, salt, a cloth garment, or any other thing." (Empire of Morocco, pp. 272-81)

Frederick Moore says, "There can be no mistake about the records of history, which state that thousands of Christian slaves, many of them British, were sold in the great white market of Sallee." (Passing of Morocco, 133-34, 1908). Voltaire, who lived that time, tells in the eleventh chapter of Candide of the color of the Moors, ("blacks and mulattoes") and of their capture and sale of white people.

Mulai Ismael, Emperor of Morocco, an almost full-blooded black, had 10,000 white slaves to build his stables at Meknes and a regiment of whites born in captivity. Abbe Busnot, who went to see him on a mission sent by Louis XIV, describes his appearance and tells of the white slaves he saw. Other writers of that time as Pidon de St. Olon and Lempriere have done the same.

As late as 1810, white Americans were captured on the high seas and sold at the great

Ancient slavery: The Helvetians, a Germanic people, pass the Romans under the yoke after the battle of Lake Leman (from the painting by Gleyre).

slave port of Salee, Morocco. Some were taken inland as far south as Timbuctoo. After America won independence, she had to pay tribute to the North African powers, better known as "the Barbary Pirates," to sail the North Atlantic. In 1785, two American ships were captured and their crew made prisoners. In October and November 1793, 119 Americans were captured. (Wright, L. B. First Americans in North Africa, p. 23-24. 1945). In 1821, Commodore Decatur freed many Americans there.

(Further details of European captives as far north as Sweden taken to Africa are in "Nature Knows No Color-Line, Chapter Five).

Slavery among the ancients—These white slave-girls who were sold in the slave-markets of Greece and Rome came sometimes from even royal families. Such were usually captives. Horace, Roman poet, 65-8 B.C. mentions three of this kind. He says, "Briseis, though a slave, had power to move Achilles' heart with her white beauty; "Tecomessa"; and Phyllis of royal blood. Think not, at least that e'er from tainted breed thy darling is sprung." (Book II, Ode, iv). (Painting by Girard).

49

A 15th Century conception of Africa with white people held as slaves.
(Dapper's Naukenrige Beschryvinge der Afrikaensche (frontespiece))

Emperor of Morocco, whose mother was an unmixed Negro slave had tens of thousands of white slaves. From a painting of 1670. See John Ogilby's Africa (p. 264, 1670).

Africans treated their white slaves much better than white Americans their Africans. "The meanest Christian slave on becoming a Mohammedan," says Blake, "was free . . . and he and his descendants were eligible to the highest offices in the state." Acceptance of Christianity made no difference in the status of the African slave in America. General Eaton, American consul at Tunis, said in 1799, "Truth and justice demand from me the confession that the Christian slaves among the barbarians of Africa are treated with more humanity than the African slaves among the Christians of civilized America." (Quoted by W. O. Blake, "History of Slavery In Northern Africa," p. 79. 1857).

For centuries also and well into the last century, the Arabs, a Negroid people, had been raiding what is now Russia for white slaves,

51

White slave in Egypt. (Drawing by Sichel).

mostly women,—the Circassians. One Arab writer declared that Arabia is such a hard country to live in that but for the importation of African and Circassian slaves its population would soon be extinct.

SLAVERY OF WHITES IN AMERICA

It happens, too, that the first slaves in what is now the United States, were white Englishmen. The earliest warrants banishing convicts to a life of servitude in Virginia were signed by James I in 1617 and the first hundred arrived in 1619 (that is, the same year the Negroes did), and were sold.

The Greek Slave by Hiram Powers.

52

Scene on a slave-ship bound for America from a French lithograph of 1802. Similar scenes existed on ships bringing white slaves from Europe a little earlier.

53

Charles V of Germany freeing white slaves held in Africa after his victory there in 1535. (From painting by Nicoles de Keyser).

Freed whites returning to France from slavery in Africa.

One gets an idea of how the sale of white people was regarded in colonial America by what Cotton Mather, famous New England divine, said should be done with William Penn, founder of Pennsylvania, a Quaker. Mather called that faith, "very horrible idolatry." (Diary, Vol. 1, p. 572). Hearing that Penn, whom he called "the chief scamp," was on the high seas with his settlers, he urged the authorities to send a ship to capture him. "Make captive Penn and his ungodly crew," he urged, "so that the Lord may be glorified. Much spoil can be had by selling the whole lot to Barbados, where slaves fetch high prices in rum and sugar."

Act V, 1680, of the Laws of Virginia, reads, "For the encouragement of trade and manufacture, it is provided that all goods, wares, English servants, Negroes and other slaves imported after September 29, 1681, shall be landed and laid on shore, bought and sold at appointed places and at no other places under penalty."

They were advertised for sale along with Negroes. The Boston News Letter, September 13, 1714, offers "several Irish maid-servants;

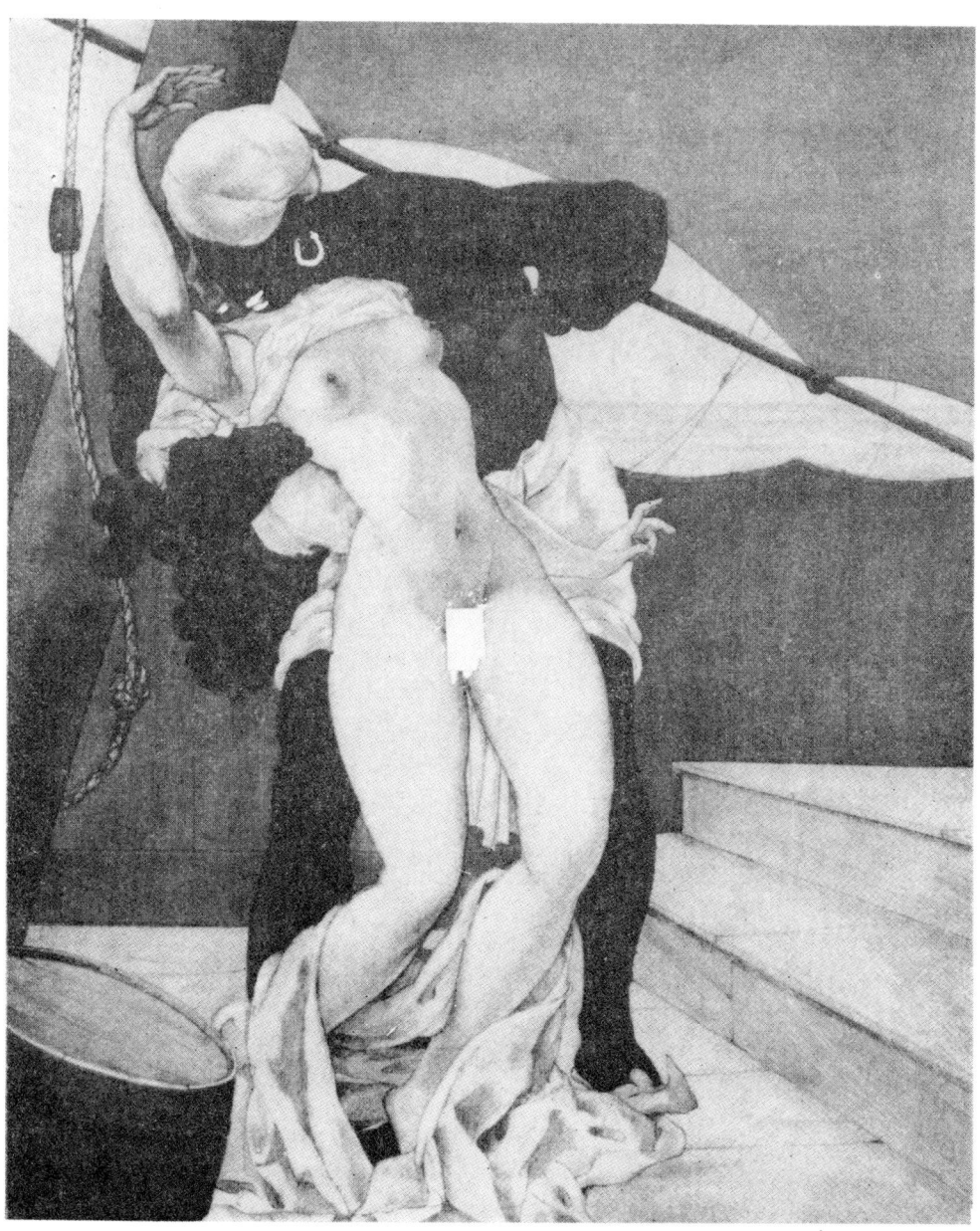

European girl captured by Moorish sea-captain. From Voltaire's Candide. Daughter of the Princess of Palestrina. (Illustration by Bruneschelli).

one Irishman, good barber and wigmaker; and five likely Negro boys." The New York Gazette, September 4 and 11, 1732, offers "Welshmen, Englishmen, Negroes, a Negro girl, and Cheshire cheese." Wall Street was then a slave market. A Philadelphia advertisement of 1728 reads, "Lately imported and to be sold cheap, a parcel of likely men and women servants." They were mostly German.

Johann Buettner, one of those who came under these conditions tells how men and women were stripped naked on board on arrival and examined like cattle by prospective buyers. He says that on the voyage the women slept indiscriminately among the men. So much the better if they became pregnant. They would fetch more.

G. Mittelberger, who came to America in 1750, wrote, "Many parents must sell and trade away their children like so many head of cattle." He estimated that during the four years he was in Philadelphia, 25,000 of his compatriots were sold there. Children from nine to twelve went for from $30 to $40; and over eighteen from $60 to $69.

William Eddis in "Letters From America, 1769-1777" tells how badly these white slaves were treated by their masters. In that of September 20, 1770, he compares their treatment with that of the Negro slaves: "Negroes being a property for life the death of slaves in the prime of youth and strength is a material loss to the proprietor . . . they are therefore under more comfortable circumstances than the miserable Europeans over whom the rigid planter exercises an inflexible severity. They are strained to the utmost to perform their allotted labor . . . generally speaking they groan beneath a worse than Egyptian bondage."

"White servants," says Bancroft, "came to be a usual article of traffic. They were sold in England to be transported and in Virginia resold to the highest bidder; like the Negroes they were to be purchased on shipboard as men buy horses at a fair."

J. B. McMaster says, "They became in the eyes of the law a slave and in both the civil and the criminal code were classed with the Negro and the Indian. They were worked hard, were dressed in the cast-off clothes of their owners and might be flogged as often as the master and mistress thought necessary. . . . Father, mother, and children could be sold to different buyers. Such remnants of cargoes as could not find purchasers within the time specified were bought in lots of fifty or more by speculators, known as 'soul-drivers,' who drove them through the country like so many cattle and sold them for what they would fetch." (Acquisition of Political, Social, and Industrial Rights in America, pp. 32-35). Some whites served under Negro slave overseers.

White slaves who ran away were advertised for in the newspapers. If caught, they were branded with the letter "R" (runaway). Those who "stole flour and meal given out for baking" had their ears clipped. George Washington advertised for two white runaways.

No wonder Moreau de St. Mery, who spent five years in America (1793-98) wrote as regards the sale of white people, "It is, therefore, not the goodness of the soil, nor the excellence of the laws which are responsible for the growth of the population of the United States, but the traffic in men from Europe." He estimated that in one year alone, 13,000 of these whites were sold at ten pounds sterling each, or a total of some $650,000. (Voyage, etc. pp. 321-22). There is a translation of this work by Kenneth Roberts.

One reads of the horrors that Negroes suffered on slave ships from Africa but eyewitness accounts of what white slaves suffered on their passage sound as awful. Mittelberger wrote in 1750, "During the voyage there is on board these ships terrible misery, stench, fumes, horror, vomiting, many kinds of sea-sickness, fever, dysentery, headache, heat, constipation, boils, scurvy, cancer, mouth-rot and the like all of which comes from old and sharply salted food and meat, also from the bad and foul

Detail from "The Slave Market" by J. L. Gerome (1824-1904). Negroes and Whites being sold together.

water . . . lice abound so frightfully, especially on sick people, that they can be scraped off. . . . During a storm that closely packed people tumble over each other both the sick and the well. . . ." (Journey to Pennsylvania, p. 20). Geiser's "Redemptioners," Chapter "The Voyage" gives equally harrowing tales of those sufferers.

Like the black slaves, they were packed like sardines. "Packed like herrings and sold as slaves," says Pastor Kunze. Christopher Sauer in his petition to the Pennsylvania legislature in 1775 asserted that at times "there was not more than twelve inches room for each person at night."

These unfortunate whites, mostly Irish and German, died like flies. Caspar Wisler said in 1752, "Last year a ship was twenty-four weeks at sea and of the 150 passengers on board more than 100 died at sea." Sauer estimated in 1778 that 2,000 of those on the fifteen ships arriving that year, died during the voyage. On one ship with 400 passengers, 350 died at sea. (Henninghausen L. P., History of the German Society in Maryland, pp. 120-28. 1949).

James Oneal, writing of a sale of whites in 1826, says "A half a century had passed since the adoption of the Declaration of Independence which declared all men free and equal and yet the purchase of white flesh had not become extinct." (Chapter on "The White Slave Trade" in Workers in American History). But the sale of white orphans continued in New York until as late as 1858. They were put up for sale in a church at $10 each. Congressman W. Jacobs writing in 1859, quotes an advertisement of these children in the New York Journal of Commerce, May 6, 1858. One sale is described thus: "The price of each slave was $10. The Free Church was then thrown open, the young females occupying the front seats in rows, some of them crying. Customers walked among the ranks with perfect coolness examining their condition, one by one, as they found one suitable they plaked the cash and carried off the piece." The Journal of Commerce of October

reports that "4,000 of such children have been sold and fifty will be sold every two months." More details and sources are given in "Sex and Race" (Vol. 2, p. 210).

Kidnapping of whites in Europe for sale as lifetime slaves in America was common. Richard Hildreth wrote in 1848, "Just catch a stray Irish or German girl and sell her."

The very high price of slaves induced many to kidnap white children and sell them as Negroes in the South as late as the 1850's. Instances of such abound. I have reproduced in "Sex and Race" Vol. 2, an engraving of 1838, showing a tanning pit in which white children were dipped to blacken them. This was hardly necessary as due to racial intermixture, some of the Negroes were so white that real white people held as slaves couldn't prove what they were. The best known case is that of Sally Muller, German-born, whom the Supreme Court of Louisiana ruled was a Negro and was proved to be white only when her birth-certificate was dug up in Alsace. George W. Cable writes of her in his "Strange True Stories of Louisiana. A motion picture of some years ago showed white women being kidnapped in the Eastern states and sold on the block to white men in the West. This was far from being mere fiction.

FIRST AFRICANS NOT SLAVES

Strong documentary proof that the first Africans in America were not slaves and that chattel slavery of them did not start until about 1659 or 1682 is given by competent researchers, four of whom are J. H. Russell, M. P. Andrews, Mary Standard and Helen Catterall.

Russell, in his chapter "Origin of the Free Negro Class" calls the belief that the first Negroes were slaves "a popular error maintained and supported by a large number of writers." M. P. Andrews says, "The evidence clearly points to the customary indenture for Virginia archives show that throughout the

The King of Dahomey giving presents to his subjects in annual ceremony. Note the variety of facial types. Present are the envoys from Louis XIV of France. Kings of Dahomey were for centuries great sellers of their people into American slavery.

59

Raid on an African village for slaves.

second quarter of the seventeenth century Negroes were being released at the end of the period of indenture." (Virginia: The Old Dominion, pp. 88. 1937.)

Mary Stanard says, "The common belief that all Negroes brought to Virginia in the early period were slaves is an error." (Virginia's First Century, p. 159. 1928.) And Helen Catterall in "Judicial Cases Concerning American Slavery and the Negro," a Carnegie Institution publication, gives instances of the first Negroes serving for only a number of years. One is a court order of September 1625, ordering Lady Yardley, wife of the governor, to pay a Negro "40 pounds of good merchantable tobacco per month, as long as he remained with her." She adds, "In 1661 occurs the first reference in the statutes of Vir-

ginia to Negroes in the quality of slaves." (Vol. 1, pp. 16-41, 76-77. 1926). Some of these Negroes were from England itself. There were tens of thousands of Negroes there then. One such was Benjamin Lewis. Catterall names others.

The slaves for life were white convicts shipped from Europe. There were no prisons in that part of Africa from which the blacks came. Hence there were no convicts among them. The word "slavery" was at that time loosely used, too. Argall's proclamation of June 16, 1617, reads, "Goods to be sold for 25 per cent and tobacco for three shillings per pound — and not under or over — penalty three years' slavery to the colonies."

EARLY VIRGINIA NEGROES BOUGHT WHITE PEOPLE

Finally, Negroes bought white people in America as early as the 1640's. The United States Guide to Virginia, says, "In the 17th Century in Virginia, Negroes used to import white servants and received head rights to land. One of them, Richard Johnson, imported two white servants and received 100 acres of land on the Pungoteague River. In 1651 Johnson imported eleven and received 550 acres adjoining. About 1650, Benjamin Dole imported six and received 300 acres in Surry County, while others did the same." (p. 11, 1950.) About 1650, when Johnson's house was destroyed by fire and he claimed that he and his wife were "Inhabitants of Virginia" for thirty years, he was freed from county taxes.

J. H. Russell (white) in his doctor's thesis, "The Free Negro in Virginia," says, "Indeed for more than twenty years after the Negroes first appear in the courts there was no restriction upon their right to own white indentured servants." (p. 91).

E. S. Abdy, an English visitor to America in the 1830's, mentions two German families, who "were bought by free Negroes of which there is a fairly large number in Baltimore." (Journal, etc. Vol. 2, p. 56, 1835. Also Henninghausen, L. P. German Society of Maryland, p. 28, 1909).

These first Africans were variously called, Niger (from River Niger), Nigra, Neger, Ethiopian, Moor. Niger was pronounced not Ni-*jer* but Ni*gger*.

Virginia, as we see in Hening's Statutes, passed laws five times prohibiting the purchase of white people by free Negroes. Act 5, 1670, reads, "No Negro or Indian, though baptised and enjoying their own freedom shall be capable of any such purchase of Christians but yet not debarred from buying their own kind." By "Christian" was meant white. That a Negro was a Christian made no difference.

Other such laws were Act V, 1680; Act 49,

(xi) 1705; Act 9, October 1748; and Chapter 67; 1792. That of 1748 included Jews. "No Negro, Mulatto, Indian, although Christian, or any Jew, Moor, or Mohammedan . . . shall purchase any Christian servant." Statutes of Louisiana, Section 13, March 20, 1818, makes the same provision. Whites so bought should be set free immediately.

That these first Negroes could buy white people shows that in earliest America there was equal treatment for white and black according to class, that the first Virginians did not regard Negroes as a "race of slaves," or that as Thomas Carlyle, a great advocate of slavery said, "God has put into every white man's hand a whip to flog the black."

Discrimination came later. Why? There were at least two causes: the indispensability of the Negro and the humane attitude of some of the white colonists. And later, as the opposition of these latter — the abolitionists — grew, so tightened the laws to hold the Negro down. This, too, was the reason for using the Bible to prove that the blacks, "sons of Ham," were cursed by God and doomed to eternal servitude to whites, "sons of Japhet." Biblical argument was then the most powerful that could be used to alienate sympathy from any one group, white or black, as Jews and Catholics. In the case of the blacks here was a spectacle of the masters belittling and reviling their most useful and prized possession, a thing they wouldn't have done to a prize bull or horse.

THE SLAVE-TRADE NOT A RACIAL ISSUE

It is clear that the enslavement of Africans did not start as a racial issue. The great need then was for human beings to develop a new world and Africa had an unused reservoir of them. Had the Africans been white, instead, it would have made no difference, as we see from the captive whites of Europe, also shipped to the Americas. In fact, it was rather a religious issue. Chief Justice York, in restoring

Negro slavery in England, itself, in 1749, ruled that Africans and Indians were pagan and therefore bondsmen of Satan, thus it was right for Christians, who were servants of God, to enslave them. There was also the belief that by taking them out of Africa, they were being saved from eternal punishment in hell. Very pious Peter Faneuil, the richest American slave merchant, thanked God he was the instrument of bringing so many heathen into the light of the Gospel.

The abolitionists, on their part, asked whether the rum was "helping those heathen" still in Africa.

Of course, what was America's gain was Africa's great tragedy. The millions taken from her for 420 years (1440-1860), estimated by some at fifty millions, set her back tremendously. And that was not all, millions more were killed in slave raids. But it was a cruel age, an age when White Christians, in their excessive zeal, did not hesitate to inflict the most horrible barbarities on their fellow-whites to enforce "the word of God." In Puritan Massachusetts, the penalty for denying the word of God was death. Habitual non-churchgoers had their ears nailed to the church door. White women (Quakers) were stripped nude to the waist, tied to a cart's tail and whipped out of town; others had their tongues pierced by red-hot skewers, three were hanged on Boston Common. Albert Bushnell Hart gives a list of these tortures practiced by the devout.[7] "Witches" were hanged.

With white people treating other whites like that, what could be expected for Negroes and Indians? There were whites like John Woolman and Judge Sewall, who were deeply touched by their plight and fought for them. The latter said, "I essayed to prevent Negroes and Indians from being rated with cattle and I could not prevent it." Woolman said, "A heavy account lies against us as a civil society for the oppressions admitted to a people who did not injure us." The fact is that Negroes were better treated than poor whites since they were property.

Furthermore, the slave trade could not have

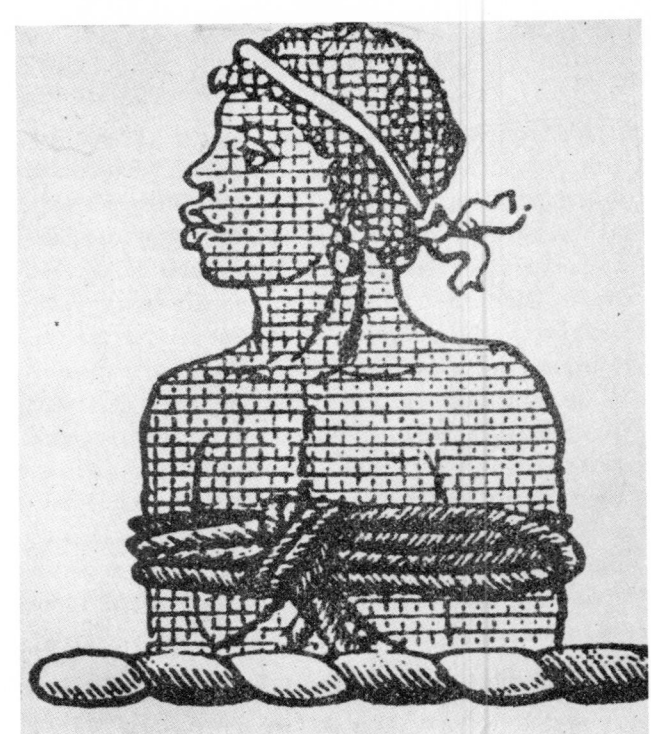

A bound African, Coat-of-Arms of Sir John Hawkins, 1532-1595, father of the modern slave-trade.

flourished as it did but for the cooperation of the Africans themselves. They were as eager to sell as the whites to buy. Stronger chiefs made war on the people of weaker ones for captives. Some grew very rich and lived in great luxury.

Two of the most notorious, Norbert Da Souza and John Ormond, were mulattoes with Christian rearing. Da Souza, prince of slavers, better known as "Cha-Cha," was born in Brazil; John Ormond had been educated in England. Da Souza lived in a palace in Dahomey like a maharajah. He had a harem drawn from many parts of the world. Captain Drake, American slave-dealer, said that Cha-Cha offered him the pick of them. "You shall have French, Spanish, Greek, Circassian, English, Dutch, Italian, Asiatic, American," or any other kind. (Autobiography of a Slave Smuggler, 1807-1856. See also Mayer B. Adventures of an African Slaver, Chapter 33; and Dow, G. F. Slave Ships and Slaving).

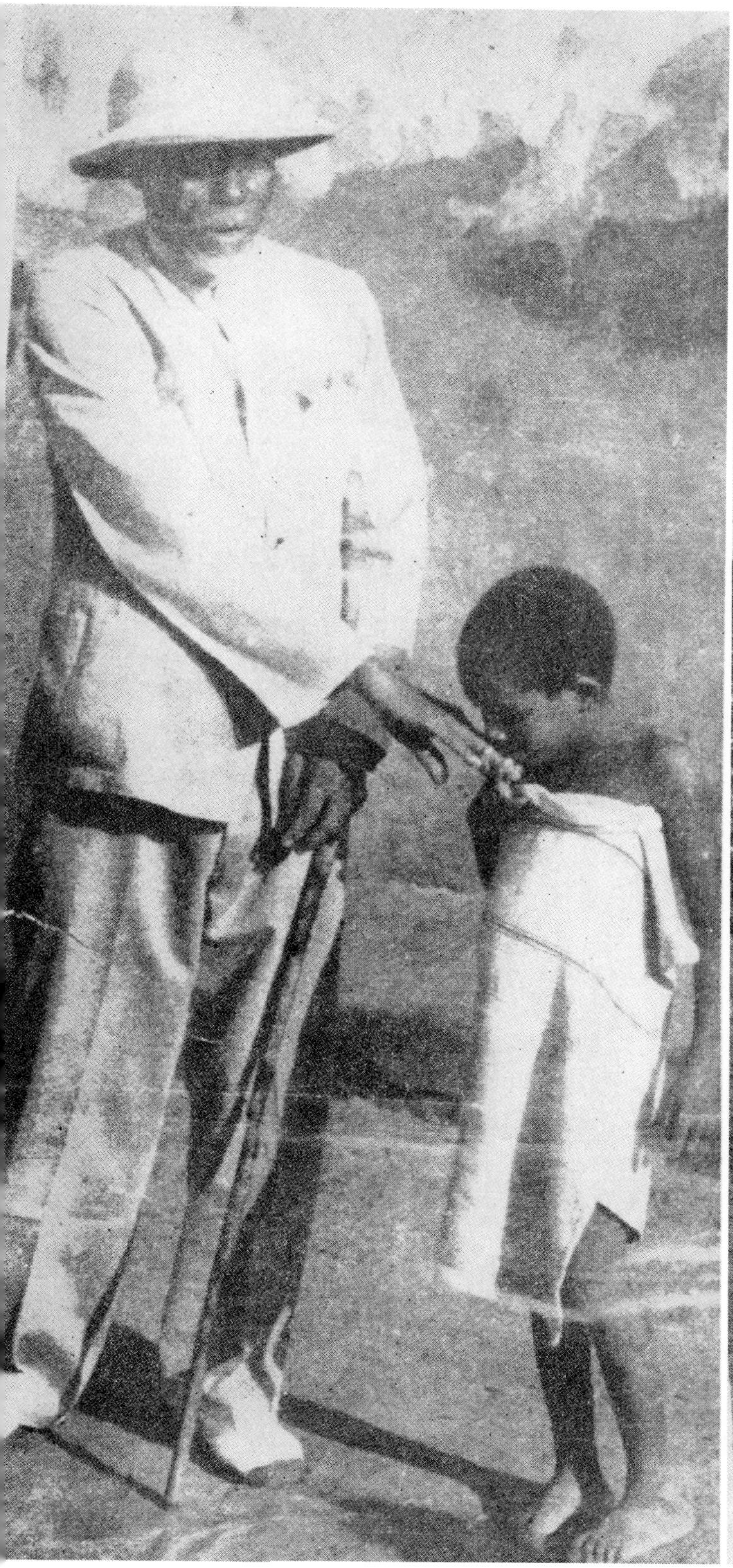

Souza (Cha-Cha) of Brazil, slave mogul of West Africa (see text).

Sebehr, most notorious of the slave-raiders.

Towing away the dead executed after a revolt in Senegal. Frenchsarcasm on the handiwork of civilization in Africa. (L'Illustration, Paris, April 11, 1891.) Scenes far more horrible than this occurred during thecenturies of the slave trade to America, which lasted until the 1860's.

"This Work of Civilization in Africa." Revolt against the French in Senegal. (L'Illustration, Paris, April 11, 1891.) Scenes like this occurred in Kenya during the recent Mau Mau revolt.

65

On this side of the Atlantic was Zephaniah Kingsley (1765-1843) of Florida with his East African Negro wife, Madegigne Jai. Both made an immense fortune from smuggling slaves.

Kingsley, who was related to Whistler's mother, was not only the richest man in Florida, but one of the richest in America, and a powerful political figure. His ships brought in many thousands of Negroes bought at $25 each in Africa and sold in America and the West Indies for $1,500. Once when U. S. coast-guards captured 350 contraband blacks on Kingsley's ships, the government not knowing what to do with them, turned them back to him. (Florida Historical Quarterly, Vol. 23, no. 3, p. 157, 1944-5; Corse, D. Key to the Sea Islands, p. 115, 1931; Kingsley Z. Treatise on Slavery 1829; and N. Y. Times, August 6, 1950).

Negro masters in the South weren't any kinder to their slaves than were the whites. Some had the reputation of being worse. They fought with the Confederacy to hold them and were bitter at their loss. When William Lloyd Garrison felicitated a Negro slaveholder in Charleston, South Carolina, over the emancipation, he replied, "What me happy at the freeing of me niggers."

Had the people of Africa been white and as poorly armed as the black then were, they would have been seized as slaves just the same. As we said, they were kidnapped by thousands in Europe and sold in America, a practice that continued in spite of the death penalty, after England restricted the exportation of white servants in order to counter the growing objections to the convicts she was sending.

Slavery was a cruel apprenticeship for all peoples in all ages. It was for the impoverished white immigrants to America and even more so for the African, since his difference in color permitted him to be set aside for continued exploitation even after his emancipation.

Incidentally, a very good reason why the slavery of the African succeeded and that of the Indian did so poorly was that the Indian was on his own soil with his people about him. The African wasn't. Brought from lands, as far east as Madagascar, he found himself isolated in a land to which he was a total stranger and among people of whose language he was utterly ignorant. Even other Africans on a plantation might be total strangers to him in ways and language. He had, therefore, almost no choice but to adapt himself to the new life forced on him. Furthermore, the masters, while keeping him illiterate, took care to pour into his mind such Christian doctrine and promise of the hereafter that would make him submissive. Slavery of the African in South Africa had succeeded only because the slaves had been brought from distant parts, even as far as Malaya. Native South Africans as the Zulus and Basutos fought the Europeans even more fiercely than the Indians did American whites.

In short, slavery of itself was no disgrace to anyone, white or black. It is no more a disgrace than it is to hand over your money to an armed robber; or to pay ransom to a kidnapper. And when the descendants of such a violated individual or group are considered debased because their forefathers were so treated that sums up to the last word in idiotic thinking. Moreover, some of the greatest white men were once slaves. Plato was slave to Anniceris; Epictetus to Epaphroditus; Captain John Smith, real founder of Virginia, was a slave in Africa; and so was Cervantes, author of the immortal Don Quixote. For the Aframerican to have arisen from slavery and its harsh aftermath to his present position, such as it is, is a real credit. One is reminded of a story told by Dan Crawford, famous missionary, of an ex-slave he met in Africa, who by his own energy had risen to a position of power and affluence. Once, when a white man proud of his country and ancestry boasted of them to him, the former slave replied, "Oh, white man, you're proud of your *descent;* I'm proud of my *ascent."* The man who boasts of his ancestry is, as Josh Billings said, "like a potato plant; the best part of him is underground."

COMING OF THE AFRICANS

Popular history starts the Negro in the United States in 1619. In 1919 there was a tercentary observance of it at Jamestown. But this date, based on a letter by John Rolfe, to Sir Edwin Sandys, is 107 years too late. Negroes first came with the Spaniards, who were the real founders of the United States. The first of them was Ponce de Leon, who landed in Florida, Easter Sunday, 1512. There seems to be no record of the number of persons in his expedition or of their ethnic origin. But Salvador Brau does mention one Negro, Pedro Mexia.[1] Mexia, he says was a "mulatto" and "one of the companions" of Ponce de Leon.

However, it is safe to assume that there were other Negroes in that expedition as there is abundant evidence of their being with later Spanish explorers as De Aviles (1523), Hernando de Soto, Narvaez, d'Ayllon, Coronado, Tristan de Luna, and Menendez.

Another important fact: Spaniards of that time were much mixed with Negroes and had been from before the Moorish invasion of 711 A.D. Simon Bolivar reminded Spanish-Americans of his time that they were not "pure" European to begin with. "Spain, itself," he said, "had ceased to be European by its African blood, its institutions and character."[2] Napoleon, or someone before him, had rightly said, "Africa begins at the Pyrenees." In short, the United States was not founded by a "pure" Nordic race.

THE RACE FOR A CONTINENT

Spain, in its efforts to head off the English, French, and Dutch, began a feverish attempt to be first in all parts of North America. In 1526, d'Ayllon, with a party of 500, mostly Negroes, and a few women, landed at St. Elena, in the Carolinas and started northward till they reached the mouth of the James River, Virginia, where they started the colony of San Miguel, the exact site on which the English founded Jamestown eighty-three years later. But the colony was a failure because the Negroes revolted. Justin Winsor in his "Narrative and Critical History of America" says, "Ayllon . . . began the settlement of San Miguel where the English in the next century founded Jamestown . . . The Negro slaves first introduced here" did the "heaviest portion of the toil, cruelly oppressed," they revolted. "Such were the stormy beginnings of Spanish rule in Virginia."[3]

At this point, two assumptions are in order. First, since the Negroes revolted they might have stayed behind in Virginia. John Rolfe, if he knew of the Spanish attempt, did not mention it. He was speaking of the English colony. And had the Spaniards succeeded in establishing their colony, the English might not have been able to settle there later. And with success there, the Spaniards might have been able to hold on to the Carolinas, Louisiana, and Florida. Virginia was to be for the next century England's chief foothold in North America. This revolt of the Negroes was undoubtedly instrumental in shaping the destiny of the English-speaking peoples in North America.

The next Spanish expedition to the United States was that of De Narvaez in 1527. Shipwreck, attacks by Indians, and privations, killed all but four of its members. One of these was a Negro, Estevanico, who was to write his name high in the history of the South-West. Starting from Florida, after nine years of incredible hardships, they crossed the continent and reached Lower California. One of them, Cabeza de Vaca, told the story. In this journey they crossed the Mississippi 150 years before it was "discovered" by La Salle. Following this expedition, Cortes sailed up the Gulf of California and Cabrillo and Ferrer claimed California for Spain, 1542-43.

Estevanico's next exploit was to lead an expedition from Mexico City that discovered Arizona and New Mexico in 1540. Two years later, Negro settlers are recorded in New Mexico, one of them a Franciscan monk, who taught Christianity to the Indians.

Spaniards and Negroes continued their exploration to the west. Into Colorado, Missouri, Kansas, Utah, they went. Coronado reached Utah in 1540, or 307 years before the Mormons. Cabrillo and Ferrer claimed all that region for Spain. In 1541, DeSoto reached Tennessee and camped on the site of Memphis, then into Kansas, which he called Quiviria. Here the Negroes saved the horses during a terrific hailstorm by holding blankets over them. On the return trip to Mexico, one Negro member of that expedition stayed behind with the Indians in Alabama, and was the first settler from the Old World in that state.[4]

The settlers in these areas were mostly Negroes, half-breed Indians, and a few Spaniards. What Priestley says of New Mexico was true of most of the others. "Here a handful of Indians, half-breeds and mulattoes, led by a few civilians, missionaries and soldiers were engaged in a highly dramatic episode in Spain's long effort to subdue and hold a continent." He adds, "All the cities of Spanish America had such origin. Little farms — small self-sufficing empires — filled with a half-breed and mulatto element."[5]

In 1565, when Menendez started the building of St. Augustine, Negroes did most of the hard work, the Indians being unfit or unwilling for it. They built the houses, the fort, the streets. "This most ancient city of our modern Black Belt owed much to the labor of Negro slaves," says Priestley. ". . . A small party of them engaged for two years in making wooden platforms for the artillery of the fort of old St. Augustine. Black hands set up the first smith's forge and there made needed repairs while two of the best Negroes were sent to St. Elena to help the soldiers saw out the boards." The United States Guide (Florida) says also, "Negroes have had an important place in St. Augustine's history. In the first hospital built here in 1597, a Negro woman waited on patients . . ."

Fort Marion, oldest landmark in the United States was also built by Negro labor brought from Cuba.

With the soldier settlers into California went Negroes "to perform the hard tasks." In 1769, San Diego and San Francisco were founded, San Jose in 1770, and Los Angeles, September 1781. Of the forty-six persons in the founding of Los Angeles, twenty-four were Negroes, according to Bancroft. "A strange mixture of Indian and Negro," he says, "with here and there a trace of the Spaniard."[6] The Negroes remained a power in California.

We shall later see the Negroes and the part they played in bringing California into the Union.

NOTES

1. Le Colonisación de Puerto Rico, p. 215.

2. Blanco Fombona R., Simon Bolivar: Discoursos y proclamos, p. 47. 1913.

3. Vol. 2, p. 241, 1886.

4. Pickett, A. J., A. History of Alabama, Vol. 1, p. 20. 1851.

5. Coming of the White Man, 1492-1848, pp. 73-4, 51, 58m 98. 1939.

6. Bancroft, H. H. Works. Vol. 18 (History of California, Vol. 1, p. 345, 1884), gives their names: Jose Antonio Navarro, mestizo, wife, 42, mulatress, 3 children; Basilio Rosas, Indian, 68, wife mulatress, 6 children; Antonio Mesa, Negro, 38, wife, mulatress, 2 children; Manuel Camero, mulatto, 30, Spanish and Negro; Luis Quintero,

Negro, 55, wife, mulatress, 5 children; Jose Morano, mulatto, 22, wife, mulatress; and very likely also, Antonio Miranda, Spanish and Negro. Other sources of Negroes with the Spaniards are: Narrative of Cabeza de Vaca; reprinted 1922; Negro Companions of the Spanish Explorers, American Anthropologist, n. s. 4, 217-228. 1902; Hodge, F. W., Spanish Explorers in the U. S., p. 333. 1925; Colonial Records of Florida No. 5, Vol. 2, p. 323; Hosmer, J. K., Short History of the Mississippi Valley, pp. 25-27. 1906; Bolton H., Spanish Borderlands p. 16, 1919-21; Bandelier, A F., History of the Southwestern Pacific, pp.

107-77. 1891. Original Narratives of Early American History—Spanish Explorers in the Southern States.

See also: Dispatches of Spanish officials on the Free Negro Settlement of Gracia Real, Fla., 1688-1759. April 1924.

Note: Capt. John Smith said the Indians who came to attack him in 1607 had "black and partly-colored" men among them. They could have been the descendants of the Africans that rebelled in 1526. (Nat. Geog. Mag., May 1957, p. 593.)

VIRGINIA, NEW ENGLAND, AND NEW YORK

The first batch of Negroes under the English arrived in Virginia in 1619. They were exchanged for food (victualles). The story is that they were brought by a Dutch ship but this was to hide the fact that they had been smuggled from the West Indies by an English ship, the *Treasurer,* owned by Lord Warwick. This was resented by the Spaniards, the Dutch, and the French, from whom the English had been stealing Africans. Historians, as Alexander Brown, have gone into this matter carefully.[1]

Who were these first Negroes? One thing is certain they weren't slaves for life, because we find some owning white servants. It is likely they were refugees from the Spanish colonies and had gone on boar dor were inveigled on the *Treasurer.* On arriving in the colony, they were probably forced to serve a number of years just as most whites. At that time "slavery" was used for anyone sentenced to serve a time for offenses.

At that time, too, nearly all in the colony were practically "servants" manipulated in the interests of the London Virginia Company and held to a certain number of years of seritude. Thomas Jefferson thought these first Negroes lived on "the same footing as the whites, who, as well as themselves, were under the absolute direction of the president" of the company. In the muster-rolls of the colony, taken after the Indian massacre of 1622, the Negroes are listed as "servants" like the whites. One freeman was

William, son of Anthony and Isabel Tucker, born 1624, the first known Negro child born under English rule in America.

NEW ENGLAND

Negroes reached New England soon after the arrival of the Pilgrim Fathers. John Josselyn, an English ship captain, tells how on October 2, 1638, he heard an African woman, the property of Mr. Maverick, came under his window and cried in a loud voice against her being forced by her master "to go to bed" with his young Negro man, as Maverick was "desirous of having a breed of Negroes." It appears she was a queen in her own country and didn't want to bed with one of inferior birth.[2]

A French Protestant refugee, in Boston, wrote in 1684, "You may also own Negroes and Negresses; there is not a house in Boston, however small be its means, that it has not one or two. There are those that have five or six and all make a good living."[3]

The New England slave merchants used to bring home those of their cargoes that the West India and Southern planters would not take and sell them at reduced prices. In 1770, New England had 16,034 Negroes with Boston having the largest number.

Whites and blacks worked in the New England fields together. Some of these whites had been sold on the block beside Negroes. An advertisement in the Boston Gazette, September 7 & 14, 1741, reads, "Just imported from Ireland and to be sold on board the ship, *Virtue,* John Seymour, master, in the harbour of Boston, a parcel of menservants, chiefly tradesmen."

There are several noted Negroes of whom we shall hear later, among them Jethro, who saved the Plymouth Colony from massacre, during King Philip's War, on July 11, 1676; Lucy Terry, first Negro poet, and one of America's earliest, whose description of the massacre of the people of Deerfield, Massachusetts is said to be the most vivid account of that affair extant; and Onesimus, an African, slave of Rev. Cotton Mather, who gave information that checked smallpox, the worst evil of that time (1721) and had a great effect not only in America but in England.

Another prosperous Negro in New London, Connecticut, Robert Jacklin, did not fare so well in 1717. He bought land which entitled him to have a voice in municipal affairs. The townspeople petitioned the General Assembly to prohibit Negroes from buying land without first getting its consent.[4]

In Providence, R. I., Eleanor Alldridge, born a slave in 1785, who bought her freedom and then a home, was so well-liked that several whites wrote poems in praise of her while still alive. Her autobiography went into three editions.[5]

Pomps Pond, Andover, Mass., was named after a Negro who had served through the Revolution and was given a discharge.

More about the prosperous Negroes of the period—caterers, mechanics, artists, and others—of New England and elsewhere will be given in a later chapter.

NEW YORK

Negroes might have been with the Dutch in the founding of New Amsterdam (New York) in 1623. It was a colony of the Dutch West India Company with its base in the West Indies. The Dutch were in Surinam (Guiana) as early as 1598. It is possible that they brought Negroes from the West Indies with them at its settlement. One Negro, Black Harry, declared that he knew New York when it had only three houses in it, according to a newspaper of 1758. It was said that he was then a hundred and twenty years old and could do a good days' work when he was a hundred.[6]

A more certain instance of an old resident is a petition, April 9, 1663, for freeing "an old and sickly black woman who had served as a slave since the year 1628."[7] Another record is that of the arrival of nineteen Negroes in 1633. Still another is that of a bill sent in by five Negroes, November 19, 1635, for work done for the colony. These, it is clear, were not slaves.

An order of October 25, 1634, allots "to each patroon twelve black men and women . . . for the advancement of the colonies in New Netherland." The strongest Negroes were used as defense against the Indians. One order reads, "The Director shall employ hereunto as many of the strongest and most active Negroes as he can conveniently spare."

Negroes helped grow the crops, felled the trees, and built the fort at what is now the Battery. They lived at what is now Seventy-Fifth Street and the East River and sailed down in canoes to Wall Street to grow the wheat, cabbage, and potatoes. They swept the streets, and cleared them of dead hogs.

They were also the hangmen. They lashed offenders, white and black, male and female. One Pieter sent in his bill for whipping two Dutchmen, January 31, 1662, for stealing cabbages. Jan de Neger sent in his for 38 florins for hanging Wolf Nyssen.[8]

In 1644, nineteen Negroes were freed, to be followed by others, but their children remained in bondage. These freed ones were given land. Among them was Emanuel de Groot, who with ten families founded an agricultural settlement in 1635, now known as the Bowery, but then as

Manhattan Indians as the Dutch found in New York in the 1620's. (Museum of the City of New York).

the "Negro's Cagee." This was the first extensive clearing outside the original settlement. New York, foremost metropolis in the world, was then largely wilderness. Another early settler was Francisko.[9] He was one of the first property owners of Brooklyn in the area called Boswick. He is listed as one of the original patentees.

The names of Negro landholders as given by A. Phelps-Stokes in his "Iconography of Manhattan Island," and by other historians are many. Domingo Antony owned land on Canal Street, west of the Bowery; Cateline Antony on what is now Pell Street. Much of the land about Canal Street, Astor Place, City Hall Park, and the Woolworth Building was owned by them. Annie d'Angola owned the site of the original

Madison Square Garden. Simon Congo was allotted land, December 15, 1644. Solomon Pieters owned thirty acres at Twenty-Third and Fifth Avenue,[10] now the site of the Flatiron Building in the heart of New York. So many patents were given in the vicinity of the Fresh Water Pond, the area became known as "The Negro's Land." The Angolas were the richest Negro family. A marriage in this family, Antony van Angola and Lucie d'Angola, on May 5, 1644, is the first in Negro life to be recorded. There was no color discrimination. Negroes drank in the same bars with the whites, worshiped in the same churches and were buried in the same graveyards. At Pinkster (Pentecost) when the Negroes had a full week's holiday parading and dancing in the streets and taverns, the whites

Fort Amsterdam, now New York. From a rare print made in 1651. (Museum of the City of New York).

joined in.[11] Permission had to be asked of the authorities to flog a slave. On January 4, 1659, Pieter Vander Veen received permission to flog one of his female slaves, but changed his mind about doing it. In August 1664, the Negroes of Brooklyn and New York grieved along with the whites at the departure of their white pastor, the Rev. Samuel Drisius. On January 6, 1640, several Negroes confessed to killing a white man, probably in self-defense. Lots were drawn as to which of them should be hanged for the deed. It fell on one Manuel de Gerrit, called "The Giant," but under Manuel's huge bulk the rope snapped. The Negro hangman started to string him up again, when the audience, white and colored, pleaded so hard for him, he was pardoned.

The Negroes were highly trusted, and the colony prospered by their diligence. Peter Stuyvesant was already quoted as saying, "Everything is by God's blessing in good condition and in consequence of the employment of Negro slaves." In 1660, he wrote his secretary, "Let the free and the company's Negroes keep good watch on my bowery."

So far, Negroes had been coming from the West Indies, but in 1652 merchants were given the right to bring them direct from Africa. A fatal step this was for the Dutch — one that was to lead to direct surrender of the colony to England in 1664. When the *Gideon* arrived with a cargo of blacks, there was a shortage of food and with these extra mouths to feed, the supply ran out for everybody. The Dutch were forced to surrender, when a British fleet arrived in the harbor. Peter Stuyvesant, himself, gave

Africans in the building of New York under the Dutch. From an old print.

Francisko, first settler of Brooklyn, N. Y. (From reproduction in the Brooklyn Eagle).

this as the cause. He said, "the 300 to 400 half-starved Negroes alone, exclusive of the garrison, required 100 skepels of wheat."[12]

Here, again, as in Virginia in 1526, the presence of the Negro favored the English.

And now, "the dark aspect of slavery, which had been softened to a smile" underwent a change. Self-respecting Negroes, who had been made to feel they were members of the colony, found laws restricting their freedom. They were forbidden to engage in any sport, to ride a horse, carry any weapon, to appear at night without a lantern, all under penalty of forty lashes. None was to enter a white church; nor four weeks from October 1682 was "to be buried in Trinity Churchyard," where all, regardless of color, were formerly interred. They were given their own cemetery at Broadway and Centre Street.

Manumitting a slave was made very difficult. It was ordered, "No Negro, Indian, or mulatto, that shall hereafter be made free, shall enjoy, hold or possess any Houses, Lands, Tenements, Heriditaments within this colony, but the same shall escheat to Her Majesty, Her Heirs and Successors." Anyone who freed a slave was "required to pay the slave twenty pounds a years during the slave's lifetime."[13] The reason was, "The free Negroes of this colony are an idle, slothful people and prove very often a charge on the place where they are."

Edward Thompson, a naval officer, wrote at that time, "The laborious people in general are Guinea Negroes who lie under particular restraint from the attempts they have made to massacre the inhabitants for their liberty." J. G. Wilson rightly says, "Slavery has nowhere presented itself in a more odious form than in early New York."[14]

From a gay, laughing people, the Negroes had become angry and revengeful. Judge Saffron called them in 1701, "Cowardly and cruel those Blacks innate . . . Libidinous, Deceitful, false and rude. The Spume, Issue of Ingratitude." One of them struck the mayor. But the English continued to bring them by the thousands from Africa and the West Indies.

The Negroes, who had made common cause with the Dutch against the Indians now began to plot with the latter, and an order of 1705 forbade Negroes to go north of Saratoga, where the Indians were. Actual fear of the blacks began and with cause. Of the some 880 families in the city, nearly everyone had from one to five Negroes.[15] The weapon of the blacks was fire. Homes went up in flames sometimes three in a night. One, Lysbeth Anthonissen, was strangled for setting her master's home afire. The fort, principal defense of the city, was burnt to the ground. On April 7, 1712, the Coromantees, a fierce African people, seized what guns, swords, and hatchets they could, and rushed about the city setting fires and killing the white occupants as they ran out. Quaco, the leader, and twenty others, were broken on the wheel and then burnt at a slow fire.

A
JOURNAL
OF THE
PROCEEDINGS
IN
The Detection of the Conspiracy
FORMED BY

Some *White* People, in Conjunction with *Negro* and other *Slaves*,

FOR

Burning the City of NEW-YORK in AMERICA,
And Murdering the Inhabitants.

Which Conspiracy was partly put in Execution, by Burning His Majesty's House in Fort GEORGE, within the said City, on Wednesday the Eighteenth of *March*, 1741. and setting Fire to several Dwelling and other Houses there, within a few Days succeeding. And by another Attempt made in Profecution of the same infernal Scheme, by putting Fire between two other Dwelling-Houses within the said City, on the Fifteenth Day of *February*, 1742 ; which was accidentally and timely discovered and extinguished.

CONTAINING,

I. A NARRATIVE of the Trials, Condemnations, Executions, and Behaviour of the several Criminals, at the Gallows and Stake, with their *Speeches* and *Confessions* ; with Notes, Obfervations and Reflections occasionally interfperfed throughout the Whole.

II. AN APPENDIX, wherein is fet forth some additional Evidence concerning the said Conspiracy and Confpirators, which has come to Light since their Trials and Executions.

III. LISTS of the several Perfons (Whites and Blacks) committed on Account of the Conspiracy ; and of the several Criminals executed; and of those tranfported, with the Places whereto.

By the Recorder of the City of NEW-YORK.

Quid faciant Domini, audent cum talia Fures? Virg. Ecl.

NEW-YORK:
Printed by *James Parker*, at the New Printing-Office, 1744.

TITLE-PAGE OF THE PROCEEDINGS AGAINST THE NEGROES

VOL. III. 5

Oppressed whites and Negroes join in reprisals against their masters in a great conspiracy, New York City, March 1741.

The Negroes also found ready allies in some of the white semi-slaves who were very badly treated, too. The latter were also sold on the block at the slave-market in Wall Street.

The white masters were kept in constant fear. Then, in 1741, came the discovery of "The Great Negro Plot"[16] to set the whole city afire and massacre the whites. Four white plotters were hanged; 14 Negroes burnt alive; 18 hanged; and 71 shipped to the West Indies. The city,

thankful for its narrow escape, proclaimed September 24 that year as a day of thanksgiving. The great efficiency of the New York Fire Department started then. The firing of homes continued. The next year, Tom, a slave, caught setting fires, confessed another plot to burn the city, and was burnt alive. In 1775 came another big plot, this time aided by the Indians. Orders were given to shoot any Negro or Indian out at night, on sight. Possession of any arms meant

Burning alive of Quaco, leader of a plot against slavery, in New York in 1741. Soldiers are keeping back the crowd.

death. In the militia they could serve only as drummers.

A notable exception to this treatment was Dr. Luycas Santomee of the rich Pieters family, and the first Negro physician in the United States. Already a big landowner under the Dutch, he was allotted more acres for his services by Governor Nichols, October 18, 1667.[17]

Unable to keep them in check, the authorities started to christianize and educate incoming blacks, especially the fierce Coramantees. The first school for them was founded September 15, 1760. But the resentment of the blacks continued and when the British troops arrived during the first days of the Revolution, they went over to them in thousands. The British offered them freedom and kept their word. At the end of the war they took them to Nova Scotia and settled them there. Incidentally, the British later had to pay indemnity to their American owners.

But some did side with the Americans, foremost among them one of the richest and most influential New Yorkers, Samuel Francis (later called Sam Fraunces), a West Indian Negro, who was thanked by Congress for his services in the Revolution and of whom more will be said.

Another was Mary Simpson, who is credited with being the first to celebrate Washington's birthday publicly. She had a little store in the Wall Street district, where she sold milk, butter, eggs, and home-made cakes and pies. Washington used to pass her place daily. On his birthdays she would bake a cake — the Washington Cake — put his picture in her window and invite the neighborhood to join in the celebration.[18]

76

NOTES

1. Genesis of the United States, Vol. 2, p. 824. 1890; and First Republic in America, p. 218, 1898; Penna. Magazine of History, Vol. 9, pp. 154-55, 1865.

2. Two Voyages to New England, Mass. Hist. Coll., ser. 3, Vol. 3, p. 231. 1833.

3. Winsor, J., Memorial History of Boston, p. 488. 1888.

4. Morgan F. Connecticut, Vol. 1, p. 504, 1904.

5. McDougall H., Memoirs of Eleanor Alldridge. 1938. Green, L., Negro in Colonial New England. 1942. Negro in New England, Harvard Graduate Maga., Vol. 34, pp. 583-89. 1926.

6. Watson, F., Annals of New York, p. 268. 1846; Yates and Moulton, History of New York, p. 373. 1824.

7. Calendar of Historical Documents (Dutch MSS.) N. Y. State, Vol. 1, p. 216.

8. For extensive documentation on Negroes in all their activities see: I. N. Phelps Stokes, Iconography of Manhattan Island, 1498-1909, Vol. 6 and index in Vol. 6, p. 502-3. 1915-28.

9. Priestley, N. I., Coming of the White Man, p. 328. 1929.

10. Stokes, Iconography, Vol. 6, p. 107.

11. De Voe, T. F., The Market Book, pp. 922, 344-5, 370. 1862. Roosevelt, Theo., Historic Towns (N.Y.), p. 96, 1891.

12. New York Colonial Documents, II, p. 430. Answer to the West India Company.

13. Stokes, Iconography, Vol. 4, April 7, 1713. Colonial Laws of New York, I, 761.

14. Wilson, H. G., History of New York, Vol. 2, p. 252.

15. Valentine, J. G., gives the names of these families and the number of Negroes with them. History of the City of New York, pp. 344-365. 1851.

16. Horsmanden, D., Negro Conspiracy of New York, 1851.

17. Stokes, I. N. P. Vol. 6, p. 75, 502. Santomee was better known as Pieters.

18. Moss, F., The American Metropolis, pp. 154-5. 1897. N. Y. Herald Tribune, February 23, 1942.

Other works on New York:

The Negro in New York prior to 1860. Howard Review, Vol. 1, June 1923, pp. 1-64.

Ottley, R., New World A-Coming. 1943.

THE FRENCH-LOUISIANA TERRITORY

Negroes were with the first French pioneers in Louisiana and Florida. In 1580, two with them were killed in a skirmish at San Mateo, Florida, one of whom "fought very well." They were with La Salle in 1682 when he claimed Louisiana for France. In 1712, Louis XIV granted to Anthony Crozat the right to send one ship annually to Guinea for slaves. In 1719, 250 were landed and thereafter came in numbers. They were at the founding of New Orleans in 1718 and accompanied the voyageurs in the exploration of the Louisiana territory, which extended from the Gulf of Mexico to the Great Lakes and westward to the Rockies, and was 880,000 square miles in extent.

Of the early Negroes, the most historically significant is Jean Baptiste Pointe de Sable.[1] Leaving Haiti at a time when France's ambition was to occupy the basin of the Mississippi and to make that together with Louisiana and Canada one vast empire, he landed in Louisiana and made the long trek to the borders of Lake Michigan, where he started trading with the Indians and later built the first house on the site of what is now Chicago, in 1778. He laid out a considerable estate and married an Indian woman by whom he had two children. He is in reality the founder of what is now America's second largest city. Of his ancestry there is no doubt. The Indians said, "The first white man who settled here was a Negro." A model of his cabin was featured in the city's international exposition of 1932. A tablet erected by the Daughters of the American Revolution reads, "Site of first house erected about 1778 by Jean Baptiste Point de Sable, a Negro from Santo Domingo" (Haiti's first name). R. Shackleton says, "The first settler of Chicago as distin-

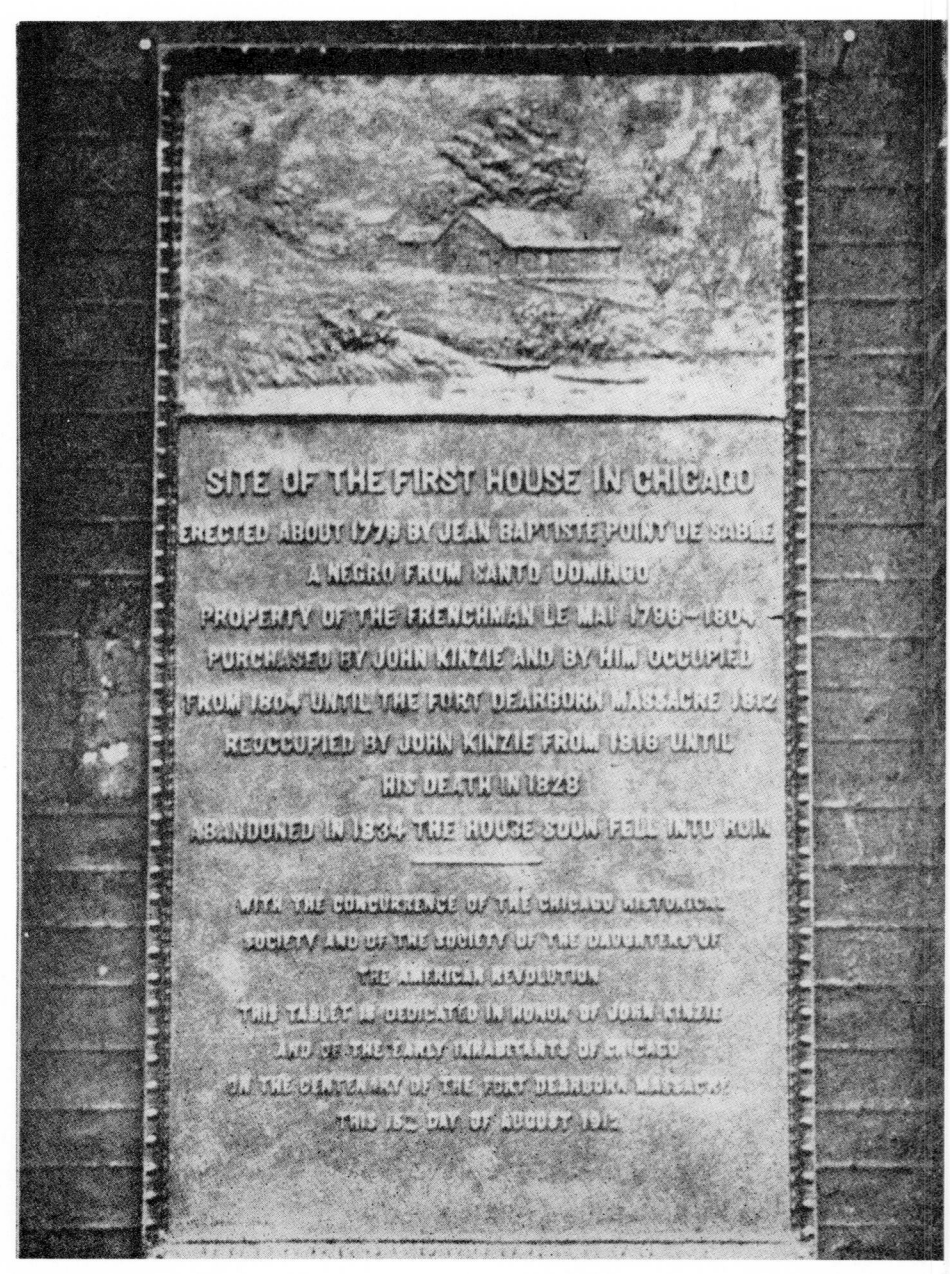

SITE OF THE FIRST HOUSE IN CHICAGO
ERECTED ABOUT 1779 BY JEAN BAPTISTE POINT DE SABLE
A NEGRO FROM SANTO DOMINGO
PROPERTY OF THE FRENCHMAN LE MAI 1796–1804
PURCHASED BY JOHN KINZIE AND BY HIM OCCUPIED
FROM 1804 UNTIL THE FORT DEARBORN MASSACRE 1812
REOCCUPIED BY JOHN KINZIE FROM 1816 UNTIL
HIS DEATH IN 1828
ABANDONED IN 1834 THE HOUSE SOON FELL INTO RUIN

WITH THE CONCURRENCE OF THE CHICAGO HISTORICAL
SOCIETY AND OF THE SOCIETY OF THE DAUGHTERS OF
THE AMERICAN REVOLUTION
THIS TABLET IS DEDICATED IN HONOR OF JOHN KINZIE
AND OF THE EARLY INHABITANTS OF CHICAGO
ON THE CENTENARY OF THE FORT DEARBORN MASSACRE
THIS 15th DAY OF AUGUST 1912

Tablet marking site of first house in Chicago. (For picture of reproduction of house see Sex and Race, Vol. 2, p. 174).

Portrait said to be that of Point de Sable, founder of the City of Chicago.

Negro-Indian Chief, Oshkosh. Oshkosh, Wisconsin is named for him.

guished from explorers and temporary abiders was, as Chicagoans, themselves, express it, "a black man, a West Indian Negro." De Sable's great-grandson, Joseph Jeremie, distinguished Haitian statesman, who died in 1958 at the age of ninety-eight, has written about him.[2]

In 1723, 500 Negroes from Haiti were sent to work the lead mines of Missouri.[3] These, with others later sent, were, with 200 whites from France, the first settlers of that state. They were among the first in Wisconsin, too. Jesuits there and in Illinois used them as farmers, blacksmiths, carpenters, brewers, and masons. These blacks amalgamated with the Pawnee Indians,

who were also reduced to slavery. The word "Pawnee" (Pani) came to be synonymous with "slave". The great Indian chief, Oshkosh, who gave his name to a Wisconsin town, was of this Negroid stock. His son-in-law, John DuBe (DuBay) was described as a "black Ethiopian."[4]

Count Arese, who visited the Middle West in 1837 tells of the voyageurs he saw there and describes them as "well-assorted for giving an idea of the shades of human skin in Europeans, creoles, mulattoes, half-breeds and what not."[5] In 1791, more than a third of the population of upper Louisiana, exclusive of Indians, was Negro—698 to 1998 white. In Louisiana, itself,

Negroes predominated. A census of 1785 gives 14,215 white, and 17,847 mulattoes and blacks. Octoroons and even quadroons were then counted as white. In 1762 in New Orleans, those of Negro strain predominated, about 1,300 white to 3,065 Negroes of whom 1900 were free.

MARYLAND

Maryland's history begins with her first 200 pilgrims who arrived in "The Ark and The Dove," from Gravesend, England, in 1634. They came by the way of Barbados, where they picked up one or more Negroes, one of whom was Matthias Sousa, or Tousa "mulatto," ship captain.[6] It is believed that he piloted the ship from there to Chesapeake Bay. In any case, he was a man of some importance in the colony, and was later given a ship to trade with the Indians. In a painting at the State House in Annapolis he is shown standing beside George Calvert, the first Lord Baltimore. Semmes[6] mentions him as one of the captains of that time. Two other Negro settlers were John Price, "black" and Francis Peres, "mulatto." They were not slaves. Slavery was first introduced about March 7, 1642, when John Skinner delivered "fourteen Negro men slaves and three women slaves."

Negro Mountain, highest point on U. S. Route 40 in Maryland, is named for a Negro who fought the Indians there under a company commanded by Colonel Thomas Cresap and was killed.

It is possible that Barbara Bladen, wife of Governor Bladen, was of Negro ancestry. She was described by William Black in 1744 "as of a black complexion . . . but very agreeable."[7] Of course, very dark persons were called "black" at that time in England, but this is significant as it was happening in Maryland, where there were so many black Negroes around. She was the daughter of Sir Thomas Janssen of Surrey, England. At that time, there were many Negroes in England and they intermarried freely with

Maryland Drummer Boy. Detail from portrait of Charles Calvert by John Hesselius in 1761.

whites. Judge Montfaucon, who is described as "an indisputable mulatto," was the founder of "a grand English family" of the 18th century, and very rich.[7a]

80

WASHINGTON, D. C.

The earliest history of the Negro in the District of Columbia belongs to Maryland and Virginia of which it was then a part. One of its most distinguished citizens at this time, regardless of color, was Benjamin Banneker[S] (1731-1806), well-to-do grandson of a white mistress, Mollie Welsh, who had married one of her slaves. He was one of the leading mathematicians and astronomers of the new nation. He published an annual almanac prepared by himself and correctly predicted the eclipse of 1798. Thomas Jefferson thought so highly of his almanac that he sent a copy to Marquis de Condorcet, president of the Academy of Science in Paris. William Pitt, then Prime Minister of England, exhibited it in the House of Commons as proof of what Negroes could do when given an opportunity.

In 1789, George Washington appointed him to assist Major Pierre L'Enfant in laying out the capital. Thomas Jefferson in a letter, August 30, 1791, tells how "he procured him to be employed in laying out the new Federal City." But before the work was half finished, L'Enfant left in a huff, taking all the plans with him. Major Ellicott was appointed to succeed him. On Banneker fell the task of drawing up a new set of plans, which were so well executed, that he won Ellicott's highest praise. The Georgetown Weekly Ledger, March 12, 1791, called him "an Ethiopian, whose abilities as surveyor and astronomer already prove that Mr. Jefferson's concluding that that race of men were void of mental endowment, was without foundation." Jefferson had said that earlier.

Banneker was a pioneer in another field, also —Peace. In his Almanac of 1793, he proposed that the United States appoint a Secretary of Peace. He wrote: "A Plan for A Peace Office of the United States. Let a Secretary of Peace be appointed who shall be perfectly free from all the present absurd and vulgar European prejudices . . . The Son of Man came into the

Benjamin Banneker's
PENNSYLVANIA, DELAWARE, MARYLAND, AND VIRGINIA
ALMANAC,
FOR THE
YEAR of our LORD 1795;
Being the Third after Leap-Year.

BANNAKER.

PHILADELPHIA:
Printed for WILLIAM GIBBONS, Cherry Street

Benjamin Banneker, leading American astronomer and mathematician of his time. Completed plans for the laying-out of Washington, D. C. (see text).

world not to destroy men's lives but to save them."

In 1955 that was the unofficial title given Harold Stassen, when appointed by President Eisenhower as roving ambassador to promote friendlier relations among the nations.

SOUTH CAROLINA

Negroes, as was said, were with the Spanish pioneers in the Carolinas. When Charles Town was settled in 1670, there were only three Negroes with the English. But the chance gift of a bag of seed rice to a Carolina planter by a ship captain was to bring them in thousands. By 1699, a letter of Edward Randolph says there were 5,000. By 1710, they had so outnumbered the whites, that the latter began to be afraid and passed an act to encourage the bringing in of white servants. A letter of the time says there were "40,000 Negroes in South Carolina, a fierce and strong race whose constitution adapted to the warm climate, whose nerves were braced by constant labor and who could hardly be supposed to be content with that oppressive yoke under which they groaned."[9] The chief fear was that the neighboring Spaniards would urge them to revolt—a fear that was justified by several insurrections especially one at Stono.[10] However, in 1715, 500 of the Negroes who had been entrusted with arms, saved the whites from massacre by the Yemassee Indians. It was not until 1930 that the white population caught up with the black.

The state has two monuments to Negroes. One at Woodward—at the entrance to Fortune Park to the Negro who served Lafayette; the other to faithful Negroes who protected white women and children while their Confederate masters were away at War.[10a]

GEORGIA

Edmund Burke has already been quoted on how Georgia was on the point of its fourth failure when Negroes were imported to save it. One of its earliest free Negro settlers was Austin Dabney,[11] a hero of the Revolutionary War. Gilmer tells how Dabney's master, Aycock, "fearing to face the danger of death during the war, offered as a substitute his mulatto boy (Dabney), who was accordingly enrolled in a captain's company . . . No soldier under Clark was braver or did better service during the Revolutionary War. In the battle of Kettle Creek, the hardest ever fought in Georgia between the Whigs and the Tories, Austin Dabney was shot down and left on the ground dangerously wounded."

He was found there by a man named Harris, who carried him home and cared for him. Later, he sent Harris' son to college and law school and paid all expenses.

The Georgia Legislature, by special act, gave him a farm. He became one of the wealthiest and most highly respected men in the state. Once, in Savannah, Gen. James Jackson, the governor, seeing him riding by, ran out into the street, drew him off his horse and carried him into his house and had him as a guest whilst business kept him in Savannah.

He owned some of the finest race-horses, and was favorite at the race-track. Upper-class whites treated him as an equal.[11]

NEGRO PIONEERS IN THE WEST AND MIDDLE WEST

After the Spanish and the French in the exploration of the West and the Middle West, came the English. When Colonel James Smith set out to explore the rich lands that are now Tennessee in June 1776, at least one Negro was with him. Several also were in the party of Donelson and Blakemore when they reached Nashville.[12] At least one accompanied Washington on his surveying expeditions. Another, Marcos Lopez, was with Captain Gray at the discovery of the Columbia River in 1792, which gave the Oregon territory to the United States. Winslow Anderson and James D. Saule were among the first settlers in that state.[13]

Several Negroes were in the Lewis-Clark expedition which left Virginia in 1803 on the first overland journey to the Pacific. One of them, York,[14] a giant in size and strength, and

Slave women returning from the fields.

very good natured, was a marvel to the Indians, who brought him wives and presents. Wheeler, a member of the expedition, wrote of him, "His color, kinky hair, size and prodigious strength were a revelation to the Indians and he was looked upon as a very god. He was the greatest kind of great 'medicine' and the tribes from the north of Missouri to the mouth of the Columbia took particular pains to propitiate his sable majesty. And he was overwhelmed with feminine attention." The Indians, by all accounts, regarded him as the leader of the party. He was the interpreter.

Another member of the expedition, Pompey, had Pompey's Pillar in Montana named after him.[15]

George William Bush, another Negro, is really the founder of the State of Washington.[16] A trapper and friend of the Indians, he led the first party of white people there from Missouri in 1843. Thanks to his friendship with the Indians, he made it possible for the whites to live there in peace. As J. E. Ayer says, "The history of the Northwest settlement cannot be fully written without an account of George Bush, who organized and led the first colony of American settlers to the shores of Puget Sound . . . He was a Negro."

"Mr. Bush was a farmer and having, as much live stock as possible, he at once broke up some of the best of the open prairie. He was so successful that in a very few years his farm was

Lewis and Clark Expedition to the West Pacific Coast in 1806. In the front boat is York (see text).

the main source for grain, vegetables and fruit for supplying the newcomers in that region. Let me say in passing that his memory is honored to this day among the early families. Although at times he was the only man in the country with food, he would never take advantage by raising the price nor allow anyone to buy more than his needs during an emergency." Bush Prairie was named for him. His son, William Owen Bush, of whom we will hear later, became in 1876 the leading man in the world in his field. "Nigger Creek" in Washington is also named for a Negro who made a gold strike there.

George Washington (1818-1905) was founder of Centralia, Wash. Born a slave in Virginia, he started west and reached Washington after a journey of 3,000 miles. He acquired land, cultivated it and invited people to settle on it. During the depression of 1893, he helped needy settlers, most of them white, out of his own

pocket. In 1922, the Women's Civic Club erected a marble monument in the city park to his memory.

COLORADO

The first American expedition to Colorado was led by Zebulon Pike in 1806, but as early as 1540, the Spaniards and Negroes had been in that region and had claimed it for Spain. They were there when Pike reached the mountain, now called Pike's Peak. The first white pioneers were fur trappers but preceding them were escaped Negro slaves who had made their way to the Indians, had been welcomed by them, and some even made chiefs. These were the first trappers from the East. Kenneth W. Porter gives abundant evidence on them and names some. "The earliest Negroes," he says, "known to be connected with the fur trade were among

84

those who occupied the highest functional category—that of independent entrepreneurs."[17] The white traders and trappers would seek out such Negroes and employ them to bargain with the Indians, because of the friendlier atmosphere they had created.

Foremost of these trappers, regardless of color, was James P. Beckwourth,[18] one of the founders of the city of Denver. Born in slavery in Virginia in 1798, he escaped and reached the Rockies, which he was later to know even bet-

George Washington, founder of Centralia, Wash.

William O. Bush: State Senator, Washington and winner of the first prize for the world's finest wheat.

ter than most Indians. The Crows made him their chief. His knowledge of Indian languages and ways made him of particular service to the United States for whom he was a scout and interpreter. He was in reality also the first great trail-blazer to California and helped greatly in its development by discovering a passage for wagons through the Sierras. The route is now the beautiful Feather River Canyon through which runs the Western Pacific. The pass was named for him, as well as a valley and a moun-

tain. In the pass is his monument. He led General Kearney's expedition to California through it. A. D. Richardson, a newspaperman, wrote of him in 1860, "He is a well-informed elderly man with a devil-may-care expression but a face full of character and of wonderful perceptive faculties . . . It is James P. Beckwourth, the half-breed, so long a chief among the Crow tribe but the most famous Indian fighter of this generation. His body is scarred from wounds received in worst extremes and on the perilous edge of battle'. But he is the very pink of courtesy."

Other trappers named by Porter are Pierre Bonga and his son, George; Edward Rose, Ezekiel Williams, Francois Duchoquette, John Brazeau, "a full-blooded Ethiopian," William and Charles Bent, and Cadet Chevalier. Negro adventurers like these helped greatly in building the great $30,000,000 Astor fortune which was founded on fur.

Negroes in the Colorado mines, mostly laborers, were unusually lucky. One known as Jim discovered on his claim at George Town a vein that ran $1,000 to the ton . . . Six white capitalists wined and dined him one whole Sunday, in spite of their color prejudice, in an attempt to make him sell it for $100,000, a fortune at that time.

85

Trail-Blazers of the Old West. Left, upper: James Beckwourth. Center: "Pop" Singleton. Below: George Monroe, famous pony mail-rider. Right: James Lyman Bowen (see text).

UTAH

Negroes, as was said, had been with the Spaniards in Utah in 1540. They came with the Mormons and were with Brigham Young at the founding of Salt Lake City, July 23, 1847.[19] Their names are on the Pioneer Monument there—Green Flake of North Carolina, 1825-1903; Hark Lay of Mississippi, 1826-1890; and Oscar Crosby, 1815-1870. Abel Burns was the trusted servant and friend of Joseph Smith, Mormon prophet. A Utah Canyon was named for William Granstaff, a settler of that state in 1877.

CALIFORNIA

In California, as was previously said, Negroes had been pioneers with the Spaniards and furnished more than half of the founders of Los Angeles. When the first trek to the West began, they came too. Delilah Beasley gives the names of hundreds of them.[20] They were also among the Forty-Niners. Some struck it rich like Gabriel Sims, Abraham Holland, James Cousins, and "Dick." They sent large sums home for the purchase of their wives and children. One, Moses Rogers, was a leading mining engineer and metallurgist.

Foremost among the Negroes of California at this time and one of its leading personages was William Alexander Leidesdorff.[21] Son of a white Danish planter and his Negro wife, Julia Ann Sparks, of the Virgin Islands, he arrived in California in 1843 and became a Mexican citizen. He was awarded 30,000 acres of land, elected city councilman of San Francisco, and city treasurer. He was also American vice-consul, a post he owed to the fact that he favored the United States over Mexico and openly supported General Fremont and his Bear-Flag Party. He was successful in seeing the state come under American rule in 1846.

Leidesdorff has three firsts to his credit. His ship, the Sitka, was the first steamship to enter

Monument to the founders of Salt Lake City. The names of the Negro pioneers are on it (see text).

San Francisco Bay, November 15, 1847; he established the first United States school there with Thomas Douglas, a Yale man, as principal; and he introduced horse-racing. His steamship caused a great sensation and was a fearsome sight to the natives who called it, "The boat with fire in its belly." All this was accomplished in only five years. When he died in 1848, the city gave him a public funeral and

87

named a street in his honor. Another Negro, Mifflin Gibbs, opened the first shoe-store in San Francisco.

Another noted Californian and a pioneer in the early development of San Francisco was George W. Dennis.[22] Born a slave in New Orleans, he was taken to California by his master in 1848. Buying his freedom for $1,000, he and his mother sold home-cooked meals to gamblers and made a fortune. Later, he went into real estate, bought up whole blocks, which he sold as the city grew, at huge profit. In six months he made on one deal alone $14,000, a sum worth many times that now.

Another who made a fortune in real estate was Biddy Mason, a young slave, who arrived in Los Angeles on foot in 1851 from the South, driving sheep behind her master's wagon. After purchasing her freedom, she bought two lots in what is now Spring and Broadway and at Third and Fourth Streets. Negroes also founded two towns in Southern California, Allensworth and Monrovia. The latter is now a thriving town, peopled largely by whites. In 1915, in a nation-wide contest for a name of the Panama-Pacific Exposition, a Negro girl, Virginia Stephens, won first prize with the title "The City of Light."

Alexander Leidesdorff. San Francisco street is named for him. (Picture of street. Courtesy Ebony Magazine).

Biddy Mason, early Los Angeles resident and land owner.

INDIANA AND KANSAS

Between 1830 and 1850, hundreds of Negro families migrated to Indiana in ox-carts and settled on lands bought directly from the federal government, the patents of which were signed by Presidents James Monroe and Andrew Jackson. There were some fifteen settlements, the best known of which were Greenville, by Thornton Alexander, who himself owned 300 acres; and Beach Roberts, and Snow Hill settlements. Among the settlers were some white former slaveholders who brought their children by Negro women, one of whom bought 300 acres for each of them. A memorandum book of 1830 says the "652 persons had been removed to free government, the expense thereof was $12,769.51"[23]

Persecution during the Reconstruction caused Negroes to flock westward into Oklahoma and Kansas. The chief leader of the "Exodusters," as they were called, was Benjamin "Pap" Singleton, the "Black Moses,"[24] who aranged to take them to Kansas at five dollars a head. They founded several towns, one of which was Nicodemus. At Topeka, itself, was a colony of 7000. One, E. P. McCabe, a former Pullman porter, was elected auditor of Kansas. Another, George J. Groves made a fortune on potatoes and was known as "The Potato King." He became one of the big landowners. The railroad offered him several hundred thousand dollars for his holdings.[25]

Alexander Clark (1826-1891) was one of the early Iowa pioneers. Starting as a barber there, he invested in timberlands and made money selling wood to Mississippi River steamboats. Self-educated, he became a leading anti-slavery orator and served in the First Iowa volunteers in the Civil War. He was also a delegate to the Republican Conventions of 1872 and '76. He is mentioned in the Iowa Journal of History volume 46; and in the Dictionary of National Biography, 1907.

Negroes helped further in Western expansion by building railroads and later guarding them from the Indians. Of that more will be said later.

Among noted figures were James Lyman Bowen, born in Liberty, Kentucky, 1842. Starting as a chef with Buffalo Bill, he became one of the most colorful figures of the West. Among those whom he fought was Sitting Bull. When he toured Europe, he was received by royalty, including King Humbert of Italy, Queen Victoria and the Pope. In 1932, he celebrated his 90th birthday at Danville, Ill.[26]

Isaiah Dorman[27] was another famous Western figure. Formerly a guide for Western settlers, he was appointed May 14, 1876 as post interpreter of General Custer. He escaped the massacre but was later killed in a fight with Sitting Bull.

Nat Love,[28] an ex-slave, born in Tennessee, 1854, was one of the foremost Wild West figures. Captured by the Indians, he was adopted by them. Love was the first of the noted cowboys and the original Deadwood Dick, then the most

Alexander Clark. Noted Iowa pioneer.

popular figure in Wild West fiction. In 1876, he won the championship of the West as rider, roper, and revolver shot at Deadwood, South Dakota.

Love and other noted Negro cowboys of that time as Emanuel Organ, Ellis Miller, Henry Beckwith, "Eighty" John Wallace, and Matthew "Bone" Hooks, are mentioned by W. S. Savage in, "Negroes on the Cattlemen's Frontiers" Midwest Jour. Vol. 6, No. 4, pp. 35-48, 1954-55.

A Negro cowboy, George McJunkin was the discoverer of Folsom Man, a people who lived in America some 10,000 to 15,000 years ago. While riding along an arroyo near Folsom, New Mexico, in 1926, he saw skeletons which had been washed out. The discovery was hailed as very important by archaeologists. Hibben, F. C. Treasure in the Dust, pp. 42-3. 1951).

MISSISSIPPI

Negroes, as was said, were in Mississippi with the Spaniards as early as 1540. They came later with the English and did most in building the first forts and houses. They built Fort Rosiale in 1716, Fort Peters in 1730, and Fort Adams in 1760. They came first as indentured servants, were given land and some grew rich. Among them were Tony La Far, who had real estate worth almost half-a-million. Free Harris had six hundred acres and six families of slaves. James Tilman for whom the town of Tilman was named had 500 acres.[29]

TEXAS

The first known Negro in Texas was Estevanico, a member of the ill-fated De Narvaez expedition which landed in Florida in 1527. Estevanico and his three Spanish companions were held slaves by the Indians of Texas six years. Later, Spaniards and Negroes, together with Indians, began settlements in Southern Texas, principally in the area of San Antonio. An official Spanish census of December 31, 1792 gives a total population of 2992, of which 429 were blacks and mulattoes. Later, this number was much increased by the number of escaped slaves, chiefly from Louisiana, who won freedom although slavery still existed in Mexico.

White Americans attracted by the rich soil had been moving in, as well as fugitives from justice. In 1799, Philip Nolan tried to seize the area around San Antonio. Slaveholders, a few of whom were Negroes, also came in with their slaves to avoid abolition influence. But, the Mexicans, inspired by the French revolution, and its slogan, Liberty, Fraternity, Equality, began a struggle for independence and won in 1821. Then Vicente Guerrero (1782-1831), a mulatto ex-slave, came to the presidency. One of his first acts was to abolish slavery and declare that "all inhabitants, White, Negro, Indian, are qualified to hold office."

The Americans, already discontented with Spanish and Mexican rule, were much more so now. They had come to Texas to be able to hold their slaves and now were faced with total loss of them. They revolted with alternate success and failure. At the Alamo, almost the entire American force was wiped out. At last, they were successful thanks to the fact that President Guerrero, occupied with political rivalry at Mexico City, hadn't the troops to spare. At San Jacinto, 1835, Sam Houston decisively defeated the Mexicans, and the republic with San Houston as its president, came into being. Slavery triumphed once more and free Negroes were forbidden to remain there. Thus the presence of the Negro, as in Virginia and New York, was an important factor in leading up to Texas becoming a state of the Union.

The reason given for the annexation was the wretched financial state of the republic. Its paper dollar had fallen to two cents. But the more evident one was that the Texans needed U. S. protection. The Mexicans had never become reconciled to their loss and to make it worse, the Americans regarded them as "niggers." Frederick Law Olmsted, who visited Texas both before and after the republic, tells of the almost open war between the two, of the assassinations and the burning of homes. "They (the Mexicans)", he said, "hate and fear the ascendant race, and involuntarily associate and sympathize with the Negroes." They were treated as "outlaws" and "regarded as niggers." One white man told Olmsted, "Why, they're as black as niggers and ten times as treacherous."[30]

What the whites hated most were mixed marriages. Negroes with white wives and whites with Negro wives had been migrating to Texas under Spain. Benjamin Lundy,[31] abolitionist, whose plan was to colonize Negroes in Texas and who knew it well, has much in his 1833 diary on these mixed couples. It had been "the policy of the Mexican government to unite all colors and treat all with respect," he says. The whites with their secret society, "The Regulators," attacked even mulatto families, like the Ashworths, who had done so much for the republic that they had been exempted by special mention from the law forbidding residence to free Negroes.

Nat Love, "Deadwood Dick."
First and greatest of the cowboys.

Harold Schoen[32], "Free Negroes in the Republic of Texas," mentions some of those who fought or otherwise gave generously to the cause of independence, as Greenberg Logan, who was one of the first to answer Stephen Austin's call for volunteers; William Goyan, who was interpreter for Sam Houston; Robert Thompson, who contributed arms and a horse; and the brothers, William and Abner Ashworth. Samuel McCullogh[33], a volunteer who served under Captain C. M. Collingsworth, was specially mentioned and rewarded for his valor.

MICHIGAN

The largest Negro colony in the Northwest was Chain Lake settlement in Michigan. It was founded in 1847 by Saunders, a Virginia slaveholder, who brought his slaves there, set them free and lived with them . . . Originally one square mile, it is now 38 square miles. The descendants still live there with fine large farms and homes amid the beautiful lakes from which came its name . . .[34]

POLAR EXPLORATION

Negroes were with the pathfinders of the sea-lanes, especially in the South Polar regions on the whaling voyages, beginning about the middle of the seventeenth century and extending to the middle of the nineteenth.

At least two were captains: A. F. Boston, grandson of the slave, Prince; and Peter Green, second mate, who took charge of the "John Adams" and piloted it around the Horn when the captain, John Maxey, died. Another noted navigator was Samuel Harris. E. A. Stackpole names the others[35].

Negroes also helped in polar exploration. One Peter Harvey,[36] born in Philadelphia in 1789, was a member of the crew of the Hero, Captain M. B. Palmer, at the discovery of Antarctica in 1820. Others had preceded Palmer in those frozen waters but he was the first to sight the archipelago, which was named for him. With the "Huron," a later expedition, were Cato Tobias, and a cook and a steward. In 1950, one of the crew of Admiral Byrd's expedition was a Negro.

The last great feat of land exploration possible on the planet was the discovery of the North Pole. And in this, a Negro, Matthew Henson,[37] played a role of major importance. He was in the party of the first six ever to reach the Pole—one white, one Negro, and four es-

Matthew Henson, first person to stand at the North Pole

kimos. And of the six, he was the first to stand at the Pole itself.

The party had reached the Pole, April 6, 1909. Commander Peary, sick, utterly worn-out, and with the loss of all the toes on one foot, was taken there by sled. On Henson lay the task of finding the exact location of the Pole. With his instruments, he found it and placed the American flag on it, while Peary with just enough strength left, waved his hand.

This story was told by Commander MacMillan in his lectures and later admitted by Henson, himself. Lowell Thomas in an article "First at the Pole," says, "According to MacMillan, it was Henson who placed the Stars and Stripes at the top of the world, while the leader sat exhausted on the sledge and feebly waved." Peary was criticized because in the last dash to the Pole, he took a Negro and no white man. Lowell Thomas quotes MacMillan on this, "The reason was quite simple and overwhelming. Henson was the most useful man of us all. He was the best man I've ever seen then, or in the thirty years since, in the handling of Eskimos. It was Henson who trained the Eskimos for all Peary's expeditions. Nobody could get along with them as well as Matt Henson . . . Besides Henson was the best man at handling the sledge or a dog team. And we all noticed that, whenever we encountered a difficulty, Matt Henson was the man he sent for." Henson spoke Eskimo fluently, Peary and the other whites only a few words. Hanson built the sledge that went to the Pole and which is now in the American Museum of Natural History. He was awarded the Congressional Medal of Honor.

Thus Negro exploration and pioneering which began with Ponce de Leon in 1512 and had continued through the centuries reached a glorious climax in Henson, 388 years later.

NOTES

1. The Book of Chicago, p. 141, 1920. Kinzie, J. H. W., Waubun, pp. 219-220. 1856. American Guide Series (Illinois), p. 193. 1947.

2. Haiti et Chicago. 1953.

3. Bolton & Marshall. Colonization of North America, p. 282. 1924.

4. Krug, M. E. DuBay, p. 128. 1946. Sinclair Lewis' "Kingsblood Royal" deals with this Negro-Indian intermixture.

5. A Trip to the Prairies, 1837-38, 1934.

6. Semmes, R., Captains and Mariners of Early Maryland, p. 107 (1937). Bibbins, R., Beginnings of Maryland, pp. 20, 49. 1934. Andrews, M. P., History of Maryland, p. 65. 1920. Richardson, H., Sidelights of Maryland History, p. 9. 1903.

7. Norris, W. B., Annapolis, p. 59. 1925.

7a. Curious Relations, ed. by William Plomer, pp. 82-100. 1946. See also Rogers, J. A., Nature Knows No Color Line, pp. 156-172, 1952, for mixed marriages in high life in England.

8. Columbia Historical Society Records, Vol. 20, pp. 114-120. 1917. Maryland Historical Society Publications No. 3. 1845. Atlantic Monthly, Vol. 11, pp. 79-84, 1863, has copy of Jefferson's letter. National Cyclop. of American Biography, Vol. 5, p. 36.

9. Journal of Negro History, Vol. 33, p. 62. 1948.

10. For an account of this see: Colonial Records of Georgia, Vol. 22, Pt. 2, 1737-39, pp. 232-36.

10a. South Carolina. WPA. U. S. Publications, pp. 35,36.

11. Gilmer, G. R., Sketches of the First Settlers of Georgia, pp. 212-215. 1855. Phillips, U. B., American Negro Slavery, p. 430. 1918.

12. Hale & Merrit. History of Tennessee. Vol. 2, p. 291.

13. Carey, C. H., History of Oregon, p. 134. 1922. White, E., Ten Years in Oregon, p. 228. 1850.

14. Trail of Lewis & Clark, pp. 134-5. 1921.

15. Journal of Negro History. Vol. 12, pp. 347-8. Washington Historical Quarterly. Jan. 1916, pp. 40-45. (George Bush the Voyageur).

16. Hines, H. K., History of the State of Washington, pp. 378-79. Journal of Negro History. Vol. 8, p. 333. Atlantic Monthly, Vol. 39, p. 676.

17. Negroes and the Fur Trade. Minnesota Historical Journal, vol. 15, pp. 421-33. 1934.

18. Autobiography of James Beckwourth. 1892. Colo. Magazine, Vol. 26-7, pp. 165, et seq. 165-176. Byers, W. N., Encyc. Biog. of Colorado, I, pp. 20-21, 134-39. Bonner, T. D., Life and Adventures of James Beckwourth, 1931. Dictionary of American Biography, Vol. 2, p. 122. Chapman, A., Story of Colorado, p. 54. Bancroft, H. H. Works of, Vol. 25, p. 352 (History of Nevada, Colorado, and Wyoming). 1890.

19. Utah Historical Society Journal, Vol. 2, p. 122, Oct. 1929. Americana, Vol. 7, 1912, p. 686. (History of the Mormon Church). New York Sun, Nov. 15, 1903. U. S. Guide (Utah), p. 425.

20. Negro Trail-Blazers of California. 1919.

21. H. H. Bancroft, History of California. Vol. 44, 711. 1884. Lockwood ,W., The Amazing Career of Wm. Leides-

dorff. Los Angeles Daily Mirror, Feb. 9, 1953; San Francisco Chronicle, April 21, 1947.

22. Thurman, S., Pioneers of Negro Origin in California. 1952.

23. For names of pioneers see Indiana Magazine of History, Vol. 27, 1931, pp. 291-306.

24. American Journal of Sociology, Vol. XV, #1, 1909.

25. Negro History Bulletin.

26. Abbot's Monthly, April 1932.

27. Journal of Negro History. Vol. 33, pp. 344-52. 1948.

28. Love, Nat, Life of Nat Love, better known as "Deadwood Dick." 1907.

29. Mosley, C. C., Negro in Mississippi History, pp. 25-30. 1950.

30. Olmsted, F. L., Journey Through Texas, pp. 324-5, 387, 456. 1857.

31. Lundy, B. Life, Travels, and Opinions, pp. 48, 57, 77, 110, 113, 116-7, 129, 143. 1847.

32. Southwest Historical Quarterly. Vol. 39, pp. 292-308; Vol. 40, pp. 26-34, 85, 113, 169-99; 267-289; Vol. 41, pp. 83-108.

33. Harmon, J. H., Free Negroes in Old Texas. Crisis Magazine, Vol. 45, pp. 6-7. 1938.

34. Voice of the Negro, p. 555. 1906. Corrothers, J. D., In Spite of the Handicap, pp. 17-18. 1916.

35. Stackpole, E. A., The Sea Hunters, pp. 286, 288, 328, 332, 399. 1953.

36. Antarctica Discovered. Geographical Review, Vol. 30, p. 540. 1940. "The participation in polar exploration is a truly interesting achievement on the part of our Negro citizens," it says.

37. This Week, April 2, 1939. Henson, M. A., A Negro at the North Pole. 1912. Hampton's Magazine, January 1910. Liberty Magazine, July 17, 1926.

Note: *Two Negroes also were in the Nautilus that made the first underwater journey to the North Pole. In the account of the trip by Commander William R. Anderson one of them is shown presenting a chunk of polar ice to Admiral Rickover. (Picture 56).*

Author's Note:

Considerable confusion and even heated **argument** exist today over what the dark-skinned, mixed-blood citizens of the United States **shall be called**. Discrimination makes a name or names necessary. The nearest to a correct one would be African-European-Amer.-Indian, since their ancestors are from three continents. But that name has never been used. The one most common has been, and is, Negro. But we are told by some that "Negro" originated among white people and means slavery. This is historically incorrect. It comes from "Niger" (River Niger) was introduced into ancient Rome and eventually came into Spanish and English as "Negro." The Latin declension of the word is: niger, nigra, nigrum.

We have a parallel example in the word, English. The Angles, a German people, brought it into Britain. They called the part of the island they settled, Angleland, hence England, English. Niger, which eventually came to **mean black**, was not a term of disgrace as even Roman emperors, as Pescennius Niger, bore that surname.

Another popular term is "colored." But certain native African leaders do not like it. They say they aren't mixed-blood but pure black and that the jim-crow car in America is marked, "Colored." But black fares no better. Many persons, especially of mixed blood, consider it most disgraceful. It is from the Anglo-Saxon, blaec, and means dismal, gloomy, foul, outrageously wicked.

Another name is African. This, too, was also considered objectionable. Africa, called "The Dark Continent," stood for centuries as a symbol of cannibalistic, savage, ignorant, naked people. But in the past twenty years or so the white powers have re-discovered the value of Africa, has given it immense publicity, and with it a cleansing of the name. The Africans today are fighting for their freedom and their descendants in the New World, who once vigorously objected to being identified with Africa, are more and more wishing to be known as African.

However, the value of a name depends upon the power behind it. Once "English" was far below what "Negro" now is. At that time the English were slaves to the Normans. "The ordinary imprecation of a Norman gentleman," says Macaulay, was 'May I become an Englishman.' His ordinary form of indignant denial was 'Do you take me for an Englishman.'"

As I said the correct name would be "African-European-Amer.-Indian." This is too cumbersome and a waste of time and printer's ink. No one is going to use it. I do not intend to. I cannot please everybody or be partisan of any single group, therefore I shall use all the prevailing names, Negro, colored, black, African-American. It is not the name but the treatment that hurts. Changing a name will not change the color of one's face, the inciting cause of this prejudice.

Part Two

THE AFRICAN-AMERICAN IN THE MAKING OF AMERICA

DEFENDERS OF FREEDOM AND INDEPENDENCE

Negroes were used as Indian fighters in all the colonies from the start. In Massachusetts in 1643 all men capable of shouldering a musket were made to do so, including Negroes. There is a record of at least one "blackamore" among them then. In 1652 an Act read, "All Negroes from sixteen to sixty years of age, inhabitants, and servants to the English be enlisted and hereby enjoined to attend trainings." In 1660, the order was repeated. And while Negroes were welcomed and treated almost as comrades, some whites were barred, namely, the Irish, because of their religion, and the Quakers.

Negroes were held in even higher favor after 1676. That year, Jethro, a slave, saved the Plymouth colony from what might have been total massacre of that and other settlements. Captured by King Philip in an earlier raid, Jethro, who knew the Indian language, heard the king and his chiefs planning the attack and escaped and warned the colony. Thus prepared, the whites easily fought off the Indians.

For this great service, Jethro was stingily rewarded. He was to remain a slave "until two years and then be freed and set at liberty" at which time he was to be given "apparel fitting to one of his degree." Hubbard in his "Indian Wars", says, "I do not find anywhere else any adequate acknowledgment the English of Plymouth colony were under to this Negro for saving Taunton from destruction," (Plymouth Colony Records, Vol. V, p. 216. 1676; Indian Wars, Vol. 2, p. 256. 1865).

In Virginia, they helped so well against the Indians, that in April 1699, the Earl of Egmont wrote the Lords of Trade in England, suggest-ing that more be brought from Africa for defense of the colonies, "But rather than spare more soldiers from England," he said, "I would advise the sending for Negroes from Guinea." Their cost, he said, would be two-thirds cheaper than English ones.

In 1704, South Carolina ruled, "Whereas among the several slaves belonging to this colony, there are a great number of them, who, by care and discipline may be rendered serviceable towards the defense and preservation of this province" that they be trained for that purpose. Any Negro killing a Spaniard or an Indian enemy would be purchased and freed. In 1715, 500 of these armed blacks saved the Carolina whites, who were in a minority, from what seemed certain extinction by the Yemassee Indians.

In the four major wars of that time against the French and their Indian allies, principally along the Canadian-New England border, Negroes also gave valuable service to the English. In 1775, at the battle of Lake George, September 10, the Negroes probably saved New York from capture. The whites, outnumbered, evidently did not show much stomach for the fight because a report of that battle says, "Our Blacks behaved better than our Whites (New York State Documents Relative to Colonial History, Vol. 6, p. 1005). Negroes helped General Wolfe capture Quebec for the English, 1759, and also Fort Duquesne, Pennsylvania, under General Braddock and his successor, George Washington. Braddock, who was fatally wounded in the fight, gave Bishop, his bodyguard, a Negro, to Washington. The names of the many indi-

Death of Crispus Attucks, March 5, 1770.

vidual Negroes who distinguished themselves in these four wars are on record.

CRISPUS ATTUCKS

One Negro, Crispus Attucks, probably an escaped slave, took the lead in the event that led most directly to the War of the Revolution, and through that to American independence. It *is* known as the Boston Massacre, March 5, 1770.

The city of Boston, angry over taxes and other impositions by England, was particularly so in 1769, when two British regiments, the 64th and 65th, were brought into the city to overawe its citizens. There were soldiers every-

where. Boston Common was filled with their tents. Some soldiers were quartered in private homes. On the streets, they challenged citizens and insulted and even attacked the women. "Our wives and daughters, and even our grandmothers are no longer safe," they complained. Clashes betwen civilians and soldiers were frequent. Soldiers were hooted and boys threw snowballs at the hated "lobsterbacks," as the red-coated British soldiers were called.

Tension increased until March 5, 1770, when it ended in the death of five citizens and the wounding of others. On that day a tall, powerfully built mulatto was standing at the busy corner of King Street when a little boy came towards him crying. Asked what was the matter, the boy said that a British officer, Captain

98

Crispus Attucks Monument, Boston, Mass.

African slaves pulling down the s

...eorge III in New York City, 1775.

Goldfinch, had come into his master's barber-shop and had left without paying, and that he had been sent after him to remind him. The captain ignored him and he followed him to the guard-house into which the captain went. He started to follow him when the guard pushed him back with the butt of his musket.

The tall mulatto was Crispus Attucks. He was then, or had previously been a member of a whaling crew. It happened also that he was very indignant at how the citizens were being treated. As the sobbing boy told his story a crowd gathered and angrily demanded punishment for the sentry. Attucks, taking the boy by the hand, led the way to the guard-house.

There are conflicting stories of what happened then but a clash followed. The crowd, armed with sticks of firewood, shouted angrily at the sentry, who shouted for the guard. The latter, headed by Captain Preston, rushed out. Preston ordered them to disperse. Attucks, seizing the musket, struck down the soldier with his fist. A soldier fired and Attucks fell mortally wounded. The crowd, shouting angrily, advanced on the soldiers. Preston gave the order to fire and four others were killed.

The bodies of Attucks and Caldwell, one of the four whites killed, were picked up and carried to Faneuil Hall, "Cradle of Liberty," where thousands from Boston and outlying towns flocked to see them. All five were placed in the same grave in the Granary Burying Ground.

Anger against Britain spread to all the colonies. The cry for independence grew more insistent. The five were regarded as martyrs. The spot on which they fell became sacred ground. March Fifth became known as "Massacre Day," and "Crispus Attucks Day." John Adams, second President, said of its importance, "Not the battle of Lexington or Bunker Hill, nor the surrender of Burgoyne or Cornwallis were more important events in American history than the battle of King Street, March 5, 1770." On its sixth anniversary, George Washington exhorted

his troops, "Remember it is the Fifth of March, Avenge your comrades."

Crispus Attucks Day remained the chief American anniversary until independence was won when it was displaced by July 4. Livermore says, "The anniversary of the event was publicly commemorated by exercises every year until our National Independence was achieved when the Fourth of July was substituted for the 5th of March, as a more proper day for a general celebration." (Livermore, Hist. Research on Negroes, p. 92, 1863).

That Crispus Attucks was the outstanding hero is proved by the fact that the memorial erected to the event is named after him. A bill approved by the Massachusetts legislature for its erection, October 13, 1888, reads, "Ordered that the site selected by his Excellency the Governor for the location of the CRISPUS ATTUCKS MEMORIAL be hereby approved." On the monument, erected on Boston Common, his name heads the list of those who fell.

On it is this from John Adams, "On that night, the foundation of American independence was laid." And from Daniel Webster, "From that moment we may date the severance of the British Empire."

John Fiske, noted historian, said, "It was this sacrifice that brought about the preliminary victory of the American Revolution." George W. Williams said, "When the colonists were staggering wearily under the cross of woe, a Negro came to the front and bore that cross to the victory of the glorious martyrdom."

REVOLUTIONARY WAR

As a result of the sacrifice of Crispus Attucks and his four comrades, the troops were withdrawn from Boston, but the city and the New England states continued with increasing resentment until it exploded at Lexington, April 19, 1775, in "the shot heard around the world." The next clash came at Bunker Hill, June 17, where the Americans fought gallantly against a superior force and retreated only after inflicting great losses on the foe. And here again, a **Negro, Peter Salem,** became a great hero of the day. He shot and killed the British commander, **Major Pitcairn,** as the latter leaped on the parapet to lead his men in a charge, shouting, **"The day is ours."** A subscription was taken up for Peter, and his name rang among lovers of liberty. Still another Negro, **Salem Poor,** so distinguished himself in this same battle, that thirteen officers, including his commander, **Colonel Brewer,** recommended him to the **General Court of Massachusetts.** The report said he **"behaved like an experienced officer as well as an excellent soldier."**

In the crisis there was no time for color prejudice. Negroes, who had been agitating for their own freedom and equality, joined in the fight cheerfully. At Fort Griswold, another Negro (unnamed), killed the British commander, **Major Montgomery,** with a deftly-thrown spear as he mounted the parapet for a charge. At Newport, Rhode Island, **Prince,** an African, captured, with his own hand, **Major-General Prescott,** commander in that colony.

In the provincial army, that is, of the New England colonies, Negroes were everywhere, fighting beside white men. **Ben J. Lossing,** one of America's historians, says, "In the North, from the early days of the War, Negroes fought beside whites in the patriot army. As the war went on, and the ranks of the army grew thinner, an increasing number of Negroes took the place of the whites, until it began to appear that Ethiopia as well as America was in arms." (The American Revolution, Vol. 3, pp. 508-512. 1948 ed.) Another writer of the times said "it looked as if Ethiopia had come to the rescue."

Then came the incorporation of the provincial forces, that is, those of the separate colonies, into the Continental Army and with it, the question of whether slaves and even free Negroes should be used. After the glowing words of the Declaration of Independence (which didn't apply to black men), to use slaves and members of a despised race to fight for the freedom of white men, seemed the last word in contradiction. England was making much of how Negroes had been used so far. The issue of the Boston newspaper that has carried the sacrifice of Crispus Attucks also had an advertisement of Negroes for sale. Had Americans no sense of the fitness of things? They were "so eager to abolish their fanciful slavery" to Great Britain, while they were imposing actual slavery on others. Dr. Johnson's picture of an American as one with a slave whip became more popular than ever in England. It was suggested that one way to teach Americans a lesson was "to abolish real slavery" —set all the Negroes free. Doing that, it was said, would hurt them like "a rasp drawn over a raw wound."

Among the Americans, who saw the contradiction, were Benjamin Franklin and John Hancock. Both opposed the enlistment of Negroes. The Committee of Safety, of which Hancock was head, ruled that "admission of persons, not freemen, will be inconsistent with the principles that are to be supported and reflect dishonor on this Colony," and that "no slaves be admitted into the army upon any consideration whatever." At the Council of War, October 8, 1775, Washington, Putnam, and other generals debated whether free Negroes should be used and it "was agreed unanimously to reject all slaves and by a great majority to reject Negroes altogether." On November 12, Washington ordered that "Neither Negroes, boys, nor old men unable to bear arms, should be enlisted." Returns were made of the fighters, according to "complexion" and all the colored ones were discharged.

Of course, the high-flown reason of "dishonor" was a sham. The chief one was economic. The whole economy of the South, principally Virginia, South Carolina, and Georgia, was built on property in black bodies, and the slave population was becoming increasingly restless. Some were demanding their freedom, many were running away out of reach, others had engaged in conspiracies, and even in armed attack, in which some masters and their families were wiped out. This is made clear by Herbert Ap-

Peter Salem shooting Major Pitcairn at Bunker Hill and bringing about defeat of the British.

theker in "The Negro in the American Revolution." On the other hand, New England, remembering Crispus Attucks and the valuable services of other Negroes, objected vigorously. Gordon of Massachusetts said, "A black, tawny, or reddish skin is not so unfavorable a hue to the genuine son of liberty as a Tory complexion." (Tories were white). General Thomas wrote John Adams, October 24, 1775, "I am sorry to hear that any prejudice should take place in any Southern Colony with respect to any troops raised by us . . . We have some Negroes but I look on them, in general, equally serviceable with other men for fatigue and in action many of them have proved themselves brave."

Of course, this ban on Negroes was very good news to Lord Dunsmore, royal governor of New York and Virginia. He took advantage of it to promise freedom and equality to all Negroes who would join him. Sir Henry Clinton, British commander - in - chief, announced, "I do promise to every NEGRO who shall desert the Rebel Standard full security to follow within these lines any occupation he shall think proper."

Negroes flocked to join him. Five thousand joined Dunsmore at Norfolk; 25,000 fled from the masters in South Carolina and nearly seven-eighths of those in Georgia. Some 2,000 joined Cornwallis. Even some of George Washington's slaves went over to Dunsmore. Runaway slaves, armed by the British, harassed their masters, slaughtered them and their families in their beds at night, and raided Savannah. In the Bronx, New York City, a strong garrison of blacks, known as the Negro Fort, held back

Peter Salem after shooting of Major Pitcairn. (From the painting by John Trumbull. 1756-1845.)

their former white masters. Other blacks were taken into the royal navy and helped attack coast towns. Some became pilots. One, Mungo, an African, piloted the "Experiment" of fifty guns safely through Hell-Gate into the New York Harbor to reinforce the British fleet there to the great surprise and joy of Admiral Lord Howe. He was handsomely rewarded.

The Americans loudly accused the British of starting "a race war." Southern whites, with their great number of slaves, shivered. They saw their black bondsmen under some leader, massacring them all, as the Maroons of Jamaica, West Indies, were doing the white colonists, there. Of this newest danger, Washington said, "Dunsmore's strength will increase like a snowball by rolling and faster if some expedient cannot be hit upon to convince the slaves and servants of the impotency of his designs."

Washington saw he must use the Negroes or run the risk of losing the war. He wrote, Colonel Henry Lee, December 20, 1775, "Success will depend on which side can arm the Negroes faster." Saying that he had learned that the Negroes who had been barred were "discontented," he appealed to Congress. The latter, seeing the necessity, but with still an eye to appeasing the slaveholders, decreed, Jan. 15, 1776, "That the free Negroes who have served faithfully in the army at Cambridge may be re-enlisted but no others."

But as the war dragged on, the prohibition against Negroes grew weaker and weaker. Many whites, seeing no end to it, dropped out and deserted. Others made peace with the British. General Schuyler of New York complained that when he called for more men, that mostly boys and the aged had been sent him. "The Spirit of '76" was now so weak that Washington complained, "The lack of patriotism (is) infinitely more to be dreaded than the whole forces of Great Britain assisted as they are by Hessian, Indian, and Negro allies." He wrote General Laurens, "That spirit of freedom, which, at the commencement of the contest, would have gladly sacrificed everything to the

James Lafayette, spy and soldier of Revolution under Lafayette. (Reproduced from Jackson, L. P., Virginia Negro Soldiers and Sailors).

attainment of its object, has long since subsided and every selfish passion has taken its place. It is not the public but private interest which influences the generality of mankind; nor can the Americans any longer boast an exception.

"Under the circumstances, it would rather have been surprising if you had succeeded nor will you, I fear, have better luck in Georgia."

From the South, Laurens wrote Washington urging the enlistment of Negroes as a necessity. "The country," he said "is greatly distressed and will be so unless reinforcements are sent to its relief. Had we arms for 3,000 black men

Washington crossing the Delaware. With him was Prince Whipple, a Negro. Upper left is Whipple's tomb in North Cemetery, Portsmouth, N. H.

as I could select in Carolina, I should have no doubt of success in driving the British out of Georgia and subduing East Florida before the end of July." Negroes were accepted in such numbers now that General Schuyler wrote, "Is it consistent with the sons of freedom to trust their all to be defended by slaves?" The slave states of the South had objected also to the quota demanded of them, especially Maryland. They declared it should be fixed, not on total population, but only on the white one. Furthermore, if white men left the colony in numbers, who would keep the Negroes in check, they added. Accordingly, on March 14, 1779, Alexander Hamilton recommended that "South Carolina being very weak in her population of whites may be excused from the draft on condition of furnishing black battalions." It was recommended that she and Georgia "take measures for raising 3,000 able-bodied Negroes" at once. They were to receive no pay but would be emancipated at the end of the war. White slave masters of the South, and some of the North, who didn't want to risk their lives, or those of their sons, sent Negroes to take their place. One such was Samuel Charlton of New Jersey, who fought at Monmouth and was highly commended by Washington for his courage, devotion, and his services in the commissary. After the war, his master refused to free him. To Virginia's credit, she overruled all such selfish masters and ordered Negro veterans freed.

In Washington's army," says Lossing, "there was an average of about fifty Negroes to each battalion and at the battle of Monmouth Courthouse, in 1778, at least 700 Negroes were on the American side. So many Negro troops were raised by Massachusetts, that in 1778, it was urged that a wholly black regiment be incorporated, but although Connecticut enlisted a separate battalion, Massachusetts continued to mix white and black troops in its armed forces." (Lossing on Negro troops, Vol. 3, 508-512. 1948).

A Hessian officer, Schlozer, writing home, October 23, 1777, said, "The Negro can take the

Rev. Lemuel Haynes, Revolutionary Patriot and Soldier. From painting by Bischoff in the Bennington, Vt. Historical Museum.

field instead of his master and therefore no regiment is to be seen in which there are not Negroes in abundance and among them are able-bodied, strong, and brave fellows." (Schlozer's Briefwechsel, Vol. 4, p. 365.) Chastellux tells also of the number of Negroes or mulattoes —"strong, robust," he saw in Washington's army, January 1781. Baron von Clausen says of the "20,000 men" he saw with Washington "5,000 were Negroes."

Rhode Island had a regiment composed almost entirely of slaves, whose fredom had been purchased. At the battle of Rhode Island, August 27, 1778, it clinched victory for its white commander, Colonel Greene, by repelling a force of 6,000 Hessians and British. Posted behind a thicket in the valley, it three times drove back the enemy, who charged down the hill to dislodge them. Lafayette called this battle "the best action of the whole war."

In 1777, after General Starke had captured the left wing of the British army of 700 men at Bennington, Vermont, Ben, a Negro, who had fought with great valor, was given the honor of leading them to Boston. The captives were joined together with ropes, and Ben, on a horse, led them to Boston. The story is told by Henry Stevens, who was there. New England was grateful to its black soldiers and showed it soon after the war by its stand against slavery. (Nell W. C. Services of Colored Americans in the Wars of 1776 and 1812).

It must be noted, too, that in face of death and grim necessity, white men forgot their repugnance to a black skin. They bunked, ate, and fought beside Negroes. Washington, himself, set the example. Once, on the field, he laid down to sleep on the same blanket beside his Negro servant, Primus Hall. War, even more than politics, makes strange bedfellows.

HAITI AND THE AMERICAN REVOLUTION

One must not forget the services rendered by the Negroes of Haiti. In 1779, 800 of them responded to the call of Count d'Estaing to fight for American independence. Among them were

Charles Mackey — served with the British in the Revolution but later joined the Americans.

Generals Beauvais, Rigaud, and Christophe (later Emperor of Haiti) and Martial Besse. At Savannah, they saved the Franco-American army from total disaster by covering their re-treat. Later, when Martial Besse, a general in the French Army in France, attempted to land at Charleston, he had to give bond because of his color. France had to protest to ensure proper respect for him.

THE NEGRO SAILOR

Negroes gave excellent service on the seas, and shared in some of John Paul Jones' famous victories. When Jones saw their loyalty, devotion and courage, he said, "I can no longer bring myself to a distinction based on color or misfortune." He freed all his slaves and said of Negroes who fought under him, "They are prime seamen and behaved as well as white men."

Negroes also served as pilots of vessels of war. A letter of George Washington, July 26, 1779, mentions the payment of one thousand dollars "promised the Negro pilots." Two acts of the Virginia legislature on October 30, 1789, freed Jack Knight and William Boush for having "faithfully served on board warships." The same year it purchased and freed Caesar, who "had entered very early into the service of the country and continued to pilot the armed vessels of this state during the late war."

Negroes also gave excellent service as spies. Pretending to accept the British offer, some even enlisted with them. Among them was Saul, who was rewarded for "very essential services rendered the Commonwealth during the late war." Quaco Honeyman; and an unnamed Negro, aided greatly the American victory at Edenton, N. C., December 8, 1775. Historian William E. Dodd wrote, "It was a godsend to the revolutionists of Virginia; it stirred drooping spirits as they had not been stirred since the news of Lexington."

James Armistead, also known as James Lafayette, was Lafayette's ablest spy. Lafayette, in a letter, now in the Virginia Historical Society, said in recommending him, "This is to certify that the bearer by the name of James had done essential services to me while I had the honor to command in the State. His intelligences from the enemy camp were industriously collected and more faithfully reported. He properly acquitted some important comunications I gave him."

The act of the Virginia legislature freeing him said, he entered "into the service of the Marquis de Lafayette and at peril of his life found means to frequent the British camp and thereby faithfully executed important commissions entrusted to him by the marquis.[33] He twice saved Lafayette from being captured. (The law freeing him is to be found in Hening's Statutes of Virginia, Vol. 13, p. 380).

In Georgia, Mammy Kate, a strapping Negro woman, rescued Governor Stephen Heard from a British prison during the Revolution by carrying him out on her head in a huge basket, covered with clothes. (Andrews, M. P. Women of the South in War Times, p. 334. 1920).

The most spectacular deed by a Negro spy was that by Pompey, a slave. The Americans had just suffered a great defeat in the loss of Stony Point, New York. As a result, Fort Fayette had fallen, West Point was in danger, and all communication to the north was threatened.

Pompey, with a basket of strawberries, went to the Fort and asked the sentry permission to go in with it. The sentry, seeing no harm in the laughing obsequious Pompey, allowed him in. The officers glad to get the berries bought them eagerly and gave him permission to return the next day. For the next three days he came, then he announced that he couldn't come any longer in the day as he had to work, but would come after nightfall. To do this, he needed the password and they gave it to him still thinking him harmless.

Each night there was a new password. Ten nights later, accompanied by three white men, with blackened faces, he stopped to joke with the sentry. While he was doing this, the three men knocked out the sentry. The American troops which had been waiting behind came up, scaled the rocks, while other burst through the gates. The British rushed out to be bayonetted by Americans, who lost only 15 killed and 83 wounded to 63 British killed and 543 officers and men captured. Lossing says of the event, "The storming and capture of Stony Point, regarded as an exhibition of skill, was one of the principal events of the war." Gen. Wayne, the commander was highly praised by Congress and Pompey was given a horse and excused from all work for the rest of his life. (American Revolution and War of 1812, Vol. 1, p. 744).

Individual Negroes who distinguished themselves were mentioned by hundreds. Barzallai Lew, a cooper of Groton, was the most famous drummer of the entire war. He often laid down his drum for a mushket. Drummesr and fifers were mostly Negroes. Two other famous ones were Cyrus Tiffany, and another simply named Tom.

Oliver Cromwell was one of the many Negroes in Washington's momentous crossing of the Delaware, at 3 a. m. December 26, 1776. Washington thought so highly of him, that at the end of the war, he wrote his discharge in his own hand. He died in 1853. The Burlington Gazette, wrote of him on his hundreth birthday, "The attention of many of our citizens has doubtless been arrested by the appearance of an old colored man, who might have been seen, sitting in front of his residence on Union Street . . . His attenuated frame, his silvery head, his feeble movements, combine to prove that he is very aged; and yet, comparatively few are aware he is among the survivors of the gallant army who fought for the liberties of our country in the days that tried men's souls . . .

"He was at the battles of Trenton, Princeton, Brandywine, Monmouth, and Yorktown . . . He was with the army at the retreat of the Delaware, on the memorable crossing of the 25th of December, 1776, and relates the story of the battles on the succeeding days with enthusiasm. He gives the details of the march from Trenton to Princeton and told us, with much humor, that they 'knocked the British about lively' at the latter place." He served six years and nine months directly under Washington. Both men had great affection for each other. At the end of the war, Washington, to show his esteem, wrote his discharge, himself. One writer, commenting on his death, said, "Had he been of a little lighter complexion (he was just half white), every newspaper in the land would have been eloquent in praise of his many virtues."

Agrippa Hull, said to be an African Prince, served Gen. Kosciusko, Polish patriot, through the Revolutionary War. After the war, he bought a farm at Stockbridge, Mass., where he was highly respected by his white neighbors. Lafayette visited him there on his return to America. (Wright R. Grandfather was Queer, pp. 109).

One of the most famous and earliest of the Minute Men was Rev. Lemuel Haynes (1753-1833), son of a Negro and a white female bond-servant. One of the heroes of Ticonderoga, he later pastored white churches in New York, Connecticut, and one in Rutland, Vermont, for thirty years. A picture postcard was issued of himself and his white congregation at Bennington.

Middleton, called colonel, by courtesy, commanded a company of Negroes known as "The Bucks of America," which rendered such valuable service, that John Hancock gave it a special flag. After the war he and his men were honored with a special affair at Boston.

Prince Whipple, another Negro, who crossed the Delaware in the boat with Washington, is said to be the Negro shown in the famous picture of that name. He died November 18, 1796, and was buried in North Cemetery, Portsmouth, New Hampshire. He was one of Washington's bodyguards.

Edward Griffin, a slave, served with such distinction in North Carolina, that the legislature set him free and gave him 640 acres of land. Charles Mackey, a West Indian soldier on the British side, who was captured by Colonel Vanderbilt at the Battle of Long Island, later served the Americans faithfully.

White Molly Pitcher had her Negro equivalent in Deborah Gannet, who enlisted under the name of Robert Shurtleff in the Fourth Massachusetts Regiment in 1782 and served to the end of the war. Massachusetts gave her as a reward of 34 pounds sterling, praised her ability as a soldier, and for "at the same time preserving her virtue and chastity of her sex unsuspected and unblemished . . . The said Deborah Gannet exhibited an extraordinary instance of female heroism," said the award. (Nell W. C. Colored Patriots in the American Revolution, p. 23 1855).

Testimony of those who took part in the war, on the role of the Negro, is considerable. Dr. Harris, who fought in the Battle of Rhode Island, in relating its fury, says, "there was a black regiment in the same situation. Yes, a regiment of Negroes fighting for our liberty and independence, not a white man among them but the officers stationed in the same dangerous and responsible position. Had they been unfaithful, or given way before the enemy, all would have been lost. Three times in succession were they attacked with most desperate valor and fury by well disciplined and veteran troops, and three times did they successfully repel the assault, and thus preserve our army from capture. They fought through the war. They were brave, hardy troops. They helped gain our liberty and independence."

Commander Nathaniel Shaler spoke highly of the Negroes who fought under him. In a letter to Governor Tompkins, he said of one of them, John Johnson, "He ought to be registered in the book of fame and remembered as long as bravery is considered a virtue." He also wrote highly of another Negro John Davis.

Martindale of New York said in Congress, "Slaves, or Negroes who had been slaves, were enlisted as soldiers in the War of the Revolution; and I myself saw a battalion of them, as fine martial-looking men as I ever saw, attached to the Northern Army on its march from Plattsburgh to Sackett's Harbor."

Charles Pinckney of South Carolina, who was strongly pro-slavery, said "They (the Negroes) all entered into the great contest with similar views. Like brethren, they contended for the benefit of the whole, leaving to each the right to pursue happiness in his own way. Thus they nobly toiled and bled together, like brethren. And it is a remarkable fact, that, notwithstanding, in the course of the Revolution, the Southern States were continually overrun by the British and every Negro in them had the opportunity of running away, yet few did. They were then, as they still are, as valuable a part of our population to the Union as any other equal number of inhabitants. They were in numerous instances the pioneers, and in all, the laborers of your armies. To their hands were owing the erection of the greatest part of the fortifications raised for the protection of our country. Fort Moultrie gave, at an early period of the inexperience and untried valor of our citizens, immortality to American arms. And in the Northern states, numerous bodies of them were enrolled and fought, side by side, with whites, the battles of the Revolution." (Quoted in "Colored Americans in the Revolution and War of 1812, p. 8. 1861).

Charles Miner of Pennsylvania said in Congress, February 7, 1828, "The African race makes excellent soldiers. Large numbers of them were with Perry and helped to gain the brilliant victories of Lake Erie." Later writers write as strongly in praise of them. Whittier, the poet, wrote, "Their bones whiten every stricken field of the Revolution; their feet tracked with blood the snows of Jersey; their toil built up every fortification south of the Potomac; they shared the famine and nakedness of Valley Forge and the pestilential horrors of the old Jersey prison ship." (The Black Man in the Revolution. In Literary Recreations. 1854).

H. H. Bancroft said, "Free Negroes stood in the ranks by the side of white men at the beginning of the war. They had entered the provincial army . . . " Of the battle of Bunker Hill, he says, "Nor should history fail to record that as in the army at Cambridge so also in this gallant band the free Negroes of the colony had their representations . . . They took their place not in a separate corps but in the ranks with the white men; and their names may be read in the pension rolls of the country side by side with other soldiers of the Revolution . . . "(Bancroft, H. H. Vol. 7, p. 421).

It is not known how many of the 231,959 regular American soldiers were Negroes, but their number was considerable. As for their services as in building fortifications, the commissary, and the like, they were indispensable. Undoubtedly, the Negroes provided the balance of power that brought independence. When Sir Henry Clinton saw how they had helped turn the tide, he wrote Lord Germaine, British Minister of State, "Thus, my lord, are we deprived of another principal support." It is safe to say that but for the aid of the Negro, independence would not have been won, at least when it was.

NEGROES IN WASHINGTON'S PERSONAL SERVICE

Washington with Negro helper on his surveying expeditions.

Negroes served as personal attendants to Washington during the war. Among them were Hamet Achmet, skilled as a maker of drums; Primus Hall, who once slept beside Washington; and William (Billy) Lee, who served Washington during the entire war and rode immediately behind him in reviews. Before that, he had helped Washington in his surveying. Washington gave him his freedom in his will and left him a pension "as a testimony of my sense of his attachment to me and for his faithful services in the Revolutionary War." Lee became famous. No less that five other Negroes claimed to be he. Count Arese of Italy mentions a dinner in Virginia he attended in 1826, in which a Negro was a guest of honor among the white aristocrats because he had served through the war with Washington. This might have been

William Lee. (A Trip to the Prairies, p. 27, 1834.)

Another Negro who served Washington personally was Christopher, who attended him in his last moments and was so solicitous of him that Washington several times asked him to sit and rest.

The Negro, most important in the life of Washington, was a British West Indian, probably a Jamaican, Samuel Francis, affectionately known as Black Sam. He owned the finest hostelry not only in New York but in colonial America. A man of taste, and fond of display, and a connoisseur of wines, he catered to high society. Aristocrats dined there and whenever big banquets were given, it was there. Washington and his staff ate there regularly. In May, 1783, when Washington and Sir Guy Carleton met to discuss peace terms, it was over a dinner there. After the great parade that followed the evacuation of New York by the British, November 24, 1783, the reception and banquet was held there, also it was from there that Washington bade his officers farewell on November 26.

Francis was a true patriot in spite of the risk. The English once set a shot from a warship in the harbor, crashing into his tavern. When New York called for troops, he was one of the first to enlist—as a private. Washington and his officers laid their plans there, and it was there the Sons of Liberty plotted the dumping of the cases of East India tea into the Hudson.

He helped the Revolution with food and money. Officers who couldn't afford to pay were fed free. After the war, Congress thanked him warmly and gave him a large sum. Washington considered him steward, par excellence, and begged him to take charge of the Presidential mansion. New York was then the capital. When it was shifted to Philadelphia, Francis went there, too.

Washington said of Francis, "You have in-

JOURNAL OF CONGRESS.

MONDAY, APRIL 4, 1785.

Congress assembled—Present as before.

On the report of a committee consisting of Mr. King, Mr. R. R. Livingston and Mr. Ellery, to whom was referred a memorial of Samuel Frauncis.

Resolved, That the secretary of Congress take a lease from Samuel Frauncis for his house, now occupied by the public, for the term of two years, at the rate of eight hundred and twelve dollars, and one half of a dollar a year.

That a warrant be drawn in favor of the said Samuel Frauncis, for the sum of sixteen hundred and twenty-five dollars, on account of the said rent, and to discharge a mortgage on said house.

That in consideration of the singular services of the said Samuel Frauncis, and of his advances to the American prisoners, the sum of two thousand dollars be paid to the said Samuel Frauncis, on account of the loan office certificates in his hands, and that they be delivered up and cancelled.

TUESDAY, APRIL 5, 1785.

Congress assembled—Present as before.

Congress

Samuel Frauncis, important figure of the Revolution and later Washington's steward. He wears a wig. Right. Recognition of his services by Congress.

variably through the most trying times maintained a constant friendship and attention to the cause of our country and its independence and freedom . . ."

But Francis' daughter, Phoebe, did even more than her father. She saved Washington's life. In Washington's bodyguard was an Irishman, named Hickey, an agent of the British, sent there to kill Washington. Hickey began by making love to Phoebe, who used to wait on Washington, and poisoned a dish of peas that was to be served to him. Phoebe, learning of it, warned him. Washington threw the peas out of the window to the chickens, who picked them up and fell dead.

Hickey was hanged with a great crowd looking on. This account is told by B. J. Lossing, one of America's ablest, most reliable historians,

in his "Life of Washington" (Vol. 2, pp. 175-177. 1860). Lossing says he got the story directly from an eye-witness. Also Solomon Drowne, a surgeon, wrote his sister, Sally, June 24, 1776, "A most infernal plot has been discovered here which had it been put into execution would have made America tremble and had been a fatal stroke." H. R. Drowne, head of the Sons of the Revolution, says Phoebe "was Washington's housekeeper . . . it was she who revealed the plot to assassinate Generals Washington and Putnam, which led to the apprehension of her lover, an Irishman, named Thomas Hickey, British deserter, then a member of Washington's bodyguard, of which he was promptly executed on June 28, 1776." He cites same from the Orderly Book, of that date. (Fraunces Tavern, p. 12 et seq.). The Dictionary of National Biography has a sketch of Francis. This is his

Phoebe, daughter of Samuel Francis, saving George Washington who was about to be poisoned. (From the painting by Earl Sweeting).

correct name. The change to "Fraunces" was probably to give his tavern tone. He wasn't French either, but a British West Indian, probably from Jamaica. In French his name would be Francois. He was popularly known as "Black Sam" and is so mentioned in Freneau's poem. He was much darker that he appears in this portrait and wore a wig. (See data in the "100 Amazing Facts About the Negro," p. 17.)

NEGROES IN THE WAR OF 1799

In 1799, sixteen years later, an undeclared war, known as the Quasi-War, broke out between America and her former ally, France, principally over America's commercial relations with Toussaint L'Ouverture. Again, it was an-

nounced that Negroes were not wanted. "No mulattos, Negroes, or Indians," said James McHenry, Secretary of War. But again, they were used and distinguished themselves. One, Jack Groves of Portland, Maine, was one of the heroes of the day. When his ship was captured by the French, and the crew, most of them white, made prisoners, he led them in revolt and took the ship safely to Portland. Rayford W. Logan has given the names of some of the Negroes who distinguished themselves, among them George Diggs, quartermaster of the Experiment, and Moses Armstead and William Brown of the Constellation. (Negro History Bulletin, March 1951. Battle, C. A. Negroes of Rhode Island, p. 31. 1892).

And how did Negroes benefit from these services and this devotion? Lafayette said on his return to America in 1824, "I would never have

115

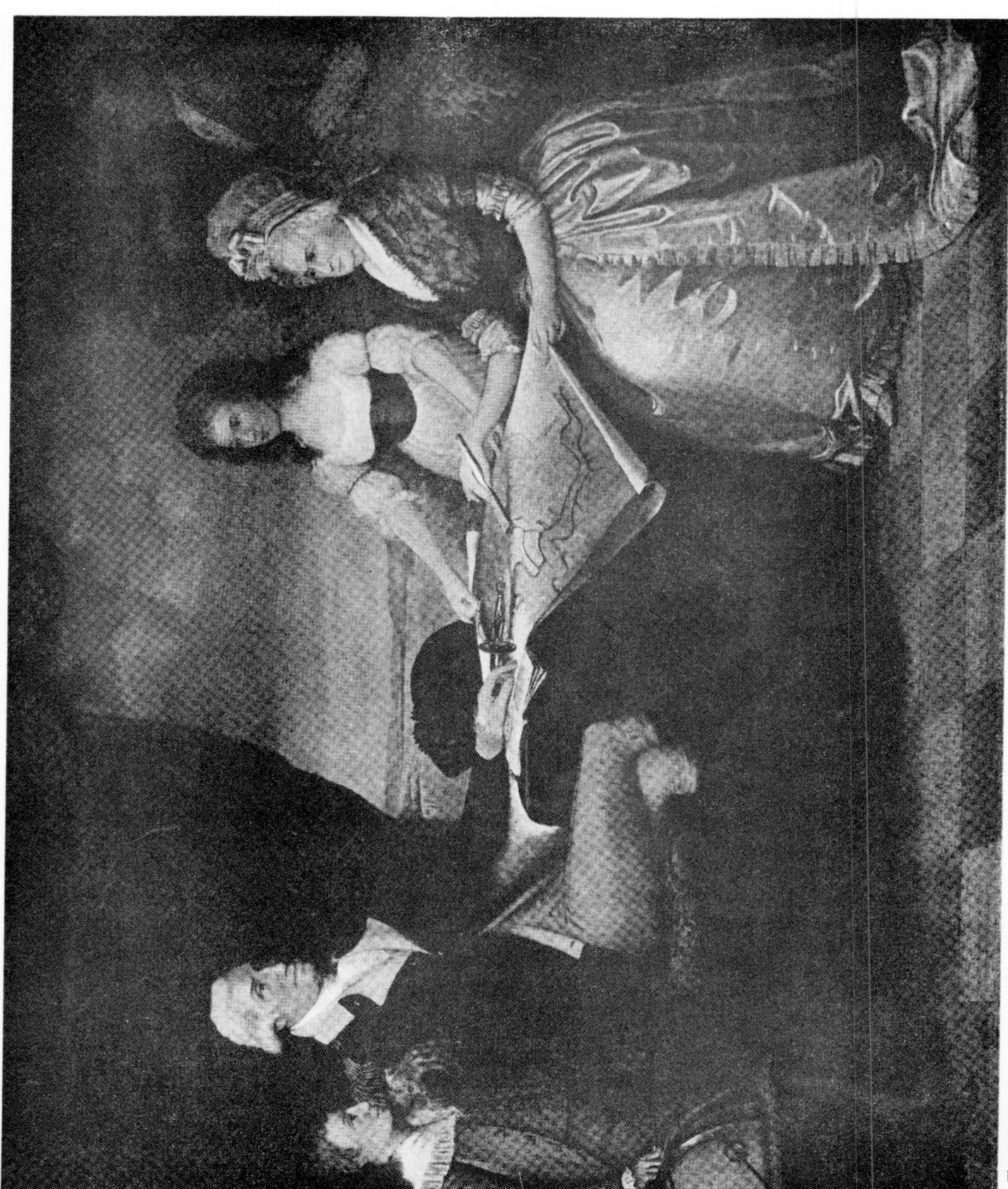

The Washington family with William Lee (right) Washington's most trusted servant. From the painting by Savage (1761-1817) N.Y. A Gall. ^

drawn my sword in the cause of freedom of America, could I have conceived that thereby I was founding a land of slavery." (Loyal Pub. Society No. 18 p. 14. 1863).

WAR OF 1812

A third war came in 1812. The issue was over "free trade and sailor's rights." England accused America of trading with Toussaint L'Ouverture, who had driven the French out of Haiti. England, then at war with Napoleon, blockaded the American coast from Maine to Georgia. Having defeated Napoleon at sea, she had the ships to spare.

Again, the Negroes came into the fight, although their services in the clash with France in 1799, like those in the Revolution, had been practically forgotten. In fact, it was the patriotism of three Negro sailors—Martin, Ware, and Strachan—that led most directly to America's declaration of war. The three, American-born, had been impressed into the British Navy, had deserted, and joined America during the war. The British had boarded their ship, the Chesapeake, and taken them off.

In this war there was again the difficulty of getting white men to enlist. Why the British were victorious at sea could be understood, but why also on land since they were in 1812 engaged in a life and death struggle with Napoleon? Negroes were accepted gladly now and regiments of them were at once provided for.

America, at the start of the war, invaded Canada. The British not only drove them out but occupied Detroit and invaded Ohio as far as the Sandusky River. In 1814, after Napoleon was defeated and sent to Elba, England, who now had the troops to spare, continued to win. America's sea-borne trade, was practically wiped out. On land the British were victorious also. They captured Florida and much of the South. Marching on Washington, they cap-

tured it and burnt the White House, and other public buildings, including the Capitol, August 24, 1814.

Single American ships won a few brilliant victories at sea but what brought about peace were chiefly victories on the Great Lakes. Much of the credit for this was due to the Negroes. Some crews had as many as one Negro to every five whites. Commodore Perry, chief hero of these battles, had the greatest difficulty getting men. Once when Chauncey sent him reinforcements, he complained, "The men that came are a motley set—blacks, soldiers, and boys. I cannot think you saw them after they were selected. I am, however, pleased to see anything in the shape of a man." (Mackenzie's Life of Perry, Vol. 1, pp. 165-6.) Chauncey replied "I regret that you are not pleased with the men sent you by Messrs. Champlin and Forrest, for, to my knowledge, a part of them are not surpassed by any seamen we have in the fleets; and I have yet to learn that the color of the skin, or the cut and trimmings of the coat, can affect a man's qualifications. I have nearly fifty blacks on board this ship and many of them are among my best men. . . ."

These blacks fought so well at the battle of Lake Erie, that Perry changed his mind. Perry's closest friend was a Negro, Hannibal Collins, who commanded his barge, at Lake Erie.

After the defeat of the British squadron under Captain Barclay by Perry, Chauncey says that when Barclay was brought a prisoner aboard the Niagara "and saw the sickly, partly-colored beings around him, an expression of chagrin escaped him at having been conquered by them."

Usher Parsons, a naval surgeon, wrote, "The white and colored men messed together. . . . There seemed to be an entire absence of prejudice against the blacks as mess-mates of the crew. What I have said applies to the crews of the other ships that sailed in squadrons."

When Captain Lawrence arrived in New York with his men after his victory over the

Battle of Lake Erie. Commander of his barge was Hannibal Collins.

Battle of Lake Champlain, War of 1812.

"Peacock", all received a joyous welcome and were feted at the Park Hotel. A news report of the affair said "a full half" of the men were Negroes.

Matthew, Perry's younger brother, also had Negroes under him. He had many on his ships when he went to Japan. In his parade through Tokyo, he had two blacks of magnificent build to walk on either side of him. (Perry, M. C. Narrative of an Expedition to the China Seas and Japan in 1852. p. 255. 1856.)

America's most brilliant victory in this war came at New Orleans. The British, having captured Florida, intended that city as their next prize. To Andrew Jackson, assigned to its defense, it all seemed a forlorn hope. Against the large and well-trained British forces, he had less than 3,000 men, white.

At that time, Negroes outnumbered the whites almost two to one in the city. They were badly treated, too, and the British, as in 1776, were offering them freedom. British victories in Florida had been much aided by them. Now they seemed the only hope of saving New Orleans. But as in 1776, the whites feared putting arms in their hands. Jackson had no choice, however. In a last desperate effort, September 21, 1814, he appealed to the blacks, thus: "Through a mistaken policy you have heretofore been deprived of a participation in the glorious struggle for national rights. This no longer shall exist.

"As sons of freedom, you are now called upon to defend our most estimable blessing." Promising them equality, he added, "To every noble-hearted freeman of color volunteering to serve during the present contest with Great Britain, and no longer, there will be paid the same bounty in money and lands, now received by white soldiers of the United States, namely, one hundred and twenty-four dollars in money and sixty acres of land. . . ." To avoid snubs by the whites, they would be enlisted in a separate corps, he said. The advantage of this would be, "As a distinct, independent battalion or regiment, pursuing the path of glory, you will, undivided, receive the applause and gratitude of your countrymen." He gave his word he said "With the sincerity of a soldier and the language of truth." Trusting to his promise the Negroes responded by thousands. Manning the breastworks, they awaited the English.

They came the second week in December up the Mississippi with 12,000 men in sixty ships and landed. The Americans mowed them down as they came on wave after wave. After two weeks and the loss of 4,000 men, they finally sailed away.

After the battle, Jackson addressed the Negro troops, "Soldiers," he said, "when on the banks of the Mobile, I called you to take up arms, inviting you to partake the perils and glory of your white fellow-citizens, I expected much from you; for I was not ignorant that you possesed qualities most formidable to an invading enemy. I knew with what fortitude you could endure hunger and thirst, and all the fatigues of a campaign. I knew well how you loved your native country, and that you, as well as ourselves, had to defend what man holds most dear,—his parents, wife, children, and property. You have done more than I expected. In addition to the previous qualities I before knew you to possess, I found among you a noble en-

thusiasm, which leads to the performance of great things.

"Soldiers! The President of the United States shall hear how praiseworthy was your conduct in the hour of danger, and the representatives of the American people will give you the praise your exploits entitle you to. Your General anticipates them in applauding your noble ardor."

The services rendered by these Negroes were soon forgotten. Jeffrey, one of those singled out for praise by Andrew Jackson and made an honorary major, was given thirty-nine lashes on his bare back for striking a white man, of which he died. He was then seventy. At the height of the battle, he had leaped to a horse, rallied a party of white men who were retreating, and led them in a charge.

It was not until 1851, thirty-six years later, that the Negroes were publicly remembered in the anniversary parade. The New Orleans Picayune said of them, "Not the least interesting, although the most novel, feature of the procession yesterday was the presence of ninety of the colored veterans who bore a conspicuous part in the dangers of the day and who by their good conduct in presence of the enemy deserved the approbation of their illustrious commander-in-chief. . . .

"The respectability of their appearance, and the modesty of their demeanor made an impression on every observer and elicited unqualified approbation. Indeed, though in saying so we do not mean disrespect to anyone else, we think that they constituted decidedly the most interesting portion of the pageant as they certainly attracted the most attention."

Among them was Jordan B. Noble, a drummer who led the attack. When he died in 1854, last survivor of the battle, New Orleans gave him a public funeral, and turned out to do him honor.

Another notable figure of this war was Richard Seavers, better known as Big Dick.

120

Born in Salem, Mass., he had joined the British Navy but had deserted to the Americans. Captured with other Americans, he was thrown into Dartmoor Prison, England. After the war he was freed and lived in Boston where he cut a big figure. He is one of the principal characters in Kenneth Roberts' novel, "Lydia Bailey." W. C. Nell in "Colored Patriots of the Revolution (p. 27. 1855) reproduces newspaper accounts of him.

Negro soldiers helped greatly in the winning of the west from the Indians. Four regiments of them—the 24th and 25th Infantry and the Ninth and Tenth Cavalry were organized to guard the railroads from Indian attack. They were especialy useful in Texas and Utah. They chased away the Indian chief, Victoria, and drove the Sioux into Canada. (Negro Hist. Bull. March 1951, p. 144.)

General Butler said of the Ninth Cavalry at Fort Myers, "For good conduct in the field against the Indians and for soldierly bearing (they) exhibited to all comers instances of the best qualities of America's cavalry." In their battles with Indians, fourteen won the Congressional Medal of Honor, America's highest decoration for valor.

NOTES ON CRISPUS ATTUCKS

Because of his name—Attucks was an Indian tribe—some assert that he was an Indian. However all the evidence points to the fact the he was predominantly Negro. The killing of the five resulted in a lengthy trial which appears in full and actual detail in F. Kidder's History of the Boston Massacre, published 1870. There we have the testimony of eyewitnesses who called him "mulatto." Moreover, the Crown Prosecutor, Samuel Quincy, in his address to the jury calls him "a mulatto" (p. 164). As was said, his body was exhibited in Faneuil Hall, where thousands came to see it, and most likely the Crown Prosecutor, himself. John Adams, who undoubtedly must have seen the body, too, in his address to the jury, called him a "mulatto."

Some writers class the "Boston Massacre" as a street brawl and quote John Adams, who said in his address to the jury, "The plain English is, gentlemen, most probably a motley rabble of saucy boys, Negroes, and mulattoes, Irish teagues and outlandish jack-tars; and why should we scruple to call such a set of people a mob, I can't conceive unless the name is too respectable for them." (Kidder, p. 255). He refers to them again as "a rabble of Negroes," and calls Attucks sarcastically "hero of the night." But that was the John Adams, lawyer for the defense; John Adams, the patriot, said just the opposite, as seen on the Attucks Monument.

Adams thought so highly of Attucks that in July the same year, he sent a letter to Thomas Hutchinson, the royal governor, and signed Attucks' name to it. It says in part: "Sir, You will hear from us with astonishment. You ought to hear from us with horror. You are chargeable before God and man with our blood. The soldiers were but passive agents, mere machines. . . ."

Signed: Chrispus Attucks.
(Works of John Adams, Vol. 2 p. 322.)

John Fiske, in his dedicatory address at the monument said Attucks was a native of Nassau, West Indies.

THE AFRICANS IN THE MAKING OF AMERICA: ECONOMIC DEPENDENCE ON THEM

The War of Independence gave Africa a respite from the American slave-trader. Business had fallen off to such extent that slavery seemed on the way out. Some colonies, as Virginia, began to agitate for the end of the external slave trade. Virginia had a surplus of slaves and their price was falling. At the constitutional convention in Philadelphia, she incurred the anger of South Carolina, because of her demand that it be ended. But six years later she was to be stronger for it than she had been against it. The invention of the cotton gin, that year (1793), gave slavery an immense spurt. The United States, which up to then had been producing cotton enough for only her own use—2,000,000 lbs. a year was, in 1801, selling to England alone 18,000,000 lbs.; and in 1811, 62,000,000, plus her own consumption. The South's demand for slaves as well as that of Central America, the West Indies, Venezuela, and Brazil, soared. America, with no England to dictate to her now, could buy molasses wherever she wished.

But, alas, for those slave states that had opposed the slave trade! Their agitation, aided vigorously by the abolitionists, had borne fruit. In 1794, Congress forbade Americans and American ships to engage in the trade. Result: the spectacle of Americans defying their own government on the same matter they had done George III. This worsened in 1808, when America, by international agreement, forbade all importation of Africans to her own shores.

Smuggling on an immense scale became the order of the day. Indeed, one can hardly call it smuggling. The trade was bringing in so much money that the federal government virtually closed its eyes for the next fifty-three years. Seward, Lincoln's Secretary of State, said, "The African slave trade continued to thrive in defiance of laws and treaties. Public sentiment was adverse but private cupidity was strong. Courts were lax and officials blind." (Autobiography Vol. 3, p. 167. 1891.)

Captain Richard Drake,[1] a smuggler of the 1830's, tells how his ship, Napoleon, made a clear profit of $100,040 on the Cuban market with 250 adults and 100 boys and girls. "Such," he said, "were the enormous profits of the slave trade in 1835, and since that period, with greater risk, have come greater average returns."

Slave smuggling was a veritable gold mine. Foner[1a] cites other fabulous figures of the times. C. A. Lamar of Georgia estimated that a cargo of 1,200 Negroes at $650 a head would bring in a clear profit of $480,000. The Journal of Commerce, Feb. 29, 1861, said the slaver, Espoir, had made a profit of $436,000 on one trip.

J. G. Spears cites, among others the case of the VENUS, American ship, built in Baltimore, at a cost of $30,000, which landed a cargo of 860 slaves in Cuba at a profit of nearly $200,000 after allowing for the cost of the ship and all expenses, including a bribe of $27.50 a head to the Cuban officials. Another American ship, LES TRES AMIGOS, delivered 1,350 slaves to Bahia, Brazil, at a fabulous profit.[2] Two hundred and two cargoes of slaves were landed at Charleston, S. C. alone January 1, 1804 to December 31,

1807, 128 of which were American ships, with a total of 39,075 slaves.[2a]

Slave-breeding became an important industry in the South but that was too slow. The demand was immediate and imperative. Savannah and other Southern ports showed very brisk trade. De Bow's Magazine said, "It cannot be denied that the Southern States—more especially those in which are grown the great staples of cotton, sugar, and rice—demand a greater number of Negro laborers than can now be acquired by natural increase or from those sources which have hitherto yielded but a sparse supply." The price of slaves, it said, "has reached that point which is beyond the means of small planters." Able-bodied slaves sold as high as $1,835, or about $10,000 now.

The "smugglers" made no efforts to conceal their activities. At a political convention in Montgomery, Ala., Spratt of South Carolina, openly boasted of his. Several conventions voted for the reopening of the slave trade.

Two of those who acted openly were C. A. Lamar of Savannah, and Zephaniah Kingsley of Florida. The Atlanta Daily Intelligencer, March 5, 1859, gave full details of a cargo of slaves landed in Savannah at that time for Lamar on the notorious "Wanderer."[3] The "Wanderer" was a fast, new 104-foot schooner belonging to Captain W. C. Corrie of the New York Yacht Club. Once, in 1858, when Corrie arrived off the Slave Coast, he found a British warship blockading the coast against slavers. With the Yacht Club's flag at his masthead, he invited the officers of the ship aboard, entertained them and when the ship was gone, loaded 750 slaves and sailed off to Savannah. He made other trips and was finally expelled from the club.

New York City, not New England, was now the center of this illicit trade. Its hundred or more slave-ships took hundreds of thousands of them to the Slave States of the South, the West Indies and Central and South America. Cuba alone took some 60,000 annually. New York became known as "the greatest slave-trading mart in the world." Between February 1859 and July 1860, some 85 new ships were fitted out there for the trade.

T. P. Kettel, writing at that time said in his "History of the Great Rebellion," New York was "the commercial centre of the Union and her acquired wealth made her its financial head. The capital of the whole country came to her for investment. Her own vast capital moved the crops of the West and the exchanges based on Southern production were negotiated in her market. She was the factor for every producer, the banker for every merchant, she was, so to speak, the negotiator between every section of the Union and foreign nations."

The origin and the chief support of this financial power was slave smuggling and the profits from slave-grown products. New York's corner on that trade made her bitterly hated in the South. In 1860 when the London Times asked "What would New York be without slavery?" James De Bow, leading Southern journalist, replied, "The ships would rot at her docks, grass would grow in Wall Street and Broadway, and the glory of New York, like that of Rome would be numbered with the things of the past."[4] It does appear as if New York got its start as the world's leading metropolis from the sale of Africans and the fruits of their enslavement.

New York State had abolished slavery in 1827, or thirty-three years earlier, but New York City remained pro-slavery. In 1860, it voted against Lincoln by 30,000 in spite of the campaign in his favor by influential citizens. The city would lose its trade if Lincoln won, the pro-slavery "Union" declared. In 1861, when Lincoln did put his foot down and Captain Nathaniel Gordon, whose ship the ERIE, with 271 adults and 621 children had been captured by the USS MOHAWK, was sentenced to death, angry mobs stormed the jail to free him. At his execution, February 21, 1862, eighty-four marines were needed to keep order. New York was so pro-slavery that Boston was advised not to send its Negro troops by rail through the state! They had to be sent South by ship. The same year, New York saw the anti-draft riot

Execution of Gordon, slave-smuggler in New York, Feb. 21, 1862.

with the greatest massacre of Negroes in American history, Negroes were lynched on the streets and a Negro orphan asylum set on fire by the mob. New York continued its smuggling to Cuba till 1886, the year of its emancipation.[5]

SACO'S QUERY ON AFRICA
APPLIED TO THE UNITED STATES

To apply Saco's question to the United States: What would have been her fate had there been no Africa? Would she have been where the other nations of the New World now are, say, like her neighbor, Mexico? Brazil is larger than the United States and with as great or greater economic resources, yet she is behind America.

Where would the New England merchants have found other primitive people they could have traded for rum? Not in East Asia. That region and Egypt, since the Pharaohs had been tapping Africa's source of labor. Moreover, the people there are Moslems and do not use strong drink. They would not have got them in India or China either, and if they did there would have been months of voyage to bring them by Cape Horn. It is safe to say that unless New England could have found something else to give her commerce so good a start, America's fate might have been much less brilliant. Fur-

124

Charlie Smith of Polk County, Texas, last known living slave brought to America. Born in Liberia about 1842, he was kidnapped. Was recently featured among living centenarians in Coronet Magazine.

presses how desire for the plundering of Africa triumphed over finer feelings, even to the extent of pressing Christian gospel into its justification. He says:

"Molasses and alcohol, rum and slaves, gold and iron moved in a perpetual round of commerce. The most enterprising and active ports only admitted the more of the fetid misery. All society was fouled in the lust, inflamed by the passion for wealth, callous to the wrongs of imported savage or displaced barbarian. The shallow sympathy expressed in the seventeenth century for Indians and native proprietors had expended itself. A new continent in possession, old Ethopia must be ransacked that the holders might enjoy it more speedily. Cool, shrewd, sagacious merchants with punctilious, dogmatic priests in promoting this prostitution of industry." (Amer. Antiquar. Soc'y Jour. pp. 107-128. 1887.)

NOTES

1. Revelations of a Slave Smuggler, p. 93. 1860.

1a. Foner, P., Business and Slavery, pp. 1-14. 1941.

2. Scribner's Vol. 28, July 1900, pp. 3-15, 304-314; The American Slave Trade. 1901.

2a. De Bow, J. D., Industrial Resources of the South, etc. Vol. 2, pp. 340-42. He gives the names of ships, 1804-1807 at Charleston.

3. Jackson, H. R., The Wanderer Case, 1851; Dow, G. F., Slave Ships & Slaving, pp. 267 et seq. 1927.

4. Quoted by Foner, p. 4.

5. An African or two of those times might still be alive. One, Cudjoe Lewis, who was kidnapped in Liberia in 1847, was interviewed at his home in Mobile, Alabama, by the Journal of Negro History in 1937. Another, Charlie Smith of Polk County, Texas, was featured in 1957 in Coronet Magazine's article on centenarians. He was born in Liberia in 1842 and brought to America at the age of twelve. He was said to look like "a spry seventy," and the pictures of him showed it. The Baltimore Afro-American, March 4, 1961 has a recent picture of him alive.

thermore, we have seen how important were the Africans in the race for the possession of North America by the Spaniards, French, Dutch and English in the sixteenth and seventeenth centuries. But for their presence, Virginia, Texas, and New York might not have become English colonies.

It must be noted that little or no humane considerations entered into this evil. W. B. Weeden, in giving precise data, correctly ex-

Part Three

THE NEGRO IN THE SAVING OF AMERICA

THE CIVIL WAR

"The destiny of the nation has the Negro as its pivot." Frederick Douglass.

That Americans of African ancestry provided the balance of power that saved the Union and makes a United States of America possible today was very definitely the opinion of the one most qualified to say it: Abraham Lincoln.

On March 26, 1863, he wrote Andrew Johnson (his successor), "The colored population is the great available and yet unavailed of force for saving the union. The bare sight of 50,000 armed and drilled black soldiers upon the banks of the Mississippi would end the rebellion at once." On March 29, 1863, he said "To now avail ourselves of this force is very important, if not indispensable."

To Governor Seymour of New York "It is a resource, which if vigorously applied will soon close the contest."

Early in the war, Lincoln saw (as did Washington in the Revolution) that the war couldn't be won without the Negro's help; that without it the United States as a single nation would cease to exist. In its place would be two countries: The Confederate States of America to the South, composed of eleven states—Alabama, Arkansas, Florida, Georgia, Mississippi. North Carolina, South Carolina, Louisiana, Tennessee, Texas and Virfiinia; and a United States of the North Texas and Virginia; and a United States of the North and West. The South was winning.

DEFEAT FOR THE NORTH

The war began with the South's seizing most of the twenty-nine federal naval and military bases in its territory. On April 12, 1861, it attacked Fort Sumter, whose undermanned garrison surrendered two days later with a loss of 15 dead on both sides.

The North regarded all this as sheer bravado. The South was not only financially dependent on the North but to its 9,000,000 souls the North had 23,000,000. And while 3,500,00o of the Southern population were slaves, nearly all of the North was white and free. When one con-

gressman shouted, "We'll crush the rebels as easily as an elephant tramples on a mouse," the North lustily agreed.

Lincoln called for 75,000 men. On July 18, the Army of the Potomac, 28,455 strong under General McDowell, crossed into Virginia.

Invasion Made Into a Picnic

So certain was the North of victory that the invasion turned into a picnic. Congressmen, their wives, and society leaders followed the army in carriages with baskets of food, whisky, champagne, and bands of music. Livery stables made a fortune renting horses and buggies. A thousand dollars was asked for one broken-down horse.

To the soldiers it was a sporting event. "On to Richmond," they shouted, singing and strumming guitars. In high glee they tore down Confederate flags, looted Southern homes, smashed pianos for wood to barbecue pigs and ogled Southern belles. They dressed in looted women's clothes and hats and strutted to the amusement of all. One dressed as a preacher read the "funeral service" over Jefferson Davis, Confederate President. Discipline was forgotten. They took off their shoes to loll in the shade and broke ranks to pick fruit. If this was war, they wanted more of it.

Union Announces Easy Victories

Advanced outposts of Confederates ran from them without firing a shot. Telegrams were sent announcing great victories. The Washington, New York, and Boston papers carried glowing accounts. The war was being a walk-over as they predicted.

Three days and twenty miles later they reached Bull Run. Here the Confederate army of some 24,000 under General Beauregard waited. McDowell, Union commander, got his men ready for battle but the Southerners, already in the best positions, held them off. When finally the Confederate cavalry charged, uttering the rebel yell, the Union soldiers ran in panic, leaving their artillery, guns, ammunition, wagons, and equipment behind. Also 481 dead, 1124 wounded, and over 1500 prisoners.

The New York World gave a graphic account of the catastrophe. Its correspondent said, "By the time I reach the top of the hill, the retreat, the panic, the hideous head-long confusion were beyond a hope."

Sir William Howard Russell, war correspondent of the London Times, wrote, "A cowardly rout, a miserable causeless panic. Such scandalous behaviour on the part of soldiers I should never have considered possible."

North Frightened; Lincoln Stunned

Washington, fed with glowing accounts of victory, was panic-stricken. Lincoln returned from his Sunday morning drive, certain of victory, to receive this telegram, *"McDowell's army in full retreat. The day is lost. Save Washington."*

News came that the Confederates were marching on the Whitt House. Thousands fled the city. Lincoln, from a window, saw his men straggling back, dropping exhausted in the streets, sleeping where they fell, oblivious to the women offering them coffee. He didn't know what to do. Neither did Congress.

Russell wrote, "The President and his Ministers, stunned by the tremendous calamity, sat listening in fear and trembling for the sound of the enemy's cannon. . . . At any moment the Confederate columns might be expected in Pennsylvania Avenue. . . . If in the present state of the troops the Confederates were to march on Washington, the Capitol must fall into their hands. . . . General Winfield Scott (head of the army) is quite overwhelmed by the affair and is unable to tsir. The Secretary of War knows not what to do. Mr. Lincoln is equally helpless. . . ."

Horace Greeley of the New York Tribune

wrote Lincoln, "The gloom in this city is funereal. . . . On every brow sits sullen, scorching despair." If it's best for the country and mankind, he said, "make peace with the rebels at once and on their own terms." McDowell reported, "The larger part of the army is a confused mob, entirely demoralized."

More Union Defeats

Another defeat at Wilson's Creek, August 10, staggered the North even more. Russell wrote, "The severest battle since Waterloo. It was Manassas (Bull Run) all over again. Once the Federal troops gave way they did not stand on the order of their going."

A third defeat at Ball's Bluff convinced Lincoln all was lost. He came out of the telegraph office tears streaming down his cheeks, groping blindly. He staggered and would have fallen had not the newspapermen caught him. General Sherman said, "Nobody, no man can save the country. Our men are not good soldiers. They brag but they don't perform. What is in store for us I don't know." The North had some little success principally on the sea and in the West, as the war dragged on. But defeat seemed certain. Russell wrote, "So short-lived has been the American Union that men who saw its rise may now see its fall. . . . The voluntary enlistments entreated by the President and sought to be expedited by bribes of bounty-money have lamentably failed. The President asked for 300,000 men and in five weeks less than 30,000 offered themselves. . . . In fact much as the North hates disunion it hates Negro emancipation still more. . . . The South gets heated as the North grows cold. Jefferson Davis takes heart as Lincoln loses it."

By July 1862, it seemed all over for the North. At least, Lincoln firmly believed so. His only hope was to win over the slaves of the South and have them fight on his side by offering them freedom. Here are his own words as told to Artist F. B. Carpenter." *Midsummer 1862 things had gone from bad to worse until*

I felt we had reached the end of our rope on the plan of operation we had ben pursuing; that we had about played our last card, and must change our tactics, or lose the game. I now determined upon the adoption of the emancipation policy; and without consultation with or the knowledge of the Cabinet, I pre- *pared the original draft of the proclamation, and, after much anxious thought, called a Cabinet meeting upon the subject."*

The Cabinet, says Lincoln, was shocked at hearing the state to which the Union had been reduced, Secretary Seward in particular. Seward said while he favored the proclamation,

Thomas W. Higginson, Colonel of the First South Carolina Volunteers, and an outstanding foe of slavery.

Eminent foes of the Slave Power.

Great foes of slavery. Left to right, Upper: John Brown, Harriet Beecher Stowe, Count Adam Gurowski. Lower: Henry W. Longfellow, Henry Thoreau, Ralph Waldo Emerson.

he did not its issuance. "I question the expediency of its issue at this juncture," he said. "The depression of the public mind, consequent upon our repeated reverses is so great that I fear the effect of so important a step. It may be viewed as the last measure of an exhausted government, a cry for help; the government stretching forth its hands to Ethiopia, instead of Ethiopia stretching forth her hands to the government." Such a step, added Seward, "would be considered the last *shriek* on the retreat." (Lincoln: Complete Works, Vol. 2, pp. 479-80. 1894.)

This view of the Union's predicament is amply supported by the dispatches of foreign correspondents as that of the Illustrated London News, August 30 and September 20. On October 4, 1862, this paper said, "Southern independence is no longer a dream but a fact."

Lincoln says that Seward's gloomy prediction caused him to postpone the proclamation another six months. "But," he said, "from time to time I added or changed a word. Well, the next news we had was of Pope's disaster at Bull Run. Things looked darker than ever. Finally came the week of Antietam. I determined to wait no longer."

With the South revealed as a foe to be reckoned with the question is: Why did the able and far-seeing Lincoln wait two years to use his trump. He knew at the start of the war that the Negro was the balance of power. On the day before the South struck, Ashmore of South Carolina, said in the House, "The South can sustain more men in the field than the North. Her 4,000,000 slaves alone will enable her to support an army of half a milion men in the field."

Karl Marx, away on the other side of the Atlantic, was able to see this. He wrote Engels, August 7, 1862, "The North, itself, has turned the slaves into a military force on the side of the Southerners instead of turning it against them. The South leaves productive labor to the slaves and can therefore put its fighting strength in the field." Lincoln knew also that the Confederates had seized most of the twenty-nine army army bases in the South. "Uncle Sam," said Russell of the London Times," has built strong places for his enemies to occupy."

Lincoln knew, too, how the South feared a revolt of the slaves. Its leaders knew what had happened to the whites of Haiti when their slaves revolted. Lincoln had letters from the South warning him against this. One, January 14, 1861, said, "The whites here cannot without endangering their lives allow you to take the Presidential chair. They, the Negroes might start a servile war. Even now many are living in constant fear of insurrection on the part of the Negroes." Another one said, "They (the Negroes) have commenced their work of poisoning and incendiarism." Still another, "Could there be a greater curse than to let loose the 4,000,000 Southern Negroes freed amongst us?"

me outstanding and able foes of slavery in the Civil War. Left to right, upper: Colonel James Lewis, Rev. Henry Highland Garnett, "Mammy" Pleasant. Lower: Bishop Henry M. Turner, William Grant Still and Sojourner Truth.

WHY DID LINCOLN HESITATE TWO YEARS TO USE NEGRO TROOPS?

"We didn't go into the war to put down slavery but to put the flag back."—Lincoln: *Reply to church committee. Sept.* 13, 1862.

"In a certain sense the liberation of slaves is the destruction of property—property acquired by descent or by purchase, the same as any other property." — Lincoln: *Annual Message, Dec.* 1, 1862.

Lincoln fully realized the decisive value of black man-power. When it comes to this forget about color, he said. "It is not a question of sentiment or taste but one of physical force which may be measured or estimated as horse-power and steam-power are measured and estimated," he said. So great was the advantage of this black man-power to the South that with its only six million whites it was beating the North with its twenty million whites.

LINCOLN'S PROBLEMS

The answer why Lincoln had not used the Negro in the war so far is that the nation, as a whole, favored slavery. Pro-slavery opinion was strong in the North and with it a great prejudice against Negroes. In the presidential campaign of 1860 all four parties were for slavery to a greater or less degree. The three principal ones were the Republicans, headed by Lincoln; the Northern Democrats by Stephen Douglas; and the Southern Democrats by John Breckenridge. Lincoln was for the South keeping its slaves but opposed the extension of slavery into the territories like Kansas and Nebraska. These, he said, are places "for poor people to go to and better their condition." They were, indeed, the only refuge of the poor whites of the slave states, who were, on the whole, worse off than a slave with a kind master. Lincoln's stand was very important, too, because these territories were slowly being admitted into the Union (as Oregon and Kansas) and if they became slave states they would increase the power of the slave bloc in Congress. At bottom, of course, was the rivalry between the industrial North and agricultural South. We shall later see how the North was exploiting the South.

Douglas was for letting the white people choose just what they wanted to do about slavery. He had made that clear in his famous 1858 debates with Lincoln. "Slaves," he said, "are property and hence on an equality with all other kinds of property. This government of ours is founded on the white basis. It was founded by the white man to be administered by white men in such a manner as they should determine." The white man, he insisted, should decide what should be done about the Negroes. If in Minnesota and New York, white men decided Negroes should vote it should be so, he said, and if in the South, they held they were to be slaves, that also should be so. "I do not acknowledge that the Negro must have civil and political rights everywhere or nowhere." He declared he would follow the Constitution in the matter of States' rights. And the Constitution did say that slavery was legal. Douglas had no slaves himself but his wife, a Southerner, had 150 and he managed her estate.

Breckenridge was definitely pro-slavery. The Confederacy wrote in its Constitution, March 11, 1861, "No bill denying the right to own property in Negro slaves shall be passed." Alexander Stephens, its vice-president, said, "Our new government is founded on slavery . . . its foundations are laid, its corner-stone rests upon the great truth that the Negro is not the equal of the white man."

Lincoln, on his part, really hated slavery. But he knew that an open attack on it would hurt his chances. He had lost to Douglas in the contest for the Senate in 1858. The nation, as a whole, was in favor of slavery. Abolitionists were being very badly treated in the North and even worse in the South. John Brown had been hanged; Elijah Lovejoy beaten to death in Alton, Illinois, and his printing-press burned. Pennsylvania Hall, meeting-place of the abolitionsts at Philadelphia, was burned to the ground. Even in Boston, anti-slavery home, there were riots. Garrison was dragged through the streets of Boston with a rope around his neck; Whittier's carriage was fired on. Had Lincoln come out wholly against it he mightn't even have been nominated. As it was he received only 40 per cent of the votes cast in the 1860 election. Of the 4,645,390, he had only 1,857,610. Douglas had 1,291,674;; Breckenridge, 850,082; and Bell of the Constitutional Union, 646,124.

Lincoln, as was said, hated slavery deep within. Thirty years before when he saw some slaves chained together, he said. "That sight was a continual torment to me and I see something like it every time I touch the Ohio or any other slave border. . . . I confess I hate to see the poor creatures hunted down and caught and carried back to their stripes and unrequited toil but I bite my lip and keep quiet." He was a man of great compassion. Frederick Douglass said, after meeting him, "I saw the tender heart of the man rather than the commander-in-chief."

The Dred Scott decision had made Lincoln angry, not alone because it made the stand of the Republicans unconstitutional but also because it said that a Negro had no rights a white man was bound to respect. He declared that all men were created free and equal "was true of the Negro, too," and that if one might say it didn't include Negroes, it could be made to apply to other men.

To this Douglas had said that Lincoln thought the Almighty made the Negro his equal and his brother, but "for my part I do not consider the Negro any kin to me nor to any other white man." He openly charged Lincoln with promoting the marriage of whites and blacks in fact that that was his express purpose. An anti-Lincoln slogan was, "Would you have your sister marry a big, black buck nigger."

Lincoln was so emphatic in denying that that at times he had seemed even to outstrip Douglas in his stand on inequality for Negroes. "There is," he said, "a natural disgust in the minds of nearly all white people at the idea of an indiscriminate amalgamation of the white and black races; and Judge Douglas evidently is basing his chief hope upon the chances of his being able to appropriate the benefit of this disgust to himself. If he can, by much drumming and repeating, fasten the odium of that idea upon his adversaries, he thinks he can struggle through. . . .

"Judge Douglas will have it that I want a Negro wife. He can never be brought to understand that there is any middle ground on this subject. I have lived until my fiftieth year, and have never had a Negro woman either for a slave or a wife and I think I can live five centuries, for that matter, without having had one for either."

At another time he said, "The judge regales us with the terrible enormities that take place by the mixtures of races; that the inferior race bears the superior down.

"I will say then that I am not, nor ever have been, in favor of bringing about in any way the social and political equality of the white and black races—that I am not, nor ever have been, in favor of making voters or jurors of Negroes, nor of qualifying them to hold office, nor to intermarry with white people; and I will say in addition to this that there is a physical difference between the white and black races which I believe will forever forbid the races living together on terms of social and political equal-

Caricature on Lincoln and the charge that he was promoting mixed marriages. At extreme left he is seen bowing to mixed couple.

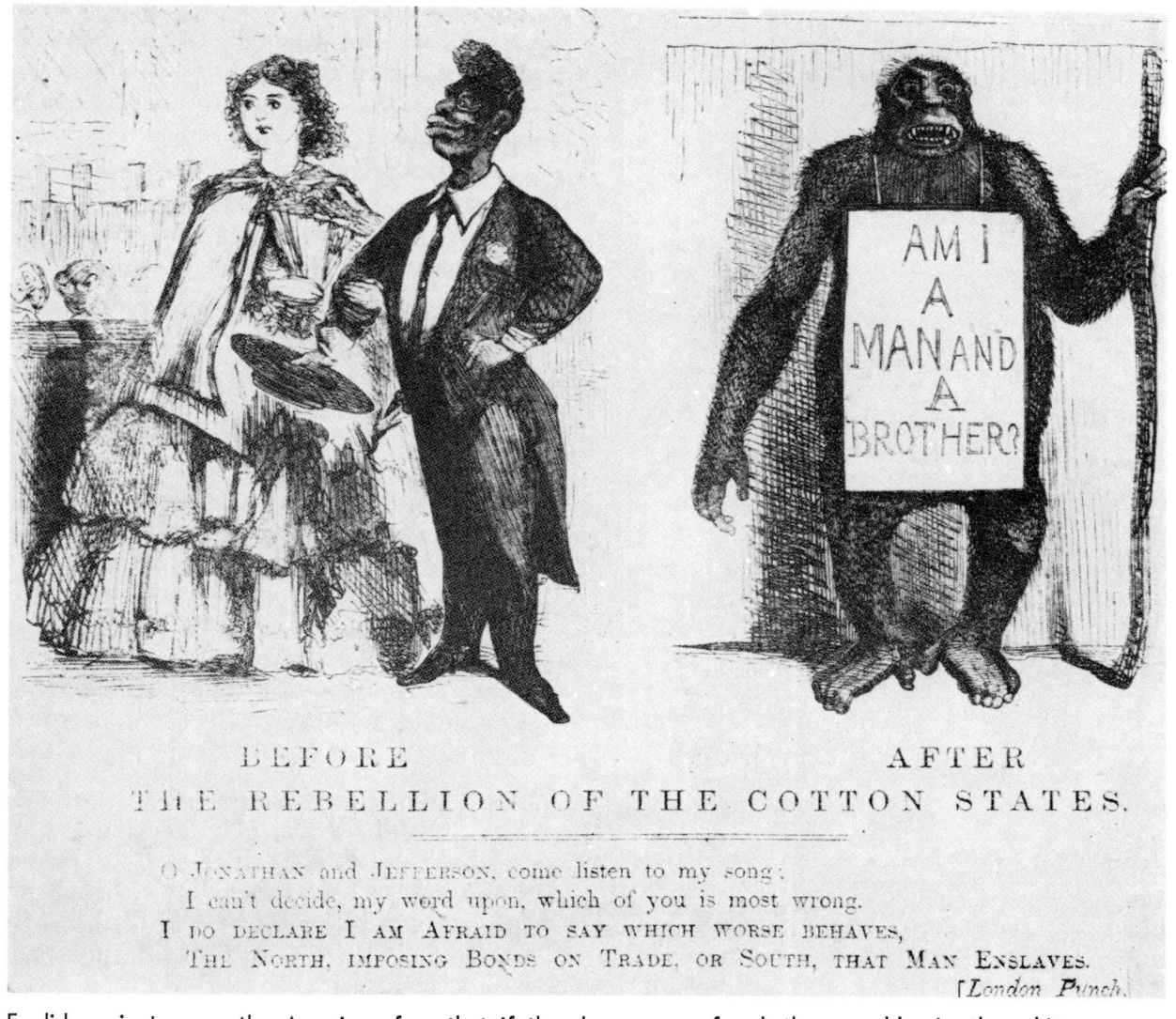

BEFORE   AFTER

THE REBELLION OF THE COTTON STATES.

O JONATHAN and JEFFERSON, come listen to my song;
    I can't decide, my word upon, which of you is most wrong.
I DO DECLARE I AM AFRAID TO SAY WHICH WORSE BEHAVES,
    THE NORTH, IMPOSING BONDS ON TRADE, OR SOUTH, THAT MAN ENSLAVES.

[London Punch.

English caricature on the American fear that if the slaves were freed they would win the white women.

ity. And inasmuch as they cannot so live, while they do remain together there must be the position of superior and inferior, and I, as much as any other man, am in favor of having the superior position assigned to the white race. . . ."

He said again, "The proposition that there is a struggle between the white man and the Negro contains a falsehood. There is no struggle. If there was, I should be for the white man. If two men are adrift at sea on a plank which will bear up but one, the law justifies either in pushing the other off. . . .

"I expressly declared that my own feelings would not admit of a social and political equality between the white and black races, and that even if my own feelings would admit of it, I still knew that the public sentiment of the country would not, and that such a thing was an utter impossibility."

Incidentally, statements like these make it

Creole Lady of New Orleans. A mixture of White, Negro and Indian, these gentlewomen were sometimes educated in France, were wealthy, had many slaves, and spoke French. Some whites of supposedly unmixed strain pretended to scorn them but they and their men were a power in the city. The word "Creole" itself is of African origin. African slaves in Peru called their children born there by that name.

clear that not the least of Lincoln's problems must have been the struggle with his own conscience—with that sense of right, logic, and humanity which he possessed to a very high degree. What he was saying on "race" politically was contrary to the evidence of his own senses and knowledge! He must have known that the South's howl against racial intermixture was rankest fraud. Not only had there been two centuries of freest, even planned mating of white men and black women in the slave states of the South but there had been legal

marriage of the two in some parts. This was especially true of Virginia. The census of 1830 names more than a few rich Negroes with white wives in the state. In fact so much amalgamation had taken place in the South that many whites were almost as white as some of the Negroes. In the North, on the other hand, there had been little such mating, even during slavery there.

Vincent G. Colyer, Lincoln's agent in North Carolina for the handling of Negro refugees said he saw men and women "so white that I could not believe they had a particle of Negro blood in their veins. Many of them were as white and as comely as any Italian, Spanish or Portuguese beauty. So remarkable is the difference in the color of the blacks in the South from those of the North that the conviction is constantly forced on my mind that slavery if left to itself but a few generations longer would have died out from this cause alone." (Services Rendered by the Colored People to the U. S. Army in North Carolina. 1864.) This was true of every Southern state.

Lincoln also saw these white Negroes around himself. William Slade, his confidential messenger and beloved friend, was fully as white, or whiter, than himself. Slade was of light olive complexion with light eyes, and straight, chestnut brown hair. His wife, according to her portrait, was also indistinguishable from white. Lincoln, on the other hand was dark and his hair "coarse" as he himself says.

Elizabeth Keckley, a Negro woman, and Mrs. Lincoln's closest friend and confidante, was quite as white as Mrs. Lincoln as seen in her portrait in John Washington's "They Knew Lincoln" (p. 229). Mrs. Keckley's son by her white master, was officer in a white regiment. This Lincoln knew.

As early as 1790, a visitor to America, Duke de la Rochefaucauld-Liancourt, wrote, "I have seen especially at Mr. Jefferson's, slaves, who neither in point of color nor features, showed the least trace of their original descent by their mother's being slaves." He also told of a rich and obvious Negro in South Carolina, who owned several hundred slaves and had a white wife and white son-in-law.

Lincoln knew, too, that Richard M. Johnson, while Vice-President under Van Buren, had a Negro mistress as head of his mansion in Washington; that he still had her; and that Johnson had had his daughters by her married to white men, because he had attacked Johnson on that score. Also, it was no secret that founders of the republic as Washington, Jefferson, Patrick Henry, had Negro mistresses and children by them.

Lincoln knew also that two of the most important figures in the war, one Northern the other Southern, were openly said to be of Negro ancestry, and that both sides were making much of it. (We shall hear of that a little later.) All of this shows how politics can make a true lover of justice and the right deny the obvious.

But now and then Lincoln, pushed too far, let his true inner feelings escape. To his tormentors, he once said, "I shall never marry a Negress, but I have no objection to anyone else doing so. If a white man wants to marry a Negro woman let him, if the Negro can stand it."

Did Lincoln consider all this political strategy? Did he really feel that what he was trying to do justified such awful logic? Here's an almost incredible act of his: His favorite solution of the question had long been colonization, that is, shipping Negroes to any country that would have them. He had written several Central and South American countries asking them to take them and several had readily agreed. One of his pet ideas was shipping some to settle on the Chiriqui colony in Panama, founded there by a capitalist, Ambrose W. Thompson. He had Congress give him $100,000 to colonize outside the United States the Negroes who had been freed in the District of Columbia, and later $500,000 to ship out still others. Eventually he intended to spend millions more for the same purpose. Accordingly, on August 14, 1862, at a time when the South,

"Black Mammy." Masterful slave women like these dominated many Southern households, including even the white mistress. Some, like this one, were indistinguishable from white.

thanks to "Stonewall" Jackson, was winning some of its most brilliant victories, he sent for Negro leaders and advised them that the best thing they could do to help America would be to get their people out of it. Telling them of the sum that had been appropriated by Congress and placed at his disposition, he said, "See our present condition—the country engaged in war—our white men cutting another's throats—

139

none knowing how far it will extend—and then consider what we know to be the truth. But for your race among us, there could not be war, although many men engaged on either side do not care for you one way or the other. Nevertheless, I repeat, without the institution of slavery, and the colored race as a basis, the war could not have an existence. It is better for us both, therefore, to be separated. There is an unwillingness on the part of our people, harsh as it may be, for you free colored people to remain with us. Now, if you would give a start to the white people, you would open a door for many to be made free. . . . If you will engage in the enterprise I will spend part of the money entrusted to me. . . . The place I am thinking about for a colony is in Central America. . . . Could I get a hundred tolerably intelligent men, with their wives and children and able to cut their own fodder, so to speak? Can I have fifty? If I could find twenty-five able-bodied men, with a mixture of women and children—good things in the family relation I think—I could make a successful commencement. I want you to let me know whether this can be done or not. This is the practical part of my wish to see you."

Instead of a hundred, more than a thousand Negroes responded. Nearly five hundred were made ready to go. Lincoln was so eager to start them off, he played right into the hands of Bernard Kock, a trickster, and continued to support Kock even after he was exposed. Kock's plan was to settle them on Ile de Vache (Cow Island) off the coast of Haiti, where they could grow cotton, tobacco, and sugar. He would take 5,000 there at fifty dollars a head. Northern capitalists fell hard for it.

Kock left Fortress Monroe, Virginia with some 431. The Negroes, glad to get away, left singing allelulia. But they were in for terrible disappointment. Kock had made no preparation for them. He had simply dumped them on that desolate, fever-riden isle. Bitten by poisonous insects, eaten by chiggers, and suffering great privation, they begged to be taken back.

On February 1, 1864, Lincoln was forced to issue the following order:

"Hon. Edwin M. Stanton, Secretary of War.

Sir: You are directed to have a transport (either a steam or sailing vessel, as may be deemed proper by the Quartermaster-General), sent to the colored colony established by the United States at the Island of Vache, on the coast of San Domingo, to bring back to this country such of the colonists there, as desire to return. You will have the transport furnished with suitable supplies for that purpose, and detail an officer of the Quartermaster's Department, who, under special instructions to be given shall have charge of the business. The colonists will be brought to Washington unless otherwise hereafter directed, and be employed and provided for at the camps for colored persons around that city."

Of the 431, about 378 returned alive, some of them seriously ill. The colony was a total failure. The Negroes returned singing alleluia.

Nearly all writers on Lincoln omit mention of this tragic blunder. Details, however, are in Nicolay and Hay's: Abraham Lincoln: A History, Vol. 6, pp. 360-65. 1890.

One cannot help but wonder in the light of what Lincoln said of the Negroes' role in saving the nation what would have happened had they left en masse?

His colonization plan at such a time was a most fantastic dream. Did he hope by it to pacify the Northern Negrophobes and to convince the South that he was after all had been said and done, a white man first? It must have been clear to him that the South wanted independence most of all, and that it had, in addition, most of the Negroes in its power. And was using them.

Still worse, his advice to the Negroes to leave America was in effect telling them there was no hope for them here, this at a time when he knew he needed them badly. A great many with their leaders were eager to serve. Suppose what he had said had so discouraged them they had decided to do nothing?

MORE OF LINCOLN'S PROBLEMS -- BIG BUSINESS

Lincoln's greatest and nastiest opponent was big business. Naturally so. Slavery and the illicit slave-trade were then America's principal source of wealth. The estimated value of the three and a half million slaves was two billions, or about five times that now. Cotton, slave-produced, was king. The North, with its huge investments, dominated Southern industry. Wall Street, then as now, was the nation's business centre. Shippers, railroad magnates, merchants and all who made money out of slavery, wanted no abolition, no agitation, and most of all no war. New York City headed the opposition against Lincoln. The city had voted against him by 30,000. It was also the center of very profitable slave-smuggling to the Southern states, and South and Central America. It was feared and rightly that Lincoln would put a stop to it. Secretary of State Seward was quoted on this illicit trade in the preceding chapter.

Congress, to reassure business passed a resolution declaring that the war was being fought to maintain the Constitution, not to end slavery. Lincoln also stressed that. In his first inaugural address, he reminded both North and South that he had said during the campaign, "I have no purpose, directly or indirectly, to interfere with the institution of slavery where it exists. I believe I have no lawful right to do so and I have no inclination to do so." The Constitution upheld slavery.

Heading the opposition was Governor Seymour, Democrat, of New York, who called Lincoln "bloody" and "treasonable." James Gordon Bennett, owner of the New York Herald, told Lincoln not to go to the White House but to yield to someone more acceptable to all parties. Lincoln, he said, would go down in history as one of the most execrated characters of all time, perhaps even be felled "by an assassin." He blamed the war on "nigger-lovers." The New York Express screamed, "Down everywhere with the Negro. Down with him as the pest of the parties and the country." A term of contempt for all whites, who favored Lincoln was "Black Republican." Sir William Howard Russell, newly-arrived correspondent of the London Times, wrote, March 19, 1861, "I was astonished to find little sympathy and no respect for the newly-installed government."

C. L. Vallandigham, Ohio congressman, was so violent that he was sentenced to prison, which Lincoln satirically changed to exile in the Confederacy. Ex-President James Pierce was almost as bitter.

Northern sentiment in favor of the South and slavery went even further. "Copperheads" in high places sent every available bit of information they could to the Confederates. As Kettell said at that time, "The new administration (Lincoln's) found itself completely in the power of the secession party and all its secrets from the cabinet debates to the details of orders were known to the South. The bureaus of the department, the judiciary, the army and the navy, and the offices were filled with persons who were eagerly watching to catch up and transmit every item of information that might aid the Confederates or thwart the government." J. R. Freese in his "Secret History of the Late Rebellion," reveals much of this. So does Gen. L. C. Baker, who was then head of the secret service, in "History of the United States Secret Service"; also the famous Alan Pinkerton. To this espionage was added an enormous amount of graft, frauds by Northern Officials, and the bounty-jumpers (those who got a bounty for joining) and then skipped. Need anyone wonder nowadays why the South with its only 9,000,000 souls could withstand the North with its 23,000,000 so long?

WHY THE SOUTH SECEDED

Business, then was the chief reason for the South's wishing to quit the Union. The Southern planter, was, on the whole, but a sharecropper for the Northern capitalist. It was the case of one exploiter putting the screws on another—of one robber forcing another to hand over most of his loot. While the Southern planter had all the trouble with his cotton, sugar, tobacco, rice, and the care and management of his slaves, the lion's share of the profits went to the Northern capitalist, who made not only the loans and investments but was also the middle-man. T. W. Kettell, writing in 1860, made this clear in his "Southern Wealth and Northern Profits."

Banking in the South, also, was negligible compared with the North. The big banks were in New York, Boston, and Philadelphia. The South, largely agricultural, was far behind in commerical activity as shown by the 1850 census. In capital invested, raw material used, etc. the South had only $351,354,312 to the North's $1,743,846,249. New York with $237,597,249 in business turnover, alone led the sixteen slave states. Sir William Howard Russell, war correspondent of the London Times, who travelled through the South told of the enormous profits accruing to the North from slavery and of the indignation of the slaveholders. He said, "The Southerners argue that by breaking up their un-natural alliance with the North they will save upwards of $47,000,000 a year."

The estimated value of the cotton crop alone in 1861 was $200,000,000, or over a billion in today's value. By selling this direct to Europe and not through the Northern middleman, all the profits would come to them, argued the planters.

Russell said that the ex-governor of a state told him that "sooner than submit to the North we will become subjects of Great Britain again."

On top of this was that the South had grandiose plans for its own expansion. This was to be a great slave empire extending below the Rio Grande as far south as Cuba, the brainchild of William L. Yancey, the South's greatest orator and the "Father of the Confederacy." His plan was a vast revival of the slave-trade. Hundreds of thousands of Africans would be

brought in the empire's own ships. Of course, federal and international law was against the slave-trade but was not the North flouting that and successfully, too, for the past fifty years? Moreover, the Africans would be brought in, not as "slaves," but as "apprentices," that is, under indenture. But what was to prevent their being held for life? Ignorant of the law, the Africans would not know the difference. Several states passed laws in its favor and this kind of importation began. In the meantime adventurers who favored the idea went into Mexico, Nicaragua and Cuba to stir revolt, among them General William Walker, who after some success, was finally executed in Nicaragua.

To appease the South the North offered it freedom within its own borders. On February 4-27, 1861, Congress in a "Peace Convention" pased a Thirteenth Amendment (better known as the Corwin Amendment), making slavery perpetual in those states that wanted it. Signed by President Buchanan, it went to the states for ratification. But the South gave it no time for that. It struck forty-one days later, that is, when only three states had had time to ratify it. Repeated attempts were made to stop the war with this as a bait. General Gordon, later head of the Ku Klux Klan, said some thirty attempts were made by the Union and that if the South had wanted to return to the Union, it could have accepted that.

ENGLISH AND FRENCH TRADE AND THE WAR

Another of Lincoln's great worries arose from foreign trade. Cotton, grown by slaves in the South, was very important to British industry. The correspondent of the Illustrated London News, wrote, June 8, 1861, "Several millions of our (English) people are as absolutely dependent for their livelihood upon this fibrous produce as they are for their lives upon an adequate supply of bread. . . . The Southern States of America are the stronghold of Negro slavery and cotton is the food upon which it principally thrives." In 1860, England used 1,115,890,608 pounds of cotton, eighty per cent of which came from the South. Karl Marx, who was living in London, wrote, "Nearly all the commercial wealth of England at this day is due to those Negroes."

England, therefore, sided with the South. The English masses, however, were opposed to slavery and had been since Magna Carta. American abolitionists, Negro and white, had been most favorably received, also. But here was Lincoln openly declaring that the war was not being fought to end slavery—a statement, which together with the need for cotton, inclined the English people generally to side with the South. England regarded the Confederacy as a legitimate belligerent, which amounted to virtual recognition. She built warships for the South. So did France. The Alabama, English-built, alone destroyed 68 Union vessels. England came near more than once to declaring war on the Union over the blockade of Southern ports, which prevented the shipping of cotton and other slave products. England also helped in the floating of Confederate bonds.

This and the foregoing show what an important economic factor the Negro was nationally and internationally.

THE LOWER-CLASS WHITES

Another part of the Northern population opposing Lincoln were the poorer, and largely unskilled whites. They held that the war was being fought to free the "nigger" who would then become even greater competitors for their jobs. Why should white men be so idiotic to risk their lives for that? This was especially true of the Europeans who were then pouring into America. The Irish, who then furnished nearly a half of the foreign-born population, were the most insistent. Of the 363,643 immigrants who arrived in 1853, 161,481 were Irish. Mostly degraded they were fit only for the lowest paid

jobs, which were then held by Negroes. These Irish, since they were white, believed Negroes ought to be ousted to make way for them. Brawls between Irish and Negroes for longshore jobs were common on the Boston, Philadelphia and New York water-fronts. Theodore Parker wote in 1854, "When the Irishman reaches America, he takes ground against the African. . . . The Irish, as a body, oppose the emancipation of the blacks, as a body" though the Irish were "the class most sinned against in Europe." (Works of Theodore Parker, Vol. 5-6, p. 307, 1863.) The Germans and the French, many of whom were refugees, were more liberal.

THE ABOLITIONISTS

Another of Lincoln's problems were the abolitionists. In fact, he had been at odds with them from his first entry into politics. In 1837, he had introduced a resolution in the Illinois legislature to the effect that while slavery was founded on "injustice and bad policy . . . the promulgation of abolition doctrine tends rather to increase than to abate the evil." In his eulogy of Henry Clay, Springfield, Illinois, July 16, 1852, he voiced his great irritation at them. He said they were so exacting they were ready "even to burn the last copy of the Bible rather than slavery should continue a single hour," adding that in consequence they "have received and are receiving their just execration."

Who were the ones he was so strongly denouncing? Some of the most highly honored individuals then and now—Emerson, Garrison, Thoreau, Whittier, Longfellow, Greeley, Whitman, Former President John Quincy Adams, Theodore Parker, Thaddeus Stevens, Wendell Phillips, Moncure Daniel Conway, and Arthur Tappan. Among the white women were Julia Ward Howe, Harriet Beecher Stowe, Susan B. Anthony, Lucy Stone, Lydia Maria Child, Angelina Grimke, and Lucretia Mott. Among the Negro abolitionists were Frederick Douglass, William Still, William Wells Brown, Henry

Frederick Douglass as Marshal of the District of Columbia. (Drawn from life by artist of the Illustrated London News).

Highland Garnett, Samuel Ringgold Ward and Samuel Cornish. Lincoln was called by many, "The slave hound of Illinois" because of this opposition.

What angered Lincoln most was that the abolitionists were clamoring for the use of Negro troops, which he was very strongly against. He once said that the whites in the Union Army were so opposed to this that they might "mutiny" if he used them. It must be noted though certain Cabinet members did not agree with Lincoln, and some of his generals in the South were actually using escaped slaves as fighting men.

The most fiery critic of Lincoln for not using Negro troops was an abolitionist we hear little of today—Adam Gurowski, a Polish count, of splendid training and education, a refugee from Czarist tyranny. So bitter were his attacks that Lincoln said, "So far as my personal safety is concerned Gurowski is the only man who has given me serious thought."

But Gurowski, a most kindly man, would never have harmed him. What impelled Gurowski was his intense hatred of slavery and injustice. Of slavery he said, "What confusion prevails about the rights of the existence of slavery! Why not establish the rights of the existence of syphilis in the human body?" He called the slave masters a "race knitted of the Devil's excrement mixed with his saliva."

He was especially angry at the fact that the North was suffering such defeats and yet Negro troops were not being used. He said, "The Africo-Americans ought to receive military training and be armed. But it ought to be done instantly and without loss of time; it ought to be done earnestly and broadly; it ought to be done at once on all points and on the largest scale; it ought to be done here in Washington under the eyes of the chief of the people. . . ."

After the defeat at Fredericksburg, he wrote in his Diary, "You cannot change Lincoln's head; you cannot fill his small but empty skull with brains." He offered again to head a Negro regiment and when he was ignored said of the administration and its conduct of the war, "A helpless imbecile in the hands of a cunning and selfish and ruthless charlatan is the sight that daily meets our eyes in Washington. . . . (The charlatan he refers to was Stanton, Secretary of War and a friend of the slaveholders.)

"The President is even worse than I had imagined him to be. . . . Poor Lincoln! As the devil dreads holy water so Mr. Lincoln dreads to be surrounded with stern, earnest, ardent, patriotic advisers. . . ."

Negroes, North and West, were eager to enlist. Everywhere they formed military clubs and waited for a call. In New York when they started drilling, the authorities drove them away calling them "disorderly persons." Groups that offered their services to the Union were rebuffed. On April 29, 1861, seventeen days after the South had struck at Fort Sumter, Jacob Dodson of Washington, D. C. offered his services and those of 300 other Negroes, but was told that the Union had no intention of using Negroes. Michigan Negroes were told the same. So were slaves who had escaped from their masters in loyal border states as Missouri. Kentucky, and Maryland. In November 1861, Negroes of Cincinnati, Ohio, who organized themselves into "The Black Brigade" with all black officers, were hooted and insulted. Later, when they helped save the city from the Confederates, they were hailed as heroes. When a delegation from the white anti-slavery press offered two regiments of Negroes equipped at its expense, Lincoln told it, "I have decided not to arm the Negroes." (Sandburg, Carl: "Lincoln: The War Years," Vol. 1, p. 581.)

Again, August 4, 1862, when a delegation of Westerners offered him two Negro regiments from Indiana, he said, he could use them only as "laborers" lest he offend the border slave states supporting the Union, like Kentucky. To arm the Negroes, he said "would turn 50,000 bayonets from the loyal Border States against us that are for us." As late as April 27, 1863, the governor of Kansas objected to having

Negro soldiers in his state and on March 10, 1864, when Negroes were helping to win some of the most brilliant victories, Colonel Woodford of Kentucky protested against having Negroes soldiers there.

At such times, Lincoln would reiterate that his sole aim was to save the Union, "I would save the Union. I would save it the shortest way under the Constitution. . ... My paramount object in this struggle is to save the Union, and is not either to save or to destroy slavery. If I could save the Union without freeing any slave, I would do it; and if I could save it by freeing all the slaves, I would do it; and if I could save it by freeing some and leaving others alone, I would also do that. What I do about slavery and the colored race, I do because I believe it helps to save the Union." "Yes, Mr. President," replied the abolitionists, "you'll save the Constitution but you'll lose the Union." In vain they told him that "God and right came before the Constitution," that the Constitution recognized slavery and that those who had put it in were ashamed of it. They reminded him that in the original draft of the Constitution they had struck out the words "slavery" and "servitude" and put in instead the more respectable one of "service." Secretary Seward reminded him that there was "a higher law than the Constitution." Thaddeus Stevens urged him "to march into the heart of slavedom not to pick cotton" but to "put guns in the hand of the slaves."

But the "copperheads" expressed such solicitude for the women and children of the rebels that Lincoln had to order Union commanders in the South to return runaway slaves to their masters.

NEGROES BLAMED FOR THE WAR

In addition to being the victim, Negroes were made the scapegoat. But for them, it was commonly said, white people would have got along without fighting among themselves. Even Lincoln felt this. As was quoted above he had told that delegation of Negroes to the White House, "But for your race among us, there could not be war," and that white men would not be "cutting one another's throats," therefore the Negroes should get out of America.

Worst enemies of the Negro were the proslavery Northerners, better known as copperheads (from a poisonous reptile of that name). They were forever declaring that this was a white man's country, what were Negroes doing in it? In vain, the abolitionists and the Negro leaders replied that it was their kind that had dragged the Negroes here, and if they left whom would they exploit?

Storke and Brockkert wrote, "The Negroes from the first had been the objects of their especial vengeance. Told by the demagogues who for weeks had been inciting them to this carnival of theft, rape, rapine and murder that the Negroes when set free would flock thither and take from them their employment, the Irish day-laborers and servants vented all the malignity of their ignorant and brutal nature upon that helpless, quiet and unoffending race." (History of the American Rebellion, Vol. 2, p. 1014. 1865.) The reference here is to the great riot of July 1863, in which hundreds of Negroes were killed and of whom we shall hear later.

These and other problems made Lincoln an harassed man, indeed. Correspondent Russell of the London Times, said, "The poor President, he's to be pitied! Surrounded by such scenes." Though unlike some of his predecessors in the White House he had no proven affairs with Negro women, filthy jokes were told of his alleged fondness for them, such jokes, said Russell "which nothing but extreme party passions and bad taste could tolerate." Mere mention of the Negro, made him nervous, said Conway. In January 1862, when Salmon P. Chase, Secretary of the Treasury (who favored the use of Negro troops) sent Edward L. Pierce, an abolitionist, to tell him how Negroes were coming into Union camps in the South, Lincoln broke in impatiently, "What's all this itching to get niggers into our lines." Albert Bushnell Hart, Professor of History at Harvard, tells this in his Life Of Chase, p. 259, 1899. Of the Presidency, he said, "If to be head of hell is as hard as what I have to undergo, I could find it in my heart to pity Satan, himself." For relief Lincoln told jokes. He once said that if he didn't indulge in a little humor he "would die."

THE SOUTH AND ITS USE OF NEGROES

While many Northerners were expressing such solicitude for the white women and children of the South and Lincoln was resolutely refusing to use Negroes as soldiers, what was the South doing? It was using Negroes for all army chores and even as fighting men. They furnished most of the cooks, mess attendants, teamsters, stablemen, builders of fortifications, brakemen, baggage-men, track-layers, and porters. Negro women were used as nurses, and Negro musicians and entertainers were used to relieve the monotony of army life. Early in the war, the Confederate Congress had provided for this. As one writer says, "Their singing, playing, and dancing were effective foes of gloom and nostalgia and their unfailing cheerfulness gave powerful fillip to army morale."

And it was easy to get Negroes to enlist. The Southerner, even with slavery around him, was kindlier to Negroes on the whole than the Northerner. The North was awful for all but a few of them. The fight to get and hold a job against the white immigrant was terrific. Race riots were common; hatred of a black skin great. Big Northern cities as Boston, New York, Philadelphia, had jimcrow cars; the South none (not till the 1890's). Lossing said of the New York Negroes then "They were more degraded and oppressed than when they were in bondage. They were herded in the lowest localities and because they were an enslaved race they seemed to be almost beyond human

sympathy." (History of New York, p. 463). Representative Hayne hardly exaggerated when he said, "There does not exist on earth a population so poor, so wretched, so destitute of all comforts and decencies of life as the unfortunate blacks of Philadelphia, New York and Boston."

There were, however, a select few, who were able to rise above the oppression. Mrs. Trollope wrote in 1831, "There are a great number of Negroes in New York, all free. . . . Not even in Philadelphia do the blacks appear to wear so much consequence as they do at New York. They have several chapels in which Negro ministers officiate and a theater in which none but Negroes perform. At this theater a gallery is appropriated for such whites as choose to visit it." But on the whole, free Negroes in the South, as well as many slaves, lived better than most Northern Negroes. Some had large estates and many slaves, some of them more than a hundred. The census of 1790 gave 195

ARMS of yͤ CONFEDERACIE.

Cartoon on the Confederacy and its dependence on the slave.

148

Conductor expelling Negro gentleman from white coach in Philadelphia.

Negro slave-holders, only 15 of whom were in the North. In 1830, the number was 4,500. L. P. Jackson, in "The Free Negro in Virginia 1830 to 1860" names some and the property they owned. The richest landowner in Jefferson County, regardless of color, was a Negro. Some even had white wives as recorded by the census of 1830. Of the $25,000,000 in property owned by Negroes, the far greater part was in the South. The richest ones were in Louisiana, then the center of Negro wealth and culture. In 1830, New Orleans, alone, had some 650 Negro slave-holders. J. W. DeForest, a Union officer, writing from Louisiana during the Civil War, said, "You'd be amazed to see the swarming mulattoes, and quadroons and octoroons who possess this region. . . . Some of the richest planters, men of really great wealth, are of mixed descent. . . . These are not the former slaves, observe, but the former masters. . . ." (A Volunteer's Adventure, p. 157.) These rich Negroes were treated as equals by upper-class whites. As Historian

William E. Dodd, a white Southerner, says, "Some Negroes were gentlemen with a standing among gentlemen which would scandalize good Southerners today. In New Orleans as in Charleston there were Negro slaveowners who played a considerable part in the civic life. . . ." Such Negroes voted at elections like white men in most Southern states.

These Negroes, Southerners at heart, threw in their lot with the Confederacy. Besides they were convinced that was the only way to save their property and to protect themselves and their families. They knew how those of their color were being treated in the North, a fact that the Confederate press played up to the utmost. And it didn't have to lie, either. Race-riots in which Negroes were butchered mercilessly, were rather common. To name a few: Connecticut, 1827, 1836, 1841; Pennsylvania, 1834, 1838, 1839, 1843; Ohio, 1830; New York City was worst of all, one of its worst, occurring in a church in which an anti-slavery meeting was being held. Northern cities had jim-crow cars, among them Boston, Philadelphia and New York, while in the South, free Negroes rode with white people.

Charles Dickens describes a Massachusetts jim-crow car—"a great blundering clumsy chest" —in his American Notes, Vol. 2, p. 58. 1869. On the other hand Amelia Murray tells how she travelled in the South in the same coach with Negroes: "From what we hear in England I imagined Negroes were kept at a distance. This is the case in the Northern States but in the South they are at your elbow everywhere and always seek conversation." (Letter from the U. S. Vol 2, pp. 159, 177. 1856).

LINCOLN PICTURED AS THE ENEMY OF THE SLAVE

The Yankees were said to be coming on a great slave-hunt to sell even free Negroes to Cuba and Brazil. They would also be har-

STRONG'S DIME CARICATURES.—No. 3.

Never had no father, nor mother, nor nothing! I was raised by speculators! I's mighty wicked, anyhow! "What makes me ack so?" Don no, missis—I 'spects cause I's so wicked!

Hand us over to ole Abe, eh? Ize off!

So, Topsey, you're at the bottom of this piece of wicked work—picking stars out of this sacred Flag! What would your forefathers say, do you think? I'll just hand you over to the new overseer, Uncle Abe. He'll fix you!

Entered according to Act of Congress, in the year 1861, by T. W. STRONG, in the Clerk's Office of the District Court of the United States for the Southern District of New York.

SOUTH CAROLINA TOPSEY IN A FIX.

Abraham Lincoln being used to frighten Negroes in the South

nessed to carts like mules. In short, the damyankees were going to make everything worse for them. "Echoing their masters," says Coulter, "slaves talked vengeance against the Yankees." One South Carolina slave, he says, gave five dollars to help build a gunboat "jes sech a boat as can whip Ole Blunkum (Lincoln) an' dose no-Count Yankees." Some slaves sold watermelons to raise money for the war; and one group, the Confederate Ethiopian Serenaders, gave the proceeds of one of their concerts. Rich Negroes gave sums large for that time. Thomy Lafon, real estate dealer of New Orleans gave five hundred dollars; Jordan Chase a like sum; others, horses and large quantities of food.

In Charleston, New Orleans, Richmond,

150

Negroes flocked to join and were gladly accepted. Some came even before the war began. On January 1, 1861, 153 Negroes of Charleston, S. C. offered their services and were used on building fortifications and defenses. June 28, 1861, Tennessee offered $8 a month and rations and clothing to Negroes who would join. Many did. Early in 1861, free Negroes of Louisiana, declared "they were ready to take arms to fight shoulder to shoulder." Louisiana had at least two Negro regiments. In November 1861, in New Orleans, 1,400 blacks marched in a review to the loud cheers of white women who gave them a flag. Virginia Negroes made patriotic speeches. May 1, 1861, 120 free Negroes wearing red shirts and dark trousers, carrying a Confederate flag, which had been presented by the white women of Petersburg, Virginia, responded to the call of General Gwynn for 600 Negroes to work on the fortifications around Norfolk.

Charleston Evening News reported. "They were all in the finest spirits and seemed anxious to catch Ole Linkum (Lincoln). They certainly deserve great credit for their disinterestedness and will find it appreciated." The Memphis Avalanche told of the zest with which the Negroes worked on the fortifications. "A merrier set were never seen. They were brimful of patriotism, shouting for Jeff Davis and singing war-songs." A correspondent to the New York Evening Post said of Charleston, "The thousand Negroes busy in building batteries, so far from inclining to insurrection were grinning from ear to ear at the prospect of shooting Yankees."

The New Orleans Picayune said of the grand review of Confederate troops in that city, February 9, 1862, "We must also pay a deserved compliment to the companies of free colored men, all very well drilled and comfortably uniformed. Most of these Companies, quite unaided by the administration, have supplied themselves with arms without regard to cost or trouble. One of the companies, commanded by the well-known veteran, Captain Jordan, was presented a little before the parade with a fine war flag of the new style. . . ."

Nashville Negroes sent a Negro company equipped at their expense. The Negroes fought bravely, too. The New York Tribune, January 8, 1862, reported that 700 Negroes fought the New York German Rifles at Newport News, Virginia. Negroes also served as spies and gave valuable information about the Union armies. Virginia offered $20 cash and $20 for life to any Negro who killed a Union soldier. In 1862, Virginia drafted all free Negroes between eighteen and fifty as soldiers. Other states did likewise. In fact, even slaves were later drafted as soldiers.

Negroes were a decisive factor in more than one Confederate victory. Samuel Clayton wrote Jefferson Davis, "Some people say Negroes will not fight. I say they will fight. They fought at Ocean Pond, Honey Hill, and other places." W. W. Davis wrote, "The experience of this war has been so far that half-trained Negroes have fought as bravely as half-trained Yankees."

B. I. Wiley said, "Their relation to the fighting force was so vital and so intimate as to merit consideration as a part of the army. . . . Some became so imbued with the martial spirit as to grab up muskets during battle and take pot shots at the enemy. There are several instances on record of servants thus engaged and killing and capturing Federals." (Life of Johnny Reb, pp. 328, 330.)

Frank Leslie's Weekly (July 12, 1862) tells of one Confederate Negro marksman who had "done more injury to our men than a dozen of his white compeers in the attempted labor of reducing the complement of our sharpshooters. Our men have known him a long time. . . ."

Horace Greeley, celebrated editor of the New York Tribune, rightly observed at the time, "For more than two years, Negroes had been extensively employed in belligerent operation by the Confederacy. They had embodied and drilled as rebel soldiers and had paraded with white troops at a time when this would not

Slaves hoisting cannon for Confederate attack on Fort Sumter.

Drumming up Recruits for the Confederate Army.

have been tolerated in the armies of the Union." (American Conflict, Vol. 2, p. 524.)

The Confederate press and public made heroes of Negroes. Marvelous stories were told of some to spur others on. One was Ol' Dick, a drummer of the 18th Virginia Regiment, and a veteran of the Mexican War. Dick was praised for his skill in slashing out Yankee guts with his famous bowie-knife. He once captured a scouting party under Colonel Wood of the 14th Brooklyn. The Richmond Examiner

called him "a gentleman and a true patriot." (War of the Rebellion, Vol. 4, p. 32.)

Another Confederate Negro hero was Preston Roberts, quartermaster for General N. B. Forrest, noted Confederate leader. Roberts contributed much to Forrest's success. Enlisting at the first rebel call in 1861, Roberts had a corps of 75 Negro cooks under him. Money for the purchase of food was entrusted to him. At times he served as a spy. He was awarded the

Cross of Honor, the highest Confederate decoration.

Still another was John Tinsley, a free Negro, one of the principal telegraph engineers of the Confederate Army. With a staff of Negroes and white men, he kept the telegraph lines in repair.

Many Negroes, too, served out of sheer loyalty to masters who had been kind to them, one of the most noted being Vallery, servant of Confederate general, Governor Watkins.

How did the copperheads of the North react to this most extraordinary situation? They still opposed the prosecution of the war and particularly the use of Negro troops! Lincoln, to placate them, went so far as to reverse steps his commanders in the field had found necessary. One of them, General Hunter, had raised regiments of slaves and was using them as soldiers. To encourage the Negroes, he had proclaimed emancipation in captured territory. Lincoln annulled the order. He said, "General Hunter is an honest man. He proclaimed all men free within certain states. I repudiated the proclamation." That is to be found in the "Complete Works of Abraham Lincoln, Vol. 2, pp. 155, 205. 1920.

Lincoln said also, "When early in the war, General Fremont attempted military emancipation, I forbade it, because I did not then think it an indispensable necessity. When, a little later, General Cameron, then Secretary of War, suggested the arming of the blacks, I objected because I did not yet think it an indispensable necessity."

Nevertheless, thousands of Negroes were being used as soldiers. Commanders like Butler, Meade, Phelps, and Hunter quietly ignored Lincoln's order not to use them. As soon as Butler arrived in Louisiana, he organized a Negro regiment, officered by Negroes. Salmon P. Chase in Lincoln's Cabinet secretly supported all this. It is hard to believe that Lincoln, himself, didn't know of it.

Most of the slaves did not favor the Con-

federacy, however, and they showed it as the war went on. Wherever the Union army appeared, they bolted to it. Seward said that as soon as the Union troops arrived in Virginia, 5,000 slaves ran to it. In South Carolina, 9,000 came at once. "Although the war has not been waged against slavery the Army acts immediately as an emancipating crusade," he said.

The slave masters became more severe. More than three slaves were forbidden to congregate except at religious services, which whites would attend sometimes disguised in Union uniform. There were strict curfew laws. One white male was exempted from military duty for every fifteen slaves. Home guards totalled 100,000 of which Virginia had 40,000. These helped watch conscripted slaves building railroads and other war work to prevent sabotage.

But secret and even open rebellion increased. The Daily News of London, England, reported, "There have been very alarming disturbances among the blacks; on more than one plantation the assistance of the authorities has been called to overcome the open resistance of the slaves." On October 3, 1862, Confederate General Daniel Ruggles reported that "pernicious influences have already been manifested upon many of these plantations." At Cherry Hill, South Carolina, it was reported, "There is a great and increasing dissatisfaction among the Negroes."

Near Charleston, S. C. an attempted insurrection was discovered and seven Negroes were hanged. Another report from Charleston says, "In some cases whole families were murdered before the slaves were subdued." In Culpeper County, Virginia, they revolted and seventeen were hanged. Slaves of Jefferson Davis, president of the Confederacy, set the official mansion at Richmond, Virginia, on fire.

Most terrifying of all were guerilla bands of escaped slaves who massacred the whites on plantations in Indian style. One of their foremost leaders was Henry Berry Lowry of Robeson County, North Carolina. Even before the

White master and family attending Negro service. After the Nat Turner revolt whites were always in to listen.

155

war, he had been a raider. Mounted on fleet horses, he and his men, would strike suddenly and escape before help could arrive.

These and many other Negroes believed that the war was being fought to end slavery. One report over which the South had raged during the last election had especially convinced them. It was that Hannibal Hamlin, Lincoln's Vice-President, was a Negro. The Chicago Democrat June 4, 1861, said, "The constant theme in the South for the last two months has been the election of the Abolitionist Lincoln and the free Negro, Hamlin, to the Presidential chair and the consequences that were to result from the events. The slaves heard all this and they have told it to their companions and the news has spread to the plantations with that celerity which is so remarkable a feature of slave life. The news has not been lost travelling. There now exists a very general belief among the slaves that an army from the North is soon to march down to the South and liberate all the slaves."

Hamlin was much more hated in the South than Lincoln. Not only was he outspoken against slavery but his skin was darker than that of many who were called Negroes. The South considered his election the crowning insult. Editorials thundered against "the dire effects of electing a free Negro to the Vice-Presidency." During the campaign, R. B. Rhett of the Charleston (S. C.) Mercury, July 9, 1860, said, "Hamlin is what we call a mulatto. He has black blood in him. The Northern people elected that man in consequence of his peculiarity. . . . They design to place over the South a man who has Negro blood. . . ." Hamlin was for emancipation from the start. Lincoln later praised him highly for it.

But while the South was raging against Hamlin's color, the Union was laughing at the South. One of its leading generals, a beaten candidate for the Presidency of the United States, looked more Negroid than Hamlin. He was John B. Floyd, former governor of Virginia, and former U. S. Secretary of War. The Springfield Republican told the story of Floyd and two Indian chiefs. "A few years since," it said, "a gentleman residing in Richmond, Virginia, gave a large dinner to some distinguished men, among whom was Floyd, then a rising man but whose personal appearance indicated neither mental nor physical superiority, he being a pursy, dark-complexioned man with crispy hair. Among the guests were two Indian chiefs—magnificent specimens of their race. Floyd thinking to compliment them and make them at their ease told them in a condescending manner that he could boast of Indian blood, being descended from Pocohantas. One of the chiefs, drawing himself up majestically and disdainfully and with a look of contempt upon his noble countenance said in broken English, "Ugh! No: No: *Nigur! Nigur!*" (Nigger! Nigger!.) The confusion and dismay of Floyd was complete and it required all the boasted politeness of Richmond to keep the other guests from laughing." (Rebellion Record, Vol. 3 (Poetry & Incidents) p. 47, 1862.)

In short, events in the South during the trying years up to December 1862, showed what could have been accomplished had John Brown's plan of inciting slave revolt been adopted. Brown, himself, was now being made a hero. Union troops going into battle sang "John Brown's Body." Later when the South in desperation conscripted the slaves, N. P. Hallowell, white colonel of a Negro regiment, said he actually regretted that that had come so late. Slaves were escaping in such numbers into Union lines he had "no hesitation in saying that the slave regiments would have deserted en masse to the Yankees and that the supposition that they would have fought for the Confederacy is hugely and grotesquely ridiculous."

THE EMANCIPATION PROCLAMATION

At last came January 1863. Lincoln saw definitely now that "he had reached the end of his rope, that he must change his tactics or lose the game." He had only one card left—a card he had been hesitating to play for six months. On New Year's Day he issued the Emancipation Proclamation.

What was the nature of this proclamation? Did it free the slaves? Definitely not. It was a gesture rather than a reality since it "freed" only those slaves Lincoln had no power to free and kept in slavery those he had the power to free. Those slave states, or parts of them, that favored the Union were excepted. These "excepted parts are for the present left precisely as if this proclamation were not issued," said Lincoln. The excepted parts were West Virginia thirteen parishes of Louisiana and the city of New Orleans; seven counties of Virginia and the towns of Norfolk and Portsmouth. Tennessee was omitted in the hope that it would return to the Union. So was Maryland, which rather favored the North and was on the way to abolishing slavery which it did the following year. Perhaps no other important document in all history has been more misinterpreted. *It was the Thirteenth Amendment that freed the slaves.* The proclamation served this purpose, however: It ended the oft-repeated assertion of Lincoln that the war was being fought, not against slavery, but to preserve the Union.

What, then, was the real purpose of the proclamation. We'll find that in its closing words, "And I further declare and make known that such persons of suitable condition will be received into the armed services of the United States to garrison forts, positions, and other places and to man vessels of all sorts in said services." The "such persons" were the Negroes.

And they were very badly needed. The war was in the third year. There was scarcely a home in the North but had lost a loved one. White volunteers were getting scarcer and scarcer. It looked as if the South would soon cut itself free.

The proclamation was a triumph for the abolitionists. How different all would have been, they said, if Lincoln had followed their advice. Think of the vast number of lives that could have been saved. Some attacked Lincoln's opportunism. Lydia Maria Child said, the proclamation was "a measure to which we were forced by our own perils. No recognition of the principle of justice and humanity surrounded the politic act with a halo of moral glory."

"At last," said Longfellow, "the slave will be given a chance to fight for his own freedom."

Having taken this step, Lincoln pursued it vigorously. Frederick Douglass made a stirring appeal to Negroes to enlist. That was hardly necessary. They flocked to join. Groups, once refused, were eagerly accepted now. A line of recruiting depots extended from Boston to St. Louis in the West and to Louisiana in the South. But even in some cities, as Philadelphia, recruiting had to be done quietly for fear of the white mob. In parts of Ohio it was regarded as a good thing because it was a good way of "getting darkies away to Boston," where they were supposed to be welcome. To please the copperheads the Senate, by a vote of 18 to 7, decreed that no one of African descent should "be commissioned or hold office in the army of the United States."

Slowly but surely the tide now turned in favor of the Union. Seven months later, August 26, 1863, Lincoln wrote J. C. Conkling that in the opinion of his commanders in the field and of himself, "The emancipation policy and the use of colored troops constitute the heaviest blow yet dealt to the rebellion and that at least one of these important successes could not have been achieved but for the use of colored troops."

The New York Times, said February 10, 1863, "We have no doubt that the whole state of Florida might easily be held for the Government in this war by a dozen Negro regiments."

The Proclamation had yet another beneficial effect. It improved the international situation almost overnight. The statement "forever free" in it convinced Europe, especially the English, that the war was now a crusade against slavery. The English workers, although many were starving because of the lack of cotton, as well as the liberals, reacted so strongly against the Confederacy that its English supporters were forced to yield. The Illustrated London News, February 7, 1863, reported at length the great meeting held at Exeter Hall and the tremendous anti-slavery feeling manifested. Lincoln's letter to the English workers had a still more reassuring effect. Public opinion swung so much in favor of the Union that a court of adjudication later forced the British to pay $15,000,000 for damage done to Union shipping by warships that England had built for the Confederacy.

But in spite of these successes, hidebound prejudices against Negroes in the North continued. The war, the copperheads, openly said, was now exactly what they had always declared it was—to free "niggers." Their catechism read:

"What is a President?

"An agent for niggers."

"Save the Union," they would cry, "but not through the nigger. This is a war of white men." N. P. Hallowell, white colonel of the 54th Masachusetts Infantry (colored) wrote, "Public opinion in the North was either avowedly hostile to the scheme or entirely sceptical of its value."

General Butler said, "The prejudice against them (the Negro soldiers) among the white officers was at first fearful, especially the regulars." Even in Boston, aristocratic ladies hooted the 54th Negro regiment. New York warned Massachusetts not to send the 54th through that state lest it be mobbed. It had to go to Beaufort, South Carolina by sea on the transport, De Molay.

Northern Democratic newspapers, like the Chicago Times, still shouted against "niggers" . . . big, black, stinking buck niggers."

Lincoln's reply to this was, "There will be some black men who can remember that with silent tongue, clenched teeth, steady eye and well-poised bayonet, they have helped mankind on to this great consummation; while I fear there will be some white ones unable to forget that with malignant heart and deceitful they strove to hinder it."

THE TURN OF THE TIDE --

As late as August 15, 1864, when victory was well on its way for the Union, Lincoln was still forced to defend his use of Negroes as soldiers. In an interview with John T. Mills, he said, "The slightest knowledge of arithmetic will prove to any man that the rebel armies cannot be destroyed by Democratic strategy. It would sacrifice all the white men of the North to do it. There are now in the service of the United States nearly 150,000 able-bodied colored men, most of them under arms, defending and acquiring Union territory. The Democratic strategy demands these forces be disbanded, and that the masters be conciliated by restoring them to slavery. The black men who now assist Union prisoners to escape are to be converted into our enemies, in the vain hope of gaining the goodwill of their masters. We shall have to fight two nations instead of one.

"You cannot conciliate the South if you guarantee to them ultimate success; and the experience of the present war proves their success is inevitable if you fling the compulsory labor of millions of black men into their side of the scale. Will you give our enemies such military advantages as insure success, and then depend on coaxing, flattery, and concession to get them back into the Union? Abandon all the posts now garrisoned by black men, take the 150,000 men from our side and put them in the battle-field or corn-field against us, and we would be

Recruiting Poster.

159

General Butler recruiting escaped slaves (called contraband) into the Union Army in Louisiana.

compelled to abandon the war in three weeks. . . ."

Again to Charles D. Robinson (two days later) "Drive back to the support of the rebellion the physical force which colored people now give and promise us, and neither the present, nor any coming, administration can save the Union. Take from us and give to the enemy the hundred, and thirty, forty, or fifty thousand colored persons now serving us as soldiers, seamen, and laborers, and we cannot longer maintain the contest. The party who could elect a President on a War and Slavery Restoration platform would, of necessity, lose the colored force; and that force being lost, would be as powerless to save the Union as to do any other impossible thing.

"It is not a question of sentiment or taste, but one of physical force, which may be measured and estimated, as horse-power and steam-power are measured and estimated. And, by measurement, it is more than we can lose and live. Nor can we, by discarding it, get a white force in place of it."

To J. M. Schermerhorn, he said, as regards the help the Negroes were giving, "Keep it and you can save the Union. Throw it away and the Union goes with it." Gideon Wells, Secretary of the Navy, wrote, "There is an unconquerable prejudice on the part of many whites against black soldiers. But all our increased military strength now comes from the Negroes."

In short, such a terrific prejudice had been built up in the North against Negroes that even the great help they were giving was regarded with the same disgust as one perishing of hunger has when he must eat rats and dogs to keep alive. It was to break out in the nation's worst race riot, before or since.

THE GREAT RACE RIOTS

White volunteering, as was said, had fallen almost to nothing. On March 3, 1863, Congress was forced to pass a National Conscription Act.

Democratic papers denounced it as "tyranny of the worst sort," and said that white men were now being driven to free "niggers" so that the latter could take away their jobs. Andrews, a New York copperhead, called Lincoln "that baboon in the White House" and shouted to a crowd in Madison Square Park "It's not a war to save our homes. It's a war of oppression against white Southerners and to free the nigger! Free niggers—the black savages lusting for our women will roam the streets. No woman will be safe nor any man. Do you want to spill your blood so niggers can be free?

Riots broke out in several large cities, New York, Philadelphia, Chicago. That of New York was the worst of all. In fact, history records no greater outburst of savagery. Worst of all were the Irish who were competing for longshore, and other miserably paid, jobs. Mobs ruled the city for three days—July 12, 14, and 15. More than a thousand persons were killed and wounded, many of them white policemen. The Colored Orphan Asylum, housing three hundred children, was burnt to the ground. The children escaped all but one who had hidden under a bed. The mob dragged her out and beat her to death. A report said, "The rioters advanced in a body upon the institution of 230 small children. . . . Chief Engineer Decker with a small body of men made every exertion to save the building. As well might have essayed to stay the hurricane. The insane mass swept into the building, heaped together the lightest furniture and saturated the floors with an inflammable material applied their matches and in 20 minutes the house was in ruin."

Negroes were hanged on lamp-posts. An eyewitness tells how after one Negro had been hanged, his flesh was cut in bits and thrown to the mob. "Then a demon in human form, taking a sharp knife cut pieces out of the quivering flesh and offered it to the greedy, bloodthirsty mob. "Who wants some nigger-meat?' " Scores of eager hands went up. And the answer came: I! I! "Carl Sandburg quotes

Burning of the Colored Orphan H

162

New York mob in July 1863.

THE RIOTS IN NEW YORK: THE MOB LYNCHING A NEGRO IN CLARKSON-STREET.

Riot in New York from Illustrated London News, Aug. 8, 1863.
Upper left Lynching a Negro. (Museum, City of New York).

Upper left: Mob chasing Negroes. (Illustrated London News, 1863).

165

Immigrants arriving in New York at rate of 235,000 a year in the 1850's. In competition for jobs they were great enemies the Negroes.

this in Lincoln: The War Years (Vol. 3, pp. 38-41.) See also Werstein's "July 1863: The Incredible Story of the New York City Draft Riots" (1957). The mob looted and destroyed over $5,000,000 in property. White troops had to be called from the front to restore order.

The answer of the New York Negroes to that riot was a crack regiment. John Jay of the Union League Club wrote, "Eight months after the week of terror, when men were hunted to death for no crime but their complexion, we reviewed in Union Square the Twentieth Regiment of the United States colored troops whose soldierly bearing and thorough discipline commanded universal admiration. After receiving the colors they marched down Broadway to the steamer at the foot of Canal Street." The New York Times, March 7, 1864, said of the departure of this regiment. "There has been no

more striking manifestation of the marvellous times that are upon us than the scene in our streets at the departure of the first of our colored regiments. Had any man predicted it last year he would have been thought a fool even by the wisest and most discerning. . . .

"Eight months ago the African race in this city were literally hunted down like wild beasts. When caught they were shot down in cold blood or stoned to death, or hung to the trees or the lamp-posts. . . . Nor was it solely the raging horde in the streets that visited upon the black man this nefarious wrong. Thousands and tens of thousands of men of higher social grade and better education, cherished precisely the same spirit. . . . "

More and more Southern sympathizers became reconciled to seeing Negroes in United States uniform. Even the white soldiers gave in, too. But true to form this did not come about through the common sense and patriotic urgings of Lincoln nor the eloquent pleas of Douglass, Emerson, Whittier and Beecher, but through a burlesque song on Negroes by Miles O'Reilly, songster of the Union Army. Entitled "Sambo's Right to be Killed," its most popular lines were:

"The right to be killed I'll divide with the nigger

And give him the largest half."

The gist of the ballad was that every bullet stopped by a Negro saved the life of some white man. It became very popular and was sung everywhere. Its success in having Negroes in uniform accepted was so great that Lincoln said, "That song is good and will do good."

C. C. Halpine wrote in 1864, "The song made them regard the enlistment of the sons of Ham as a good joke at first and next as a joke containing some advantage to themselves. Very quickly they became reconciled to the experiment and it was not long before they commenced to take in the movement and doing of their humble colored allies that sort of half-ludicrous, half-pathetic interest which a jolly-hearted, full-grown elder brother takes in the first awkard attempts at manly usefulness that are made by 'little Bub' who is some years his junior."

Lincoln was so grateful to O'Reilly that when he was arrested for writing a skit against an admiral, he ordered him freed. Another fact that helped to make the Negro soldiers popular was that they and others helped with their songs and entertainment to relieve the tedium of army life. As was said the Confederates from the start had used Negro entertainers.

DEEDS OF THE NEGRO SOLDIER

So many excellent books, past and present, have been written on the Negro soldier in the Civil War, that some of the highlights are all that is necessary here. They fought in nearly all the great battles—the second Bull Run, Manassas, Olustee, Honey Hill, Gettysburg, Milliken's Bend, Nashville, Richmond, Crater, Fort Wagner, Petersburg. Rev. J. M. Guthrie, white chaplain of a Negro regiment, names 251 of them in his "Camp-Fires of the Afro-American."

At Petersburg, 327 were killed and more wounded. General George H. Thomas, when he saw the heaps of Negro dead after the battle at Nashville, mingled with the white, he said, "This proves the manhood of the Negro."

General Dennis said after the battle of Milliken's Bend, "It is impossible for men to show greater gallantry than the Negro troops in that fight." A reporter gave this account: "White and black men were lying side by side, pierced by bayonets, in some cases transfixed to the earth. Two men, one white and the other black were found side by side, each with the other's bayonet through his body. It was a contest between enraged men."

After the battle of Petersburg, Grant told Lincoln how bravely the Negroes had fought and invited him to come and look at them. "Oh, yes," said Lincoln, "I want to take a look at those boys. I read with the greatest delight the account in Mr. Dana's despatch of how gallantly they behaved. He said they took six out of the sixteen guns captured that day. I'm glad they kept pace with the white troops in the recent assaults." He went off with Grant to see them, saying as he went, "I was opposed on nearly every side, when I first favored the raising of colored regiments. . . . When we wanted able-bodied men who could be spared to go to the front and my opposers kept objecting to the Negroes."

The Negro troops gave Lincoln an immense ovation.

The New York Tribune, June 8, 1864, said of the Battle of Port Hudson, in which all but thirty of the First Regiment, Louisiana Native Guards were killed or wounded, "Nobly done! Though you failed to carry the rebel works

Building Fortifications.

Company A of the South Carolina Volunteers (colored) taking the oath of allegiance.

Building fortifications at Savannah, Georgia.

169

Presentation of Colors

h U. S. Colored   Infantry in New York City, March 5, 1864.

Dress Review of Colore

unteers, Hilton Island, S. C.

against overwhelming numbers you did not charge and fight and fall in vain. That heap of 600 corpses lying there dark and grim and silent before and within the rebel works is a better proclamation than even that of President Lincoln. Even the Wood copperheads who will not fight themselves and try to keep others out of the Union ranks will not dare to mob Negro regiments if this is their style of fighting."

Secretary of War Stanton said of the battle of Petersburg, "The hardest fighting was done by the black troops. The forts they stormed were the worst of all. . . . General Smith says they cannot be exceeded as soldiers and that hereafter he will send them in difficult places as readily as white troops." Smith, himself, said, "There is material in the Negroes to make them the best troops in the world if they are properly trained."

Grant later told a Congressional committee, "If the black troops had been properly supported by the white troops at the springing of the mines at Petersburg that day, we should have gone into Richmond." (Quoted by General Burt, Crisis, Feb. 1911, pp. 23-25.) A few days later, April 2, 1865, 30,000 Negro troops marched into Richmond, Virginia, to the wild cheers of the Negro population.

But it was at the battle of Chapin's Farm, September 29, 1864, that Negro soldiers really covered themselves with glory. Thirteen won the Congresisonal Medal of Honor in that fight. The 3rd and 5th U.S. Colored Troops charged the white Confederates again and again, performing prodigies of valor. They lost most of their men: 543 were killed on the field and more than twice as many wounded. One soldier, whose hand was badly shattered, had it amputated, bound up and returned to charge the enemy. The official citations for valor give an idea of what they accomplished. Their names with their citations are:

Sergeant-Major Christian Fleetwood: "Seized the colors after two color-bearers

had been shot down and bore them nobly through the fight."

Sergeant Alfred B. Hilton: "In the charge when the associate sergeant was killed caught up his flag and carried it until he, himself, was shot down. Falling, he shouted, "Boys, save the colors."

Corporal Charles Veal: "Seized the regimental colors after two color-bearers had been shot down close to the enemy works and bore them through the remainder of the battle."

Sergeant Milton M. Holland: "Took command after all the officers had been killed or wounded and gallantly led the charge."

First Sergeant Powhattan Beatty: "Took command of his company when all its superior officers were killed or wounded."

Sergeant Robert A. Penn: "Took command after all the officers of his company had been killed or wounded."

Sergeant Alexander Kelly: "Gallantly seized the colors which had fallen near the enemy line of Abattis, raised them and rallied the men at time of great confusion and danger."

James Miles: "Having had his arm mutilated, immediate amputation necessary, he loaded and discharged his piece with one hand and urged his men forward to 30 yards of the enemy line."

Private James Gardiner: "Gallantly led his company after the commanding officer had been killed. Was the first man to enter the enemy's works."

Sergeant James H. Harris, "Among first to enter the enemy's works though wounded . . . "

Private William H. Barnes: "Among the first to enter the enemy's works, though wounded . . . "

First Sergeant Edward Ratcliffe: "Commanded and gallantly led his company after the commanding officer had been killed. Was the first enlisted man to enter."

First Sergeant, James E. Bronson: "Took command of Company C after all the officers had been killed or wounded and gallanty led it. (*Medals of Honor of U. S. Army, p*. 173. 1948.)

In the battle of New Market Heights, the Negro troops fought with equal valor and dash. Gen. Butler, their commander, years later in Congress, describing their charge, said, "The Negro troops rush forward and with a shout that now rings in my ears, go over the redoubt like a flash and the enemy never stops running for four miles. . . .

"It became my paintful duty to follow in the track of that charging column and there in a space not wider than the clerks' desk and 33 yards long lay the dead bodies of 543 of my colored comrades slain in the defense of their country who had laid down their lives to uphold its flag and its honor as a willing sacrifice. And as I rode along, guiding my horse this way and that lest he should profane the dead with his hoofs what seemed to me the sacred dead and as I looked at their bronzed faces, upturned in the shining sun as if in mute appeal against the wrongs of the country for which they had given their lives and whose flag had been to them a flag of stripes on which no glory ever shone for them. Feeling I had wronged them in the past and believing what was the future duty of my country to them I swore a solemn oath, "May my right hand lose its cunning and my tongue cleave to the roof of my mouth if I ever fail to defend the rights of the men who had given their blood for me and my country that day and their race forever. And God helping me, I will keep that oath." (Congressional Record, Jan. 7, 1874, p. 458).

And sad to relate that even after these heroic deeds it was still being a "flag of stripes" for them. The Negro goes into battle with a halter around his neck, said Lincoln. The Confederates were specially barbarous to them. At Fort Pillow, 300 of them with their white officers, were massacred. And they were underpaid. White privates were getting thirteen dollars a month; sergeant-majors, twenty-one; chaplains, a hundred. All Negroes, including chaplains and surgeons, got only seven. Hallowell, white colonel of the 54th Massachusetts tells of the letters his men got from home telling the privation of their families. Some proudly refused this pittance. One regiment stacked arms, declaring it would fight no longer. Sergeant William Walker of the Third South Carolinas refused to obey orders. He declared he "was released from duty by the refusal of the Government to fulfil its share of the contract." He was court-martialled and shot. Governor Andrews of Massachusetts said, "The Government which found no law to pay him as a nondescript and a contraband nevertheless found enough law to shoot him as a soldier."

The men of the 54th and 55th sent this letter to Congress, "Go tell them at our Capitol that we die for a nation that for 250 years has robbed us of all rights of men; that has taken our babes from their mothers' breasts and sold them for gain; that still insults us in continuing the distinction of the whole matter of pay between us and our white fellow-soldiers and further attempts to force us to submit to its continuance by starving our wives and children."

WHAT WHITE COMMANDERS SAID OF NEGRO TROOPS

Lincoln said, April , 1863, "I am glad to see the accounts of your colored force at Jacksonville, Florida. I see the enemy are driving at them fiercely as is to be expected."

In a Proclamation, December 8, 1863, he said also, "Of those who were slaves at the beginning of the war, full 100,000 are now in

Battle of Newbern, S. C., February 1862.

South Carolina Colored Troops repelling Confederates in Georgia.

Bloodhounds let loose on Colored troops in South Carolina.

the United States militia service about a half of which actually bear arms, thus giving the double advantage of taking so much labor from the insurgent cause and supplying the places which otherwise must be filled with so many white men. So far as is attested it is difficult to say they are not as good soldiers as any."

Lt. Colonel E. H. White, a white commander of Negro troops said, "Practical trial in skirmish and battle proved the gallantry and trustworthiness of the black soldier in the severest trials of devotion and heroism . . .

"At Port Hudson, Fort Wagner, at Olustee, The Mine Explosion, Petersburg, and Fort Gilmer, and in scores of other battles, the mettle of the colored troops was thoroughly tested and they were almost without exception most favorably mentioned in the orders of the commanding generals."

General George H. Thomas said the bravery of the Negro troops wiped from his mind "the last vestige of prejudice and doubt."

Major General David Birney, commander of the 10th Army Corps, said, August 19, 1864, "To the colored regiments recently added to us and fighting with us, the Major General tenders his thanks for their uniform good con-

The Battle of Milliken's Bend. Negro tro

...ging Confederates led by their former masters.

Negro infantry capturing Confederate guns to the cheers of white troops.

Negro troops in the trenches.

United States Colored troops entering Charleston, S. C.

Negro troops attacking Fort Wagner.

duct and soldierly bearing. They have set a good example to our veterans by their entire absence of struggling from the ranks."

He said in General Orders of the same date, "The enemy attacked my lines in heavy force last night and was repulsed with great loss. . . . The colored troops behaved handsomely and are in fine spirits."

Captain George R. Sherman, of United States Colored Infantry, wrote, "Their long service as slaves and servants made them obedient and

subject to their officers and very few deserted or became insubordinate. . . .

"Not only were the men remarkable for their temperate habits, cases of drunkenness being very rare, but they were quiet and orderly as well and their freedom from the use of profane and obscene language was remarkable."

General Butler wrote, "They instinctively and without needing so much drilling and experience as did white men, kept their camps neat and in better order." (Butler's Book, p. 494).

182

The Negro soldier lacked one important thing, however; initiative. That was the fault of slavery. Colonel Powell, white commander of Negro troops, said, "Accustomed to discipline (he) had never been taught to take the initiative and when in a moment of danger never thought of taking it." He was "the unthinking machine."

It was, however, this that helped to make him the perfect fighting machine—the soldier who obeys blindly. Sherman said, "He faced the same enemy with the same dogged persistence, storming the same fortifications with the same undaunted heroism and resisting assaults of the common enemy with the same courage.

"I have seen escaping slaves fresh from Southern plantations come into the army as recruits. We have later noticed their soldierly bearing, fidelity, and endurance. We have been with them on the march, in the bivouac and on picket and fatigue duty and have observed with deep respect and admiration their unyielding firmness and self-sacrificing valor on the skirmish line and amid the whirlwind of battle while cannons were roaring far and near . . . singing bullets were falling all around us but I have never seen one of them show the least sign of fear. . . .

"We once saw a white regiment, its ammunition exhausted just as the Confederates charged with their famous wild yell, breaking ranks in confusion and flee in disorder through the Union lines. We saw the Seventh Regiment of United States Colored Troops sent to the relief of the fleeing whites; we saw them advance in perfect order with the steadfastness of veterans without discharging a musket until the order was given and then they met the rushing charge of the foe as a rock received and rolls back the surges of the ocean. . . ." ("The Negro as A Soldier.")

General Grant said before Vicksburg, "I am anxious to get as many of these Negro troops as possible and to have them full and completely equipped. . . .

"The Negro troops are easier to preserve discipline than our white troops. . . . All that have been tried have fought bravely. . . ."

General Benjamin Butler said, October 11, 1864, "The colored soldiers by coolness, steadiness and dash have silenced every cavil of the doubters of their soldierly capacity and drawing tokens of admiration from their enemies. . . ."

In his farewell address to the Negro troops, he said, "You have shown yourselves worthy of the uniform you wear . . .

"The best officers of the Union seek to command you.

"Your bravery has now the admiration of those who would be your masters.

"Your patriotism, fidelity, and courage have illustrated the best qualities of manhood.

"With the bayonets you have unlocked the iron-barred gates of prejudice and opened new fields of freedom, liberty and equality of right to yourselves and your race."

In "Battles and Leaders of the Civil War," are also mention of Negro soldiers. Major General Samuel Jones said of the Battle of Fort Wagner, "The 7th New Hampshire moved forward into line on the right and the 8th United States Colored Troops on the left of the batteries. The fire of the latter was exceedingly effective." (Volume 4, p. 78, 1888.)

General Henry G. Thomas says of the "Colored Troops at Petersburg" where a great landmine killed many 'Hundreds of heroes carved in ebony." . . . The black men commanded the admirationan d respect of every beholder . . . (pp. 563-67)

Major General Slocum said, "During our stay in Raleigh I witnessed a scene which to me was one of the most impressive of the war. It was a review of a division of colored troops. These troops passed through the principal streets of the city. They were well-drilled, dressed in new and handsome uniforms with their bright bayonets gleaming in the sun mak-

Colored troops under General W

ing slaves in North Carolina.

ing a splendid spectacle." He added that a great crowd turned out to see them and among the spectators might have been some of their former owners. (p. 757)

As in the Revolution, a Negro was the first to shed his blood for freedom, so it was in the Civil War. Nicholas Biddle, a sixty-four year old runaway slave, had attached himself to the Washington Artilleries, better known as "The First Defenders." They had arrived in Baltimore by train and in changing trains for Washington, were marching through the city, April 19, 1861, when they were hooted by mobs. Their rage knew no bounds when they saw Biddle, the lone Negro in uniform. Someone shouted, "Kill the nigger, that damned brother of Abe Lincoln!" Someone threw a stone. It caught Biddle on the head, knocking him senseless. But he survived and died sixteen years later. Incidentally, a Negro regiment, the 62nd U.S. Infantry, fired the last shot in the war at Brownsville, Texas, May 13, 1865. (Crisis, October 1916, p. 298)

At the close of the war there were 149 Negro regiments of which 120 were infantry; 12 heavy artillery; 10 light artillery; and seven cavalry, a total of 123,156 men. The number that had served were 186,017. But these figures are only for two years, 1863-65, when regular enlistment began. Perhaps a half or more of that number had served with such commanders as Butler, Hunter, Phelps, before Negro service was regularized. And all these Negroes had served without pay since Congress had not yet provided for any. Added to this were the millions of Negroes who served as laborers and attended to the daily needs of the army.

Of the regularly enlisted soldiers, 134,111 came from the South, with Louisiana leading with 24,052, and Tennessee next with 20,133. Of that total number of Negro regulars, 78,779 were volunteers, of which Kentucky with 23,703 furnished the most.

There were some Negro officers also, although the objection to them was at first strong. One of the first was Lieutenant Pete Vogelsang, who had enlisted as a private in the 54th Masachusetts. He fought with distinction in several battles among them those of Fort Wagner, Charleston and Savannah. He was later promoted to regimental quartermaster. Another was Frank Welch, who had also enlisted as a private in the 54th. Massachusetts had a total of ten Negro officers; Kansas three; the First North Carolina had a lieutenant-colonel, W. N. Reed. Nearly all the officers of the Corps d'Afrique were Negroes. The highest ranking Negro officer was William Henry Singleton who had enlisted as a private in 1863, rose to be a sergeant and was promoted to colonel by Lincoln. He tells of his life in "Recollections of Slavery Days." In 1936, at the age of 103, he marched in the Grand Army parade at New Haven, Connecticut.

In the Department of the Gulf, 75 held commissions, one of whom was Major Martin R. Delaney.

Some wealthy Negroes, commanded the troops they raised themselves. One was Colonel James Lewis of Louisiana, who raised a regiment. He was later Chief of Police of New Orleans. Another was Dumas, also of Louisiana, who raised troops for Butler. There were at least seven surgeons, all commissioned, and seven chaplains, the best known of which was Henry M. Turner.

The killed were 36,847 with many more wounded. This figure represents only those who were regularly enlisted. The actual dead must have been many tens of thousands more. Twenty-one won the Congressional Medal of Honor, highest decoration for valor. Five of these were in the Navy.

NEGROES AS SCOUTS AND SPIES

Next to fighting men the most important ones in an army are scouts, spies and informers. Negroes rendered most valuable services in these fields. And they would have done more

Massacre of Negro troops and their white officers at Fort Pillow, Tenn., by the Confederates.

had it not been for the habit of depreciating them at first. One newspaper report of the first battle of Bull Run where Union troops were badly beaten, said, "There is little doubt that the rout was owing to General McDowel's ignorance of the Confederate position concerning which any Negro could have informed him."

One Negro, Furney Bryant, directed a whole corps of spies. Another, Sam Williams, was scout for the Third New York Cavalry (white).

His commander wrote of him, "There's no braver man alive." One of the ablest was John Scobell, an ex-slave, who served with the famous Alan Pinkerton, founder of the United States Secret Service. Pinkerton devoted two chapters to Scobell's exploits in his "Spy of the Rebellion." (1863). He said, "John Scobell, I found, was a remarkably gifted man. He could read and write and was as full of music as the feathered songsters that warbled in the

Negroes attending wounded whites on the battlefield.

tropical groves of his sunny home. In addition to what seemed an almost inexhaustible stock of Negro plantation melodies, he had a charming variety of Scotch ballads which he sang with a voice of remarkable sweetness and power. . . . No one would suspect the cool-headed vigilant detective in the rollicking Negro whose only aim in life appeared to be to get enough to eat and a comfortable place to toast his shins."

Scobel operated with the "Loyal League," a Negro secret society whose members brought him news of troop movements and other vital information.

Another very able spy was Alfred Wood (Ol' Alf), 3rd United States Cavalry, and one of the best horsemen and marksmen of that time. To him was due much of the success of the Union Army in Mississippi. Once when captured by the enemy, he said he was a runaway slave and told such a convincing tale of the cruel-

ties he had suffered, he was permitted to join the Confederates, to whom he gave much false information. Later, he joined the Texas Rangers, where he passed as white thanks to his light color and long hair. After a short service with them he deserted with valuable information.

Still another efficient spy was Harriet Tubman. She was an escaped slave and one of the most daring of all. Before the war, she aided slaves to escape. T. W. Higginson, white colonel of a Negro regiment, said of her, "We have here the greatest heroine of the age. Harriet Tubman, a black woman and a fugitive slave. Her tales of adventure are beyond anything in fiction and her ingenuity and generalship are extraordinary. . . . She had a reward of $12,000 offered for her in Maryland and will probably be burnt alive whenever she is caught, which she will probably be, first or last, as she is going again. . . . She is jet-black and can-

General Benjamin F. Butler, the outstanding military friend of the Negro in the Civil War.

Upper left to right. Lieut. Peter Vogelsang. Sergt. William Bronson. Lower:
Louisiana Native Guard, and Lieut. Frank M. Welch.

Mobbing of Union troops in Baltimore, 1861. Inset: Nicholas Biddle, first to shed blood in the Civil War.

not read or write, only talk, besides acting." Wendell Phillips in an outburst of admiration called her, "The best and bravest person on this continent." General Sexton to whom she gave valuable information praised her zeal and courage. When she died in 1913, at the age of eighty, she was given a military funeral.

One Negro informer, whose name was never mentioned, brought $800,000 (worth several millions now) into the United States treasury at a time when it was very badly needed. This sum in silver coin was taken from the Citizens' Bank of New Orleans and hidden in the cellars of the Dutch consulate. When General Butler arrived in New Orleans, one of the slaves who had helped in the transfer and had carefully

noted all, told of it. Butler seized it. An international rumpus followed with even the British and the French protesting. But the information given by the ex-slave was so accurate that the real ownership was proved. ("War of the Rebellion, U.S. War Department, ser. 3, vol. 2, pp. 116-124. Parton J., Gen. Butler in New Orleans, pp. 364-5. 1864). George W. Walker, another ex-slave, told of the hiding place of a vast cache of hidden arms and ammunition.

One informer, who received national publicity and the highest praise was William A. Jackson. Coachman to Jefferson Davis, president of the Confederacy, he listened carefully to all that was said by Davis and his officials, then stole into the Union lines at Fredericksburg. Taken directly to the White House, he gave Lincoln abundant and accurate information on the strength and positions of the Confederate army in Virginia, as well as its morale and finances. Harper's Weekly described Jackson as "an extremely intelligent man . . . who reads and writes and converses in a manner which shows he is used to good society."

NEGROES IN THE UNION NAVY

Unlike the Union army, there was never any question of using Negroes in the navy. Sea-life was so tough, most white men didn't like it. Slaves were more commonly used, their masters hiring them there. Herman Melville, celebrated author of Moby Dick, who served a year in the American navy, says in "White Jacket," "Black slaves were to be found regularly enlisted with the crew of an American frigate, their masters receiving their pay. This was in the teeth of a law of Congress expressly prohibiting slaves in the navy." These Negroes, being property, were much better treated than the white sailors. They were exempt from the "disciplining degradation" of the Caucasian members of the crew. Melville tells of one on his ship "who was actually envied by many of the seamen. There were many times when I almost envied him myself." (p. 353. 1892). As early as May 1862, escaped slaves were enlisted in the navy at eight dollars a month.

Of the 118,044 regular enlistments in the navy during the war, 29,511 were Negroes. This figure does not include the slaves, thus at least a third of the Union sailors were Negroes. They contributed greatly to the brilliant victories of the Union navy. In fact, it was the navy that saved the Union from total defeat in the earlier days of the war. Its blockade of the South crippled Confederate cotton trade with England. It captured over a thousand prizes, worth $13,000,000.

One naval exploit that encouraged the North in the darkest days of the war was that of William Tillman, cook of a Union vessel, the S. J. Waring, which was captured by the Confederate warship, Jeff Davis, July 7, 1861, and a prize-crew placed on board. Seven nights later while the prize-captain and the first mate were asleep in their cabins, Tillman crept in and with a hatchet killed them, then going to the wheel dispatched the second mate, too. The remainder of the Confederates not only surrendered but agreed to work the ship. Tillman, in full charge, sailed for New York, where he received a hero's welcome and was given a reward of $6,000 by the owners of the ship. Harper's Weekly devoted a whole page to the exploit and Leslie's Weekly mentioned it three times with pictures of Tillman. The New York Tribune reported it fully, also. It said, "To this colored man the nation is indebted for the first vindication of its honor on the sea." Another daily said it was an "offset to the defeat at Bull Run."

Barnum engaged him at a large salary and had a huge poster of him typifying "Black Action at Sea." So many people came to shake his hand that he threatened to quit.

Another event that brought very favorable publicity to the Negro concerned the Confederate iron-clad Merrimac, first of its kind, which had been playing havoc with the wooden vessels of the Union. With nothing to match it, the Union evolved a desperate plan to ram it with four vessels. The whole affair was kept secret but it somehow leaked out. When the white seamen who were to go on them, learnt of the very dangerous nature of the attempt, they walked off in a body.

The officer in charge, Colonel Cannon, appealed to their patriotism in vain. He then thought of the Negroes and selected 350 stevedores from them. But they, too, hearing of what they were to be used for, refused. Cannon appealed to their race pride. He told them he had selected them because white men had been too scared to go, on which, he said, "The whole line moved up in a solid column as though

Five of the 21 winners of the Congressional Medal of Honor in the Civil War. Upper left to right: William Penn and John S. Lawson of the Navy. Lower left to right: Sergt-Major Christian Fleetwood; Sergt. William H. Carney (above) and Sergt. Alexander Kelly.

Some famous spies of the Union Army; Left upper, Furney Bryant as scout; Right upper, William A. Jackson (see text); Left lower, James Gordon, spy; Right lower, Harriet Tubman (see text).

Union Scouts.

actuated by a single impulse. It was a thrilling response and the most remarkable and impressive scene I ever witnessed. . . ." He adds that Captain Fox, first assistant secretary of the navy, shortly afterwards issued an order that the fleets be recruited entirely from Negroes." (From Colonel Cannon's own account in the Troy (N.Y.) Record. Reproduced in the Crisis, May 1917, p. 26).

Later, the Union built an iron-clad, the Monitor, that sunk the Merrimac. Negroes took a leading part in that. A photograph of the times shows them as gunners.

Another exploit that thrilled the Union was that of Robert Smalls, Negro pilot of the Confederate steam-ship "Planter." On the night of May 12, 1862, while the white officers were ashore, Smalls and the Negroes sailed off. Meeting a Union warship, the "Onward," Smalls handed the Planter over and piloted both ships safely through the Confederate mines into Charleston harbor. The Planter with its cargo of war material was valued at $120,000. Secretary of the Navy Welles, mentioned Smalls in his report to Congress and made him captain of the Planter. Smalls was later elected to Congress.

Smalls was one of the many Negro pilots who knew well the coastal waters of the South. The Union navy eagerly employed such. One ex-slave, Prince, piloted the Ottawa, flagship of the squadron, up Cumberland Sound for the capture of Fernandina, Florida, and of St. Mary's Georgia. (Harper's Weekly, March 4, 1862). Five Negro sailors won the Congressional Medal of Honor—Robert Blake, Joachim Pease, John Lawson, Clement Dees, and Aaron Anderson.

VIEWS ON LINCOLN'S CONDUCT OF THE WAR

And so the war came to an end, May 26, 1865 —four years and 44 days after it started. It took more than a million lives; cost the North twelve billion dollars and the South, four billions, not counting the loss of its slaves. Yet, but for a fantastic prejudice based on color of skin, it could have been prevented at the start. Here were the slaves, a largely discontented element. In 1850, John Brown had tried to show that the best way to keep the South from seceding was to get the slaves to revolt. Lincoln, as was said, knew well they provided the balance of power. His generals and the abolitionists had prodded him incessantly to use them. General Sherman, who in 1861, said he wanted it "a white man's war," changed on August 24, 1862 to "We must seek the aid and make it the interests of the Negroes to help us. Nothing but our party divisions and our natural prejudices of caste has kept us from using them as allies in the war to be used for all purposes which can advance the cause of the country."

Lincoln would say to all this, "It would do no good to go ahead faster than the country would follow." Such a step would lead to

Negroes on U. S. gunboat, Darlington, shooting rebels concealed in trees in Georgia.

"mutiny in the army. We must wait until every other means has been exhausted. The thunderbolt will keep. . . .

"The powder in this bombshell will keep dry and when the fuse is lit I intend to have them touch it off themselves."

When the hour comes for dealing with slavery, he said, he would be willing to do his duty though it "cost my life. And, gentlemen, lives will be lost." Hoping that his opponents would one day see the light, he begged the abolitionists "to keep pitching" into him.

Rev. Moncure Daniel Conway, a staunch abolitionist, said, not without justification at Lincoln's death, "While recognizing Abraham Lincoln's strong personality I cannot participate in his canonization. . . . President Lincoln in disregard of the anti-coercion sentiment of press and pulpit and without consulting Congress assumed the responsibility of sending half a million men to their graves for the sake of a flag." By which he meant Lincoln's constant reference to following the Constitution in all he did; and which, as the abolitionists told him, would save the Constitution but would lose the Union.

Referring to one of his speeches in which he said he had 100,000 Negroes in the South who were now assisting in the Union army, Conway said, "The President had precisely the same right to take the 4,000,000 black laborers from the insurgent cause as the 100,000 with the million-fold advantage of preventing the war altogether."

Frank Bird, another abolitionist, thought Lincoln more a politician than a humanitarian. He

William Tillman capturing the S. J. Waring single-handed. Inset: portrait of Tillman from life. (Frank Leslie's Weekly)

Negro gunners of the iron-clad Monitor.

said, "The great defect in my judgment in Lincoln's character was that he ignored moral force as having to do with the government of the world. . . . It was the early abolitionists and anti-slavery men who aroused the conscience of the nation and set in motion the moral forces which abolished slavery and made the Union worth preserving."

Wendell Phillips in an address at Framingham, Mass., July 4, 1863, said Lincoln was "not to be trusted" because while he had called on the Negro to save the country he had said nothing of his rights. The debauched heir who kills his father the sooner to enjoy his estate is a meek-eyed and lofty saint compared with an administration which calls on the Negro to save it. . . . General Butler said to me a fortnight ago, 'I am no Negro lover as you are but before I ask a Negro to fight for me by the living God he should have his rights.' "

Lincoln had a trump—the slaves. He let it lay idle for two years while the nation was being ruined. Think what Caesar, Napoleon, Bismarck, or even Lee would have done in his place.

For those who believe with Thomas Huxley that there can no more be two kinds of right than there can be two kinds of straight lines there will always be some doubt as to the natural, spontaneous honesty attributed to Lincoln, at least when it came to putting his true feelings into action. For instance Frederick Douglass at the unveiling of the Lincoln Monument in Lincoln Park, 1876, said to the whites present, "First, midst, and last you and yours were the objects of his deepest affection and his most earnest solicitude. You are the children of Abraham Lincoln. . . . To you it especially belongs to sound his praises, to preserve and perpetuate his memory. . . ."

To the Negroes present, Douglass had said, "It must be admitted, truth compels me to admit, even here in the presence of this monument we have erected to his memory that Lincoln was not, in the fullest sense of the word, either our man or our model. In his interests, in his associations, in his habits of thought and in his prejudices, he was a white man.

"He was preeminently the white man's President, entirely devoted to the welfare of white men. He was ready and willing at any time during the first years of his administration to deny, postpone, and sacrifice the rights of humanity in the colored people in order to promote the welfare of the white people. . . . He was ready to execute all the supposed constitutional guarantees of the United States Constitution in favor of the slave system anywhere inside the slave states. He was willing to pursue, recapture and send back the fugitive slave to his master and to suppress a slave rising for liberty though the guilty master were already in arms against the Government. . . ."

In appraising Lincoln the above must certainly be taken into account. He branded them

William Morrison. Robert Smalls. A. Gradine.
John Smalls.

FOUR OF THE NINE COLORED MEN WHO CAPTURE
THE CONFEDERATE STEAMER "PLANTER."

On Monday, May 19th, 1862, in the Unite
States Senate, a Bill was introduced for the reli
of Robert Smalls and others (colored), who h:
recently delivered the steamer *Planter* to Comm
dore Dupont's squadron. The Bill provided th:
the steamer, with her armament, cargo, etc., l
appraised by a competent board of officers, and th:
one-half the value thereof should go to Robe
Smalls and his associates, who ran the *Planter*)(
of the Harbor of Charleston.

Left: Captain Robert Smalls, later a Congressman.

Prince, noted pilot of the Union Navy in the South. (Drawn from life by Artist Crane).

as inferior, said he was against their holding office, voting, or being jurors. He was always ready to use them when it served white interest, even while declaring his sympathy for them. Does this not remind one of the great Negrophobes that were, and still are, in Congress. Tillman, Vardaman, Blease, Bilbo, and their kind really did not hate Negroes in their heart and as if to compensate went out of their way to be kind and helpful to individual ones. Eastland of Mississippi who now wears the Negrophobe crown has the same reputation. The greatest of all the racial mischief-makers and a great quoter of Lincoln, was

Sergeant Clovese, last of the Grand Army Veterans.

Thomas Dixon, author of The Clansman and The Leopard Spots, yet I heard Dixon, shortly before his death, tell a large audience in the Century Theatre, New York, that he had always been a friend of Negroes, and that he was willing to risk his life against the revived Klan in protecting them. For this sort of conduct, Karl Marx' dictum of economic determinism is particularly apt. Power over one's subsistence is power over one's will. Hope for advantage stills conscience in most men.

Were Lincoln the paragon of moral honesty he is held up to be, what must be said of John Brown and Elijah Lovejoy who gave their lives for what they felt was right? Or of Emerson, Longfellow, Garrison, Wendell Phillips, Wil-

liam Cullen Bryant, Charles Sumner, Henry Ward Beecher and other whites who were furnishing the moral power that finally swung Northern opinion to Lincoln. The uncompromising opposition of these to slavery must have been always ringing in Lincoln's ears. Remember his later unstinted praise of Harriet Beecher Stowe, and how after 1863 he begged the abolitionist to attack his policies.

Between Lincoln the humanitarian and Lincoln the politician there was wide difference. He attacked the great amount of racial intermixture then taking place in the South. "It is worthy to note," he said, "that among the free states those which make the colored man the nearest to equal with the white, have proportionably the fewest mulattoes, the least a-malgamation. In New Hampshire the State which goes farthest towards equality between the races there are just 184 mulattoes while there are in Virginia how many do you think? 79,775 being 23,126 more than in all the free states together. . . . The statistics show that slavery is the greatest source of amalgamation." (Basler, R. P. Collected Works of Abraham Lincoln, Vol. 2, p. 408. 1953).

Yet, in the face of this, he speaks of the physical barrier to intermixture between white and black. "I will say in addition there is a physical difference between the white and black races which I believe will forever forbid the two races living together on terms of social and political equality."

To arguments of this kind, General Butler replied, "If there is any greater social equality than that to have one man become the father of seven children by six different colored women I do not know what an exhibition of social equality is."

As regards Negro voting Lincoln said in his debate with Douglas, "I am not, nor ever have been, in favor of making voters or jurors of Negroes, nor of qualifying them to hold office. . . ." But were not Negroes then voting in the free states, and were, or had been in some of the slave ones? Was he against this, too? And what of intelligent and qualified Negroes, and those who were large property owners. He certainly had made no exception in their case.

Between white and black, he also said, "there must be the position of superior and inferior and I, as much as any other man, am in favor of having the superior position assigned to the white race. . . ." But, he added, "There is no reason in the world why the Negro is not entitled to all the natural rights enumerated in the Declaration of Independence. . . ." *All the natural rights!* Yet, in almost the same breadth he advocated an inferior position for Negroes. Then as if to soften this immense contradiction

he added, "I agree with Judge Douglas that he (the Negro) is not my equal in many respects —certainly not in color, perhaps not in moral or intellectual endowment. But in the right to eat the bread, without the leave of anybody else, which his own hand earns he is my equal and the equal of Judge Douglas and the equal of every living man." This burst of apparent liberality when viewed with what he had advocated on inequality amounts to little more than political oratory. Or to be more exact: sophistry.

Lincoln in his daily contact with his faithful Negro servants, whom he loved deeply and confided in, could not help but see that they were as much human as any white person. When Elizabeth Keckley, a Negro woman, and Mrs. Lincoln's dearest friend, lost her son in the war, he was most deeply affected.

Another striking instance of this contradiction. He said in his letter to James S. Wadsworth, December 31, 1863, "How to better the condition of the colored people has long been a study which has attracted my serious and careful attention; hence, I think I am clear and decided as to what course I shall pursue in the premises, regarding it as a religious duty as the guardian of these people, who have so heroically vindicated their manhood on the battlefield, where in assisting the life of the Republic, they have demonstrated in blood their right to the ballot which is but the humane protection of the flag they have so fearlessly defended.

"The restoration of the Rebel States to the Union must rest upon the civil and political equality of both races."

In support of this idea, he wrote Governor Hahn of Louisiana suggesting that the "very intelligent" Negroes and "especially those who have fought gallantly in our ranks be members of the Convention." That is, the one that was to draft the new state constitution.

Yet on April 12, 1865, two years and three

months after the Emancipation Proclamation, and three days after Lee's surrender at Appomatox, when W. C. Bibb, a Confederate of Montgomery, Alabama, called on him and asked, "Mr. Lincoln, what do you propose to do in relation to the slave property?" he replied, "I am individually willing to grant either gradual emancipation, say, running through twenty years, or compensated emancipation at the option of the Southern people, but there are certain amendments to the Constitution now before the people for their adoption or rejection and I have no power to do anything at present, but if it should so happen that I could control it such would be my policy." This is quoted by Carl Sandburg in "Lincoln: The War Years, (Vol. 4, p. 239. 1939). Yet, on February 1, two months earlier, the Thirteenth Amendment had been passed and sent to the states for ratification. Bibb had called on him with important introductions and Lincoln had said that probably to soften the blow for the South, to win friends there, and perhaps even out of amiability. But it was to be used with great effect by the Negro's enemies after Lincoln's death. Had not their "greatest friend and savior" said that would have been his course? It was clearly Lincoln the politician who was talking. Here one is reminded of Weininger's statement that an innately honest and upright politician is an impossibility. His first thought usually is to win friends rather than to stand for what's right.

Enemies of the Negroes and of Lincoln, too, are fond of quoting him on his approval of an inferior position for Negroes. One anti-Negro writer in a paid advertisement in the New York Times, January 5, 1959, said, ". . . Abraham Lincoln, to whom the Negro owes more than any other man." Not only most whites believe that but most Negroes, too. *The simple truth is it is not the Negro who owes most to Lincoln but the Southern whites. Had they won independence instead of being a part of the great nation America now is they very likely would have risen no higher than any of the Latin-American states. Their proposed slave empire would have collapsed eventually. Being agricultural, it would still have been dependent on the North for capital.*

A vast amount of undue adulation has been showered on Lincoln. He was not "The Great Emancipator." This title was bestowed on him because of the Emancipation Proclamation, which was shown, freed no slaves, but was designed to use the Negro soldier. The war was won, not so much through Lincoln's policy as in spite of it. Far more was due to General Butler, Grant, and some other generals than to Lincoln. Had Lincoln survived the war, he would not be so worshipped today. Grant did and lost much of his prestige. H. L. Mencken predicted, "When this generation of history fakers dies out, Lincoln will smell to high heaven." One need not go that far but there's more than a little truth in it. Lincoln's tragic end contributed greatly to his present place in national and world regard.

There is much I admire about Lincoln and I sympathize greatly with him for the many trying problems he had to face but *in all fairness it must be said that he owed vastly more to the Negro than the Negro to him. Had he lost the war he would be in history where Jefferson Davis now is. In that case the immense blunderings of the North would have been charged to him even though the chief blame would have been on the prejudiced white public that tied his hands from using the straightest path to victory—the Negro soldier.*

What Lincoln said on inequality for Negroes must and will continue to be criticized because it has been for a century the strongest argument used by enemies of the Negroes. Were Lincoln alive, it is safe to say, he would repudiate them. Furthermore had he not gone into politics but remained a pure abolitionist like Theodore Tilton, Beecher, Sumner, and Thaddeus Stevens he would have spoken like them, there's good reason to believe, for fullest equality to Negroes.

Lincoln's political conduct of the war, forced as it was on him by Northern color prejudice and Southern slave econmy, was most blunder-

Cartoon attacking the 14th Amendment giving civil rights to Negroes. A Presidential candidate shining a Negro's shoes

ing. It showed little of the sagacity attributed to him. He had a trump—the Negro soldier—yet it was kept unused for twenty-one months while hundreds of thousands of lives were being lost and the nation faced ruin. Circumstances at last forced its use and the admission that it saved the Union.

And saving the Union permitted mankind to continue its upward path in all fields of progress. In the light of America's role since would that have been possible had she been split into two nations—a North and a South? Worst of all slavery would have triumphed in all that part of the New World south of the Mason-Dixon line. As was shown slavery had been written into the Confederate Constitution. In this turn-

ing-point in the history of mankind we see Africa again, through her descendants, in her ancient role of benefiting the rest of mankind.

With the war won, Negroes were to be ill-rewarded for their immense services. The South, once kindlier to them than the North, became a hotbed of hate. "Black" laws were passed to return the ex-slaves and even the freemen to a state as near to slavery as possible. Twice was the North forced to send troops again to the South to protect them, once against the Ku Klux Klan. Lynching, which had once been mostly that of white men in the West, now became a Southern pastime. Between 1850 and 1860 only twenty-six Negroes had been lynched, or less than three yearly. In 1883, it rose to 49, an increase of nearly 1700 per cent. In 1891 it was 113; in 1892, 162. And the great majority of these were for such trivial reasons as "talking back to a white man" and "trying to act like a white man, not knowing his place."

With the re-admission of the South to the Union, its representatives used Congress as a forum from which to attack and vilify Negroes. Ironically enough their strongest arguments were drawn from Lincoln and what he had said in his first campaign in support of inequality for Negroes and his objection to their holding political office. Had not Lincoln, their great "friend" and "deliverer" said they were "inferior"? Benjamin Tillman of South Carolina, an unregenerate rebel and Lincoln-hater, would rise in the Senate or at Chataquas, spouting Lincoln. Denouncing the Fourteenth and Fifteenth Amendments, he would shout, "To hell with the Constitution." Lincoln became the bible of the great Negrophobes and still is. Vardaman, Blease, Watson, Hoke Smith, Rankin, Bilbo were forever quoting him. In recent years we have had others as Byrnes, Eastland and Ellender. Thus it was the Negro's very saving of the Union that made it possible for these men to be in Congress and to wield such power in the nation. But for that they might have been in their own much less significant Confederate Congress. For anti-Negro venom, the Congressional Record is second to none as a source.

The end of the war also saw a flood of anti-Negro books as Thomas Dixon's "Clansman" and "Leopard Spots;" Shufeldt's, "The Negro, A Menace to American Civilization;" Carroll's, "The Negro a Beast;" and W. B. Smith's, "The Color Line." An era of great oppression with race riots followed until World War I, when the use of Negroes was again necessary. The close of that war was followed by great anti-Negro riots, one of which lasted for three days, in Washington, D.C. This continued until World War II, when there was a respite, which has lasted to the present.

The white skin, or rather pride in it, not the black one, has been America's curse. The immense woe that pride brought the South after the war, and continues to bring it, is a matter of record. In fact, this pride has distorted the whole pattern of American life as visioned in the Declaration of Independence. As a ship is thrown off its course by a piece of metal near its compass, so America's whole destiny has been changed for the worse by white-ism.

The whole trouble lies in not having the courage to do the right thing at the right time. The writing of slavery into the Constitution in 1787 led to the Civil War; and the killing of the Civil Rights Amendment and the approval of the jim-crow car by the Supreme Court in 1896 led directly to Little Rock.

However, what Lincoln said in favor of color prejudice will pass because the conditions that inspired them are passing. We will then prefer these words of his spoken at the beginning of his career when his spirit of humanity and justice was in the ascendant:

"It is the eternal struggle between two principles. The one is the common right of humanity; and the other the divine right of kings. It is the same spirit that says, 'You toil and work and earn bread and I'll eat it.' No matter in what shape it comes, whether from the mouth of a king who seeks to bestride the people of his own nation and live by the fruit of their labor, or from one race of men as an apology for enslaving another race, it is the same tyrannical principle."

THE CIVIL WAR

SOME PRIMARY SOURCES

Abraham Lincoln: A History. 10 vols. Nicolay & Hay, 1890.

Lincoln: Life and Writings. 1940.

Mearns. The Lincoln Papers. 1948.

Lincoln: Complete Works, 2 vols. 1922.

Sandburg, Carl. Lincoln: The War Years, 4 vols. 1939.

Lincoln: An Autobiography. 1925.

Shaw, A.H. Lincoln Encyclopedia. 1950.

War of Rebellion. Official Records of the Union and Confederate Forces. 128 vols. 1880-1901.

War of Rebellion. Official records of the Union and Confederate Navies. 30 vols. 1894-1922.

Moore, F. Rebellion Record. 10 vols. 1861-66.

Butler, Gen. Butler: His Book. 1892.

Parton, J. General Butler in New Orleans. 1864, pp. 364-65.

Sherman, Gen. W. T. Memoirs. 2 vols. 1886.

Sherman, G. R. Negro as a Soldier. 1913.

Freese, J. R. Secrets of the Late Rebellion. 1882.

Baker, L. C. History of the United States Secret Service. 1867.

Pinkerton, A. Spy of the Rebellion, 1883.

Higginson, T. W. Army Life in a Negro Regiment. 1870.

Brown, W. W. Negro in the American Rebellion. 1867.

Conway, Moncure D. Autobiography, 1904.

Williams, G. W. History of the Negro Troops in the War of the Rebellion. 1888.

Ayers, J. T. War Diary. 1947.

Guthrie, J. M. Camp-Fires of the Afro-American. 1899.

Halpine, C. G. Life and Adventures. 1864.

Hallowell, N. P. Negro As A Soldier, 1897.

Clark, P. H. Black Brigade of Cincinnati. 1864.

Colyer, V. Report on Services. 1864.

Basler, R. P. Collected Works of Lincoln. 1953.

Greeley, H. The American Conflict. 2 vols. 1864-66.

SOME GOOD SECONDARY SOURCES

Quarles, B. Negro in the Civil War. 1953.

Cornish, D. The Sable Arm: Negro Troops in the Union Army, 1861-65.

Werstein, I. July 1863. 1957.

Powell, E. H. The Colored Soldier. 1893.

Hughes, L. & Meltzer M. Pictorial History of the Negro. 1956.

FOR NEGROES IN THE CONFEDERACY SEE ALSO:

Conscription in the Confederate States. University of Georgia Bull. Vol. 26, March 1917.

Negro Soldiers in the Confederate Army. Journal of Negro History, Vol. 4. July 1919.

Negro Year Book, 1914-15, p. 158.

Black, C. Railroads of the Confederacy.

Russell, J. H. Free Negroes in Virginia. 1913.

Wesley, C. H. Collapse of the Confederacy, pp. 139-144. 1937.

NOTE: It is commonly said, even by some Negro writers, that there were only 16 Negro Medal of Honor winners. They omit the five in the Navy. They are John H. Lawson, Aaron Anderson, Robert Blake, Clement Dees, and Joachim Pease. (See Beyer, W. F. Deeds of Valor, Vol. 2, pp. 52, 72, 553. 1906. Also Cromwell, J. W. The Negro in American History, pp. 249, 260, 252, 253. 1914).

Negroes pay last tribute to their devoted friend, Senator Charles Sumner of Massachusetts, in ceremony at the Capitol, led by Frederick Douglas.

Part Four

SOME IMPORTANT CULTURAL CONTRIBUTIONS OF THE SLAVE ERA

"When a man is made a slave half his worth is taken away."

Homer, 900 B.C.

Thomas Jefferson was pessimistic on the innate ability of the Negro. He wrote, "Never yet could I find that a black had uttered a thought above the level of plain narration; never saw an elementary trait of painting or sculpture" in one. Yet many thousand years before Jefferson, as well as during his time, Negroes in Africa were producing sculpture, specimens of which are considered some of the world's finest today.

Frobenius tells of a Berlin newspaper that called these specimens of African art "vulgar, repulsive idols." Christian missionaries would destroy them—also calling them idols. Today similar objects are worth more than their weight in gold. In 1958, one small ivory mask from Nigeria, carved about 1520, was bought by the Museum of Primitive Art of New York for $56,000, a record price for such art. In the Transvaal Museum, South Africa, is the carving of a white rhinoceros worth many times as much as that. The Illustrated London News, July 14, 1928, in rapturous praise, called it, "A masterpiece of Prehistoric Art. An outstanding monument in the history of sculpture—the world famous South African bas-relief of a white rhinoceros with a swarm of tick-birds, hammered into a slab of basaltic rock, more probably 50,000 than 25,000 years ago by a sculptor of the Stone Age. . . . By virtue of its great antiquity and superb artistic qualities, South Africa becomes the birthplace of real art. . . ." (See reproduction in Sex and Race, vol. 1, p. 35. 1942).

This Negro art has profoundly influenced modern art. Among the great artists to whom it has done so are Picasso, Modigliani, Matisse.

Jefferson's opinion was based on sheer ignorance, therefore. Moreover, had he reflected on the life forced on the blacks about him, he certainly would have seen why they were what they were. Take the children on his estate, did he send them to school? No. At the age of ten he had them working all day, and a little above that age in his nail factory. One great horror of the slave-master was to see a Negro with a book. Teaching a slave to read was a crime. The Statutes of Virginia, Sec. 39, 1848, placed a penalty "not to exceed 39 lashes" on a free Negro who taught a slave to read; for a white person who did it was a fine of $100 and six months' imprisonment. On July 4, 1847, Martha Christian, white slave mistress, of Righteous Ridge, Virginia, was indicted for "not having the fear of God upon her eyes but moved by the Devil wickedly, maliciously and feloniously did teach a black woman named Rebecca, alias Black Beck, to read the Bible to the great displeasure of Almighty God." She

Wilson Chinn.   Charles Taylor.   Augusta Boujey.   Mary Johnson.   Isaac White.   Rebecca Huger.   Robert Whitehead.   Rosina Downs.

EMANCIPATED SLAVES, WHITE AND COLORED.—THE CHILDREN ARE FROM THE SCHOOLS ESTABLISHED IN NEW ORLEANS, BY ORDER OF MAJOR-GENERAL BANKS.

These white children were probably captured and sold as Negroes. For how this was done see picture of 1838 in Sex and Race, Vol. 2, page 213.

209

Ornamented cup from Belgian Congo. About 300 years old (Brooklyn Museum).

A famous Benin bronze. Thought to be a warrior-queen. Benin bronzes are worth their weight in gold now (Volkerunde, Berlin).

Royal pair. Bronze. King's face was damaged in the excavation. Nigeria.

Some of the bronzes found in the buried city of Ife, Nigeria of about 800 A.D. (Illustrated London News, Aug. 20, 1938).

was sent to the Richmond Penitentiary for two years. (Quoted in Journal of Negro History, vol. 18, p. 474).

Had this woman only *read* the Bible to her slave, she would have been praised instead, especially that passage where St. Paul had sent a runaway slave, Onesimus, back to his master, and also had bade all slaves, "Servants, be obedient to them that are your masters." Frederick Douglass tells, about the same time, how his own mistress was scolded by her husband when he once caught her teaching him to read.

What was expected of a slave was field-labor. And there was a slave-driver with a whip to see that he kept his thoughts and energy on that. He had to work from "can't see to can't see," that is, from dawn to sunset. Moreover, even as today, there are unmixed blacks who have come right out of the bush later to enter European universities and walk off with top prizes, so in Jefferson's day and earlier, there were unmixed African blacks of considerable attainment in Europe, especially Spain and Portugal, including some physicians to royalty. Two French kings, Charles VII (1422-1461), and Louis XI (1423-1483), had African physicians.

The heavy hand of a people stronger in numbers, brute force, and wealth was on the black man, even when free. But it is impossible to repress entirely intelligence and natural ability. As plants take root on inhospitable rocks and even grow into trees, so some Negroes did rise about the common herd, even of whites, and make substantial industrial, intellectual, and artistic contributions to the America of

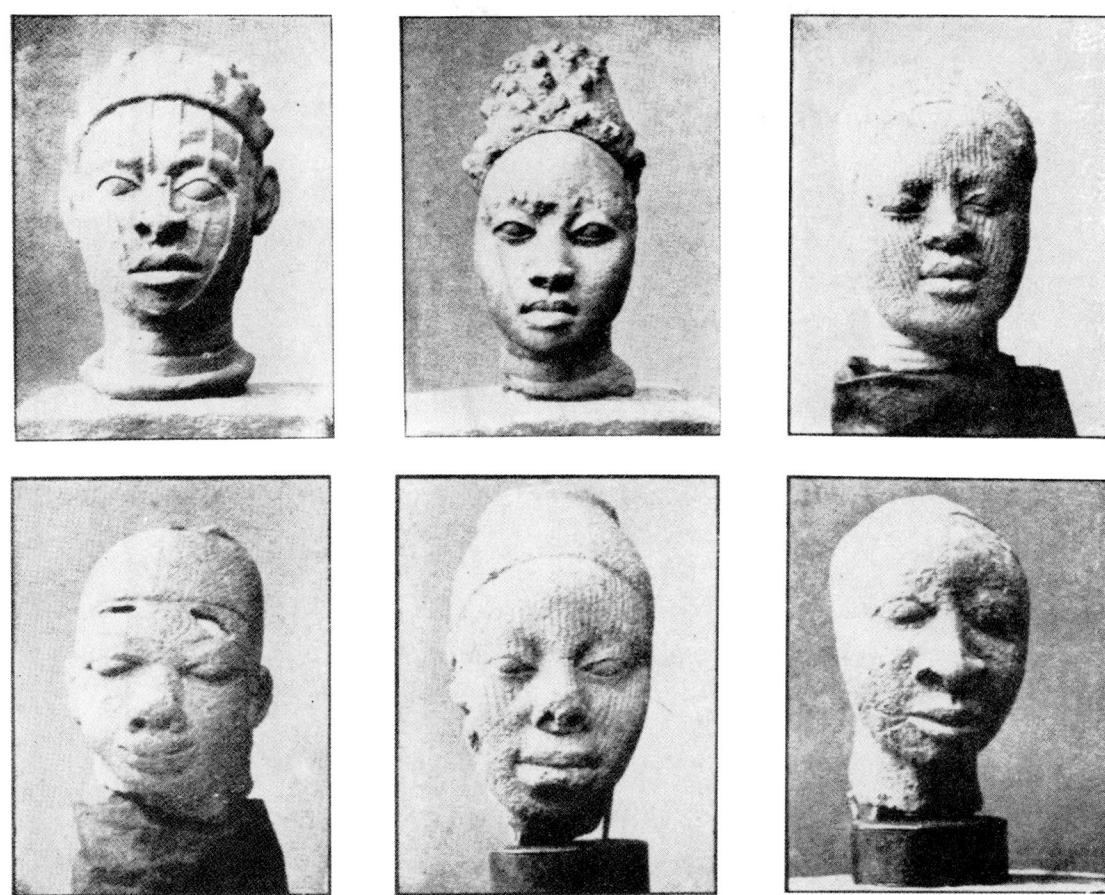

Portraits in terra-cotta found by German Inner African Exploration Expedition in 1910. (Monumenta Africana).

their day. It is important to remember, too, that even when offering America their best they had to do so under a handicap.

Africa, that is, the sale and exploitation of its people, laid the foundation of the commerce and prosperity of the United States, as was shown; and the imported Africans themselves influenced every phase of American life from cookery to religion. First and foremost was their industrial contribution.

Carved planks and beams from Yoruba Temple.
West Africa. About 1500 A.D.

Ivory mask from 16th Century, Nigeria. Purchased
by Museum of Primitive Art, New York for $56,000
in 1959. This is the largest sum ever paid for
primitive art. It is about twice the size of this
picture.

214

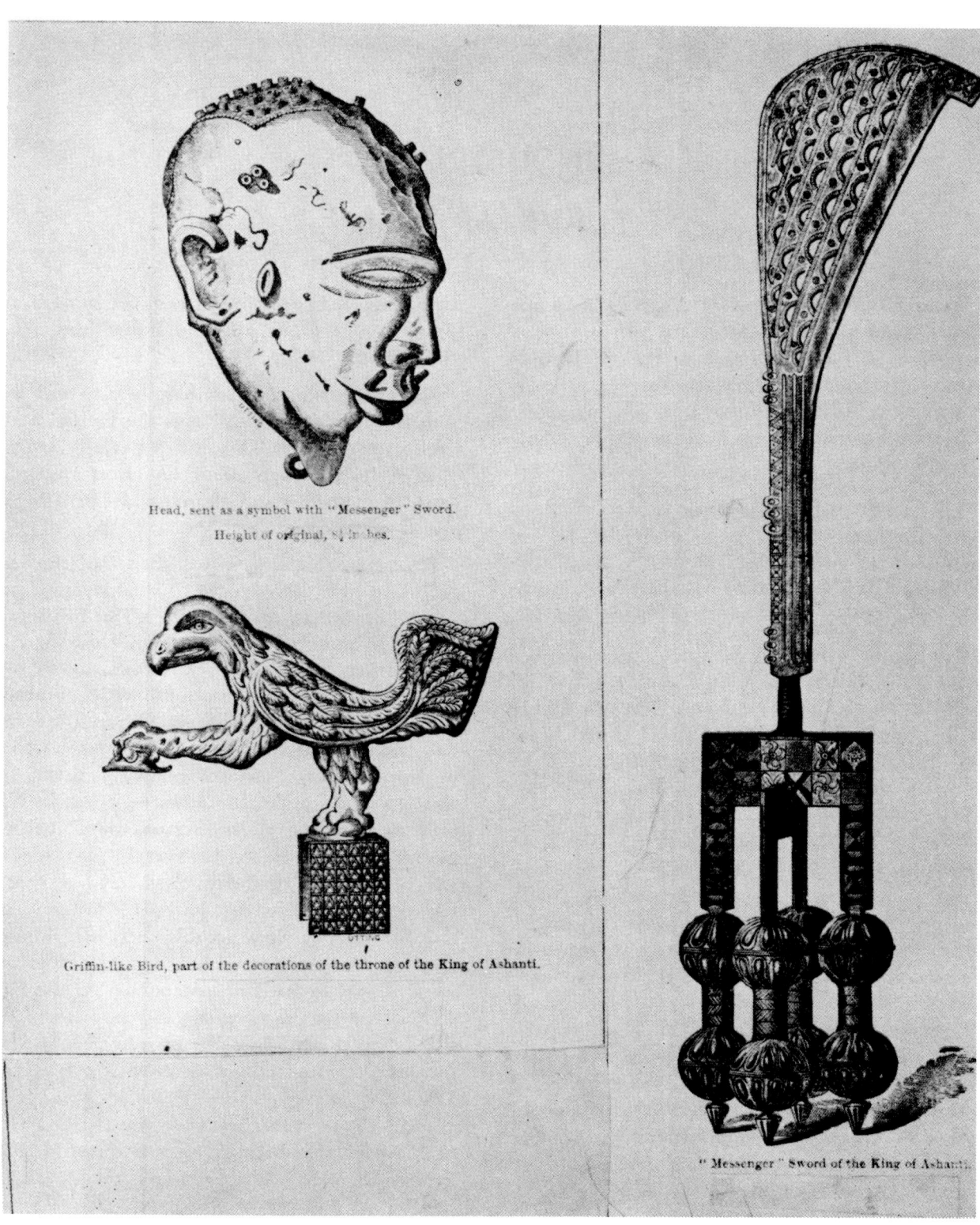

Head, sent as a symbol with "Messenger" Sword.
Height of original, 8½ inches.

Griffin-like Bird, part of the decorations of the throne of the King of Ashanti.

"Messenger" Sword of the King of Ashanti.

Some exquisite examples of Ashanti Art.

INDUSTRIAL

SLAVE ARTISANS

Among the occupations of Negroes, as mentioned in the colonial records are millers, brewers, weavers, butchers, tanners, bakers, leather workers, shoemakers, blacksmiths, carpenters, shipwrights, brick-masons, foremen, coopers, gold and silversmiths, as well as sailors, whalers and pilots.

The great colonial mansions and famous antebellum structures were built by slaves, among them Monticello, Mount Vernon, the College of William and Mary, the Wren Building and Nominy Hall, home of "King" Carter.

Most famous of the structures built by slave labor were the White House and the Capitol at Washington. It was a Negro slave, a highly skilled mechanic, who performed the delicate and difficult task of fitting the Statue of Freedom on the dome of the Capitol. The New York Tribune, December 2, 1863, in an article entitled, "The Negro Slave and the Statue of Freedom, says, "When the bronze castings were being completed at the foundry of Mr. Mills, the foreman who had superintended the work from the beginning and who was receiving eight dollars a day struck and demanded ten— a Negro took the striker's place as superintendent and the work went on. The black master-builder lifted the ponderous masses and bolted them together, joint to joint, piece by piece, 'till they blended into the majestic freedom." "A work on the "Rotunda and Dome" in the Capitol Library gives the name of this slave. It says, "Mr. Mills at that time owned a highly intelligent slave named Philip Reed who had been employed about his foundry as an expert and admirable workman. . . . Mr. Reed, the former slave, is now in business for himself and highly esteemed by all who know him. . . ." (pp. 194-95. 1869).

"Many mansions owed their beauty and durability to slave artisans," says the United States Guide to Virginia. This was especially true of New Orleans, where their fine iron and grill-work in mansions and churches, are still highly prized momentoes.

It was in this city which then had the least prejudice that the Negro made greatest progress. Charles Gayarre, writing about 1850, said, "By 1830 some of the people of color had arrived at such a degree of wealth as to own cotton and sugar plantations with numerous slaves. They educated their children as they had been educated in France. Those who chose to remain there attained, many of them, distinction in scientific and literary circles. In New Orleans they became musicians, merchants and money and real-estate brokers — a trade for which even to this day they have a special vocation; they were barbers, tailors, upholsterers. They were notably successful hunters and supplied the city with game. As tailors they were almost exclusively patronized by the elite, so much so that the Legoasters', the Dumas', the Clovis' and the Lacroix' acquired individual fortunes of hundreds of thousands of dollars." (In Grace King's "New Orleans, pp. 346-47. 1895). These colored people entertained General Butler at a banquet served on gold plate, during the Civil War.

Due to the scarcity of skilled whites, the Negro artisan was a necessity. Jernegan, in "Laboring and Dependent Classes in Colonial

Statue of Freedom on the Capitol at Washington. It was erected and put in place
by a Negro slave, Philip Reed (see text).

Negro Blacksmiths of the Union Army.

America," says, "This scarcity of artisans made it almost necessary that the planter should put forth every effort to purchase slaves who had some skill in handicraft. . . . The reference to Negro artisans in wills and inventories of the early eighteenth century is further evidence of the increase of this class.

"Indeed it is hard to see how the eighteenth century plantation could have survived if the Negro had not made his important contribution as an artisan in the building and other trades calling for skill in transforming raw materials into manufactured articles."

"The New England slave," says Lorenzo Green, "had to be equally at home in the cabbage patch and in the cornfield; he must be prepared, as will be demonstrated . . . not only to care for stock, to act as servant, repair a fence, shoe a horse, print a newspaper, but

even to manage his master's business." Some served as doctor's apprentices, he says, and more than one Negro took over his master's practice when he was ill or died. Some, with their knowledge of roots and herbs, were reported as being "extraordinarily successful." (The Negro in Colonial New England.)

One Negro, Mingo, managed his master's warehouse in Boston, and another slave, Prince, superintended the large farm of Colonel Buckminster at Deerfield, Mass. House-servants, as butlers and "mammies," occupied positions of trust and sometimes managed great mansions.

Negro pressmen were commonly used in printing offices. Thomas' "History of Printing in America," says that Thomas Fleet, noted editor and printer of Boston, Mass., had about 1729, a Negro slave, "an ingenious man," who made his wood prints for ballads and books. His sons also learned the trade and succeeded their father. (American Antiquarian Soc'y Trans., vol. 5, 1874).

The self-sufficiency of the colonies during the Revolution was in no small measure due to the Negro artisan who could make all the necessities for an army in the field, including the guns and gunpowder.

WASHINGTON HAD NEGRO CARPENTERS

In a contract George Washington made with Benjamin Butler, one reads, "The said George Washington hath several Negro carpenters which he proposes to put under said Benjamin Buckler . . . to use his utmost endeavors to hurry and drive them on to the performance of so much work as they ought to render." On December 16, 1773, Washington hired Case, a Negro carpenter, from Philip Longfit for three years.

Washington and his overseer.

Mrs. Washington watching Negro spinners.

Duke de la Rouchefoucauld-Liancourt wrote of his visit to Monticello, "I found him, (Jefferson) in the midst of the harvest from which the scorching sun does not prevent his attendance. His Negroes are cabinet-makers, carpenters, masons, bricklayers, smith, etc. The children he employs in a nail factory, which already yields considerable profit. The young and the old Negro women spin the clothing for the rest." They spun some 2,000 yards of clothing each year. Jefferson wrote, "Children 'till ten years old to serve as nurses, from ten to sixteen the boys make nails, the girls spin; at sixteen they go to the ground or learn trades."

Johann D. Schoepf, a visitor to America in 1784, said of South Carolina, in particular, "The gentlemen in the country have among them Negroes as the Russian nobility among the serfs, the most necessary handcraftmen, cobblers, tailors, carpenters, smiths, and the like whose work they command at the smallest possible or for nothing, almost. There is hardly any trade or craft which has not been learned and is not carried on by Negroes partly free, partly slaves. The latter are hired out by their owners for day's wages." (Travels, etc. p. 220).

SOME NOTED NEGROES OF THE SLAVE ERA

Cato's House. Famous New York tavern and rendezvous of New York high society for 48 years. Built in 1712. Cato was an ex-slave.

THE CATERERS

The field in which the Negroes had the freest hand was catering. Since that was some form of domestic service, there was no color prejudice against it. Their numbers were large and some made sums that would be considered good even in our day. One, Joseph Ten Eyck, of New York, left $100,000 at his death. Emanuel Bernon, who opened the first oyster-house in Providence, Rhode Island, was one of the wealthiest of its citizens at that time.

Most famous of the caterers was, of course, Samuel Francis (known later as Frauncis and Fraunces), already mentioned. His New York tavern was by all accounts America's finest in the Revolutionary period. The next most famous was Cato Alexander, an ex-slave (1771-1858). His tavern on the Old Post Road, New York City, was the rendezvous of the aristocracy. They gave special parties there. Poems were written about him. One writer said, "Those who tasted his terrapin, fried chicken, curried oysters, roast duck, or drank his New York brandy punch, his Virginia egg-nogg . . . wondered how anyone who owned him could sell him even to himself." William Dunlap, noted writer of that time, said, "Not to know Cato's is not to know the world." At Christmas he made barrels of punch in relays. Gentle, generous, obliging, he was beloved by all and made a fortune. "A sable son of Africa," says Americana, "he lived and died respected in a community far more aristocratic and exclusive than its more pretentious democratic successors." (Dunlap, "Memoirs of a Water-Drinker," vol. 1, pp. 117 et seq. 1837. Americana, April 1916, pp. 123-131, February 1946).

John Dabney (1824-1900) of Richmond, Virginia, was the most celebrated caterer of his time. He was known as "the mint-julep maker of the United States." When the Prince of Wales (later Edward VII) visited the United States in 1860, he prepared a dinner for him and made mint julep that made history. Mary Stanard wrote of him, "A Negro gentleman of

John Dabney of Richmond, Va., most famous caterer of his time.

remarkable dignity, and a chef who prepared immortal foods. . . . A very handsome and impressive man." W. P. Dabney, noted author, editor and former paymaster of the City of Cincinnati, was his son. . . .

Colonel John McKee of Philadelphia was the richest of the caterers and died a millionaire. Arriving penniless from Virginia, he found work in a German restaurant. He married the daughter of his employer and at the latter's death, took over the business and managed it. He made money, which he invested in land. He had rich holdings in Philadelphia, and some quarter million acres in coal, oil and farm land in New Jersey, Kentucky, West Virginia and Illinois. At his death in 1902, he left $800,000 to build "The Colonel John McKee College" patterned on the United States Naval Academy for white and colored youths. The value of that fund as reported in the Pittsburgh Courier, January 24, 1959, is now $1,320,614. So far, it has been giving scholarships.

COL. JOHN McKEE

George T. Downing

Still another famous New York caterer was **George T. Downing** (1819-1903). He started early and at twenty-six his place at 690 Broadway was already the rendezvous of high society. He had a summer place at Newport, Rhode Island, and another at Providence. By 1860, he had made enough from these to finance the construction of a block of business buildings. In 1865, he was asked to take over the restaurant of the House of Representatives and did. (Bartlett, I. H. From Slave to Citizen. **Story of the Negro in Rhode Island. For picture of restaurant in the Capitol with white society, see J. B. Ellis "Sights and Secrets of the National Capitol" p. 112. 1869).**

222

MEDICINE

The most noted early contribution to the physician's art — inoculation — was made by Onesimus, Negro slave of Cotton Mather, already mentioned. Thanks to him the great ravages of small pox in the colonies were greatly lessened. Mather tells the story himself in his Diary, "I had from a servant of my own an account of its being practiced in Africa. Inquiry of my Negro man, Onesimus, who is a pretty intelligent fellow, whether he ever had the small pox, he answered yes and no, and told me he had undergone an operation which

Some colored physicians of the 1860's. Upper left to right: Major Martin R. Delaney; John V. DeGrasse; James McCune Smith. Lower: Dr. Edwin C. Howard; Peter Ray and Major R. Abbott.

had given him something of the smallpox and would forever preserve him from having it, adding that it was often used among the Guaramantes. He described the operation to me and showed me the scar which it had left upon him."

This was in 1721, during an epidemic of that disease. Mather, who had studied medicine, at once wrote letters to ten physicians of Boston. Only one answered, Dr. Zabdiel Boylston, who was later to become the most famous American physician of his day. Boylston, convinced, tried it on his own son, Thomas, and two Negroes and it worked. Later, of 241 he innoculated, only six died, four of whom had the disease at the time. But some religious leaders issued a strong circular opposing it. They said inoculation was a heathen practice and Christians should not learn from the heathen. Mobs attacked the homes of Mather and Boylston. Mather wrote, "People took a strange possession on this occasion. They rave, they rail, they blaspheme. They talk not only like idiots but also like fanatics. Not only the physicians who began the experiment but I also am an object of their fury." (Mather: vol. 2, pp. 624, 631, 648. 1912 ed. Also see Boylston, G. in Dictionary of American Biography; and Ciba Symposia, "Colonial Epidemic Diseases, vol. 1, no. 12, pp. 373-74).

Later, inoculation was practised in the Revolutionary Army and helped contribute to its success. It found such favor in England that it was practised on two granddaughters of George III. Inoculation, no doubt, gave Dr. Jenner the idea of vaccination. David Livingstone later confirmed what Onesimus had told Mather of the practise of inoculation of Africa.

Earliest Negro physician in America was Lucas Santomee already mentioned. He studied in Holland. When the English took over New York City, Governor Nichols gave him land for his services. (Stokes, I. N. Iconography of Manhattan, VI, 75).

In early New England some slaves served as apprentices to physicians and in time became doctors. Lorenzo Green in "The Negro in Colonial New England, 1630-1776," mentions one of them; "Primus, who helped his master in surgery and took over his practice when he died. Primus was reported as being extraordinarily successful."

Papan, a Virginia slave, who picked up medicine probably with his master, had such a knowledge of it and made such extraordinary cures in skin and venereal disease that the Virginia Legislature as "a reward for so useful a discovery which may be of great benefit to mankind" bought him from his master in 1729 and set him free. (Virginia Magazine of History, vol. 34, pp. 103-04. 1926. See also Southern Workman, vol. 63. 1943).

In 1733, a Virginian Negro who discovered a cure for scurvy, yaws, distemper and pox, was freed by the state and given a pension of 150 pounds for life. The recipe is given in Caribbeana, vol. 1, p. 258.

Caesar of South Carolina had such a curative knowledge of roots and herbs that the assembly purchased his freedom in 1792 and gave him an annuity of $500 for life. The Massachusetts Magazine of that time carried his recipe. (Vol. 4, p. 103).

James Derham, born 1762 in Philadelphia, was a slave to James Kearsley, one of the most noted physicians of his time. Kearsley later sold him to Dr. West, a surgeon in the British army during the Revolution. He was later sold to Dr. Dove of New Orleans, who liked him and made it possible for him to purchase his freedom. During his years of slavery under physicians, he became a practical and highly skilled one, and one of the leading doctors of New Orleans. He earned from $3,000 to $4,000 a year, a large sum then. Dr. Benjamin Rush, head of a medical corps in the Revolutionary War, said of him, "I have conversed with him upon most of the acute and epidemic diseases of the country where he lives and was pleased to find him perfectly acquainted with the modern simple mode of practice on those diseases. I expected to have suggested some new medicine

to him but he suggested many more to me."
(Brissot de Warville, Nouveau Voyage dans les Etats-Unis, etc. 1788, vol. 2, pp. 31-49; Columbian Gazette II, 742-43; Earliest Colored Gentlemen in Medical Science in the United States. Bull. of the History of Medicine, vol. 8, pp. 599-620. 1940. John Hopkins Univ. Pub.).

Eight Negro physicians were commisisoned into the United Medical Corps during the Civil War. Among them were Dr. John V. DeGrasse who served on the United States Army Medical staff. Born in New York City, 1825, he studied at Bowdoin College, Maine, and Paris, France. In 1849 he visited many of the leading hospitals in Europe. He was elected to the Massachusetts Medical Society and was presented with a gold-handled sword for his services during the war.

Dr. A. R. Abbott, graduate of Toronto University, Canada; Dr. Martin R. Delaney, graduate of Harvard Medical School; Dr. Charles B. Purvis; and Dr. A. T. Augusta.

Dr. Peter W. Ray, born about 1820, was graduate of Bowdoin College and member of the New York State Medical Society. He spoke German fluently and for fifty years was one of the most popular doctors among the Germans of New York City. Nearly all his practice was white. Still another early physician was James McCune Smith, graduate of Glasgow Medical College, Scotland.

Dr. Edwin C. Howard, born 1846, was a graduate of Harvard Medical School. He was an expert in the treatment of small-pox and was one of the founders of the Mercy-Frederick-Douglass Hospital of Philadelphia.

ARTISTS

Earliest mentioned Negro painter was Scipio Moorhead to whom Phylis Wheatly, Negro poet, (1753-84), dedicated a poem. It is said that Gilbert Stuart, noted painter, got his inspiration from Neptune Thurston, a Negro slave

Edward Bannister, winner of Gold Medal for his painting at the Centennial Exhibition, Philadelphia, 1876.

who was employed in a cooper shop of Rhode Island and used to sketch likenesses on the heads of casks. Stuart thought that if Neptune had training he might have been a celebrated painter. (Peterson F. History of Rhode Island, pp. 153-4. 1853).

Earliest portrait painter of note was Joshua Johnson, who lived during the Revolution. Twenty-one of his portraits are reproduced in the Maryland Magazine of History, June 1942. All are of white society. Some of his portraits are in the Frick Gallery, New York City. Johnson was listed in the Baltimore Directory of 1796 as one of "The Free Householders of Color."

Another earlier painter of note was Robert S. Duncanson (1817-1872), of Cincinnati, Ohio, whose portraits were also of upper-class folk. He was especially admired in England. Lord Tennyson, the Poet Laureate, entertained him

225

at his home, Farringdon and told his guests that Duncanson had caught the spirit of his poems, "The Lotus Eaters" in his painting of it. Among his English patrons were Duchess of Sutherland and Duchess of Essex. His landscapes were highly praised by the critics in America and abroad. "Art in America," October 1951, devotes the whole issue to him and has some of his 65 paintings. Twelve of these are in the Taft Museum of Cincinnati, and others in art museums and the homes of private collectors. An article on him was published in the Cincinnati Daily Gazette, Nov. 24, 1865, and is reproduced in "Cincinnati's Colored Citizens" by W. P. Dabney, who owned some of his paintings.

Most noted Negro painter of the slave era, and one of the foremost then in America, was Edward M. Bannister, (1828-1901). He won the first prize in the landscape division with his "Under the Oaks," at the Centennial Exposition held in Philadelphia in 1876 to celebrate the hundredth anniversary of American independence. When it became known that it was a Negro who had carried off this high honor, there was a furore. Some insisted that the decision of the judges be set aside but the competing artists declared that Bannister had won by sheer merit since the judges did not know the identity of any of the artists. All pictures had been distinguished only by numbers.

Bannister tells his experience at that exhibition: "I learned," he said, "from the newspapers that Number 54 had received a First Prize Gold Medal, so I hurried to the committee rooms. There was a great crowd ahead of me and as I jostled among them many resented my presence.

"What is this Negro doing in here; and other remarks were heard. Finally I reached the desk and tried to get the attention of the official in charge. He was insolent. Without raising his eyes, he said shortly, 'Well, what do you want here? Speak lively.'

" 'I want to inquire concerning Number 54. Is it a prize winner?'

" 'What's that to you.'

"Controlling my self, I said, 'I am interested in the report that it received a prize. I painted the picture!'

"An explosion could not have made a more marked expression."

Incidentally, another Negro, already mentioned, William Owen Bush, of the State of Washington, took first prize at that exposition for the world's finest wheat. Bush, who was also a state senator, had the reputation of having the finest cattle in America. He was the son of George William Bush, already mentioned, who took the first party of white people to the State of Washington.

Among leading sculptors was Eugene Warbourg (1825-1861) of New Orleans. He did sculptures for cathedrals in Louisiana and Europe. His bas-reliefs of Uncle Tom from Harriett Beecher Stowe's novel won high praise in England. His principal pieces are "Le Pecheur" and "Le Premier Baiser." He had studied in France.

INVENTORS

The first known Negro to receive a patent was Henry Blair of Glenross, Maryland. In 1834, he received one on a corn-husker and in 1836, another on its improvement. Until emancipation inventions by slaves were the property of their masters.

In the history of one of the world's greatest inventions, a Negro slave must be mentioned also. He was Jo Anderson, who assisted Cyrus McCormick in the invention of the grain harvester in 1831. For years he worked beside him, making suggestions. McCormick's grandson, Cyrus, said, "Of those who helped most of all the name of his Negro helper deserved honor as the man who worked beside him in the building of the reaper." (Century of the Reaper, p. 11. 1931). The Centenary Gold Medal of the harvester shows Anderson on the reverse side.

Cyrus McCormick building the reaper assisted by his Negro slave, Jo Anderson, in Virginia, 1831. (From Harvester World, Feb. 1931).

The International Harvester in its full-page ad in the Pittsburgh Courier, September 4, 1954, said, "Back in 1831 Cyrus McCormick invented the first practical reaper. He received valuable assistance from a Negro, Jo Anderson. That was the beginning of the concern by International Harvester in the right of the Negro to economic opportunity."

Anthony Weston of Charleston, South Carolina, did valuable work in a related field in 1831.

He improved the threshing machine invented by W. T. Catto, doubling its efficiency. His master, Benjamin F. Hunt, made a fortune from it. Lewis Temple of Bedford, Massachusetts, invented a whaling harpoon that was a great improvement. Joseph Lee of Boston made considerable money on his dough-kneading machines on which he had three patents. R. B. Lewis, born 1802, in Gardiner, Maine, invented an oakum-picking machine that was extensively used in ship-building. Pierre Cazenave, undertaker of New Orleans, discovered a method of embalming that kept the body in such a state of preservation that it was believed he had resurrected the art of the ancient Egyptians. He had a mummy of his own in his show window. It is said the secret died with him.

Norbert Rillieux, a free quadroon, born at New Orleans in 1806, was one of America's first modern scientific geniuses. Educated in engineering in France, he returned to Louisiana and by his inventions revolutionized the sugar industry of the world. In spite of his inferior social status due to his color, he was the most sought-after engineer in the sugar-producing states. Tired of color prejudice, he returned to France where the government made him head of the Central School, a scientific institution. He died there in 1904 and was buried in Pere Lachaise Cemetery. The Louisiana press lauded him at his death but made no mention of his color. In 1934, at the initiative of European scientists, a tablet was placed in his honor in the Louisiana State Museum. It reads:

"To honor and commemorate Norbert Rillieux born at New Orleans, La., March, 1806 and died in Paris, France, October 8, 1894. Inventor of multiple evaporation and its application ito the Sugar Industry. This tablet was dedicated in 1934 by Corporations representing the Sugar Industry all over the world." (The date of his death is really 1906.) Rillieux did for the sugar industry what George W. Carver did for the peanut. (A Negro Scientist of Slavery Days. Scientific Monthly, Vol. 62, pp. 317-326. 1946.)

Four others, who were born during the slave era but whose chief work was done later, are Lewis Latimer, Granville Woods, Elijah McCoy, and Jan Matzeliger. Latimer, associate of Thomas Edison, solved the problem of turning the electric current into illumination by inventing the incandescent lamp. He superintended the installation of electric street lighting in New York, Philadelphia, London (England), and other large cities. He was chief draftsman for General Electric and Westinghouse. He also drew for Alexander Bell the plans for the first telephone. (Sources given in My World's Great Men of Color, Vol. 2, p. 711).

Granville T. Woods was an expert in electric motors, as well as in the telephone and telegraph. He invented a telephone which he sold to the Bell Company and a system of telegraphing from train to train which was tried on the New Haven Railway. His electric railway system was used at Coney Island. (Cosmopolitan, April, 1895, p. 761.)

Matzeliger invented a machine for sewing the soles of shoes to the uppers. It revolutionized the shoe industry, lowered the price of shoes, and made several millionaires, one of whom gave $5,000,000 to Harvard to found an engineering school. The patent was acquired by the United Shoe Manufacturing Company. (See Rogers, J. A., World's Great Men of Color, Vol. 2, p. 550-53).

Elijah McCoy, born 1844, of slave parents, was one of the world's most practical inventors. Pioneer in the art of lubrication, he made possible uninterrupted motion of all kinds of engines with his cup for steadily supplying oil to them in intermittent drops. This invention was used in locomotives, boiler engines and steamers. His graphite lubrication, an improvement, made a score of 300,000 miles without having to replace cylinders. He had a total of 67 inventions and on lubrication 46 patents. These four are among the world's great inventors.

Horace King, born a slave, was one of the foremost bridge engineers in the South before and after the Civil War. Freed by his master, John Godwin, who sent him North to be educated in engineering, he returned to build bridges in Georgia over the Chattahoochee River and others in Alabama, Mississippi, and South Carolina. Georgia and Alabama passed special laws giving him standing with white builders and contractors. King, in gratitude, erected a monument over the tomb of his former master.

Thomas L. Jennings of New York (1791-

Norbert Rillieux

Four famous inventors. Upper left: Norbert Rillieux; right: Lewis Latimer. Lower right: Granville Woods; left: Elijah McCoy (see text).

229

1859), who owned one of the city's largest clothing stores, made a fortune from his patent for renovating clothes. His plucky daughter broke up the jim-crow car in New York. When she was ejected from the white car one Sunday morning, she employed Chester Arthur, later President of the United States, to take her case to the Supreme Court, and won.

MUSIC

The African brought with him his gift of music, song and dance, which gave to most of the New World a certain rhythm and flexibility to everyday living. The most popular dances of the Americas as the tango, machiche, samba, mambo, cha-cha-cha, meringue, cake-walk, charleston, jazz, rock-and-roll, are all of Negro origin. Leonard Bernstein, eminent New York conductor, on a television broadcast, January 2, 1959, mentioned some of the great modern composers who have been influenced by Negro music, especially jazz, as Stravinsky, Ravel, Darius Milhaud and Hindemith. A popular American composer who was greatly so was George Gershwin.

The basis of the liveliest expression in the amusement life of the United States is Negroid. The Negro singer on the plantation with his guitar; and the Negro peddler, basket on her head, singing out her wares, were very welcome before and after the Revolution. James Parton said of the Negro street singers of Franklin's time, "What a debt we owe to the jolly, amiable, irrepressible, indispensable Negro! All but the tradition of jollity would have fled the country long ago but for him. He is a broad grin on the face of the country." (Biography of Benjamin Franklin, p. 215. 1887.)

Negro musicians were first in popularity in colonial days and were used at balls and parties in the great mansions of the South. Advertisements for runaways or of slaves for sale tell of the skill of some. One advertised for sale in 1760 said he played "extremely well on the French horn." Some runaways were said to have taken their violins or other instruments with them. Sy Gilliat, slave of Lord Botetourt at Williamsburg, was violinist at State balls. Robert Scott, a free Negro, with his wife and three gifted sons, played for Jefferson and entertained for LaFayette when he visited Monticello.

The Confederacy, as was shown, provided special sums for Negro musicians to cheer its men. Negro singers were very popular also in the Union Army; also New England had some succesful Negro music teachers of whites.

Most noted of all the slave musicians was Thomas Bethune, "Blind Tom" (1848-1908), greatest untaught pianist, and improviser in the recorded history of mankind. All the gift of music with which Negroes are said to be endowed seemed to have been poured into him with an incredibly lavish hand so that to many he seemed more like a miracle than a man. Born blind and unable to read or write, he could play by heart thousands of selections from the great masters. He could set to music any sound he could hear—the wind, the waves, the roar of the ocean, the ripple of a brook, the songs of birds. He created an immense sensation in Europe. Vast crowds turned out to hear him. For his master, Colonel Bethune, he was a veritable gold mine. In one London season alone, he made $100,000. Musical experts tested him. One report, signed by sixteen of them, said, "Whether in his improvisation or performances by Gottschalk, Verdi, and others, in fact under every form of musical examination—and the experiments were too numerous to mention—he showed a capacity ranking him among the most wonderful in history."

One said, "Those who have observed him most closely and attempted to investigate him most fully, pronounce him a living miracle, unparalleled, incomprehensible, such as has not been seen before and probably will never be seen again.

"BLIND TOM."—THE CELEBRATED NEGRO PIANIST.—[PHOT. BY BENDANN BROTHERS, BALTIMORE.]

TOM, THE BLIND NEGRO PIANIST.

THIS extraordinary boy, who has for several months astonished and delighted the thousands who have had the good fortune to witness the astounding demonstrations of his wonderful genius, was born near the city of Columbus, in the State of Georgia, about the 25th of May, 1849. Shut out from all knowledge of the external world but such as could be acquired by hearing and by touch, his whole being seemed to be open to and occupied by touch and sound. No matter what its character; the moan of pain, the cry of anger, the harsh grating of the corn-sheller, the roar of the thunder, and the soft breathings of the flute, all were music to him.

Before he was two years of age BLIND TOM sung every thing he heard. When the young ladies of the family, upon their return from school, sat upon the steps and sung, TOM came and sung with them; and such were the facility and correctness with which he took up the air, that they were impressed with the belief that he did not have to learn the tune, but that upon hearing the first note he knew intuitively the balance. Soon without knowing, but from the promptings of nature, that there was any such thing, he began to sing seconds.

At about four years of age he heard the sound of a piano for the first time. Upon the arrival of the instrument he was amusing himself as usual in the yard. The first touch of the keys brought him into the parlor; he was permitted to run his fingers over the keys simply to gratify his curiosity, and to indulge his propensity to make a noise; this luxury he enjoyed occasionally only, as he could chance to find the parlor empty and the piano open. Very soon, however, between midnight and day, he found his way into the parlor, the piano having been left open, and the young ladies were awakened by the sound of the instrument. To their astonishment they heard TOM playing one of their pieces; and the coming of morning found him still at the piano. After this he was allowed to play occasionally, and his powers were so rapidly and so astonishingly developed that in a little time he was permitted to go to the piano at his pleasure. From that day he has played every thing he has heard. He is still developing new and startling powers, the existence of which has been heretofore unknown to the musical world, and the possession of which seems to have been vouchsafed by the power of God to TOM alone.

Seventeen teachers of music in Philadelphia spontaneously testify over their own signatures as follows:

"The undersigned find it impossible to account for these immense results upon any hypothesis growing out of the known laws of art and science. In the numerous tests to which TOM was subjected in our presence, or by us, he invariably came off triumphant. Whether in deciding the pitch or component parts of Chords the most difficult and dissonant, whether in repeating with correctness and precision any pieces, written or impromptu, played to him for the first and only time, whether in his improvisations or performances of compositions by THALBERG, GOTTSCHALK, ASCHER, VERDI, and others—in fact, under every form of musical examination (and the experiments are too numerous to enumerate), he showed a power and capacity ranking him among the most wonderful phenomena recorded in music history."

BLIND TOM plays with wonderful effect some pieces of his own composition. One of these he composed when he was not yet five years old. It was immediately after a storm, and he called it, "What the wind, the thunder, and the rain said to him." Another he composed after hearing the various excited accounts of the first Bull Run battle. The imitation of the setting out and approach of both armies, the skirmishing, the fight, the whistle announcing the approach of KIRBY SMITH's reinforcements, and the terrible retreat, is wonderful, and brings tears to the eyes of his audience. He plays a variety of the most difficult music of the great authors, with a delicacy of touch and a power of expression such as is rarely heard. BLIND TOM, we are informed, goes to Europe in Spring.

Thomas Bethune, most amazing pianist in recorded history.

"In the numerous tests to which Tom was subjected in our presence, he came off triumphant. Whether in deciding the pitch or component parts of chords the most different and dissonant, whether in repeating with correction and precision pieces written or impromptus played to him for the first and only time."

John Law, a professor of music, said, "I may say without the slightest exaggeration that Tom's execution of all kinds of music from the classical works of Beethoven, Bach, Mendelssohn, and others down to the simplest plantation melody of the sunny South is unsurpassed by that of the best professional performers of the day.

"He would invite any member of the audience to play any piece of music unknown to him and would at once replay it with utmost accuracy, however intricate or elaborate. . . .

"As an additional proof of his remarkable powers, he gives recitations in Greek, Latin, German, French, Spanish, imitate the Scotch bagpipe, the music box, the American stump orator, in short, any sound he can hear."

His press notices were the most lavish possible. The Dundee (Scotland) Advertiser said in 1866, "The extraordinary prodigy gave two performances yesterday and on each occasion the powers displayed by him were so marvellous as to verge on the miraculous. History affords no parallel to Blind Tom. His ability would be marvellous even if he had his eyesight; when it is considered he is blind, it is beyond measure strange. Unless one sees or hears him play he is unable properly to understand the extent of his ability. Test him how you may, he never fails. His memory is as miraculous as his unusual powers and he plays over a piece he has never heard with infallible exactitude. Yesterday, several gentlemen went to the platform and played over pieces and during the time they were so occupied it was amusing to witness Tom's contortions of his body and his movements generally. He swayed himself; his eyes rolled; his fingers twitched and he seemed like one possessed. On being allowed to seat himself at the piano, he repeated from memory the various pieces played to him . . ."

The Orchestra of London, July 4, 1866, said, "His execution of the most difficult music is a perfect marvel." The Manchester Guardian, September 24, 1866, "To give in writing anything like an accurate discription of him is utterly impossible. The fingers fly over the keyboard and he seems like one possessed. Did not Shakespeare conceive this being when he describes Caliban with the magical sound in Prospero's island?"

He could play two distinct tunes at the same time while singing a third in an entirely different key and time, which, said the Philadelphia Press, December 29, 1865, "implies a three-fold exercise of the mind at the same time. No amount of skill or practice by any mind can accomplish that." The Albany (N. Y.) Argus said, "As an exhibition of incomprehensible genius excelling in its simplest manifestations we never saw the performance of this prodigy equalled." (The Marvellous Musical Prodigy: Blind Tom. 1867.)

Another, not quite so famous, was Blind Boone.

THE THEATRE

More than a century before the coming of the motion picture the most popular theatrical entertainment in America was Negro minstrels. In 1830, Thomas Rice saw a Negro boy on a Cincinnati street, singing and shouting as he danced, "Jump, Jim Crow." Rice, struck by its possibilities, copied him, blackened his face, took it on the stage and won fame and fortune. Another Negro imitator was Daniel Emmett (1815-'904), who organized the first minstrel show and became more famous than Rice. Emmet, author of "Dixie," marching song of the Confederacy, got his idea of that from Negroes. Some of Stephen Foster's Negroid songs, as Swanee River and My Old Kentucky Home,

"Daddy" Rice (white) greatest of early minstrels. English Copperplate of 1830.

White Comedians in Black Face.

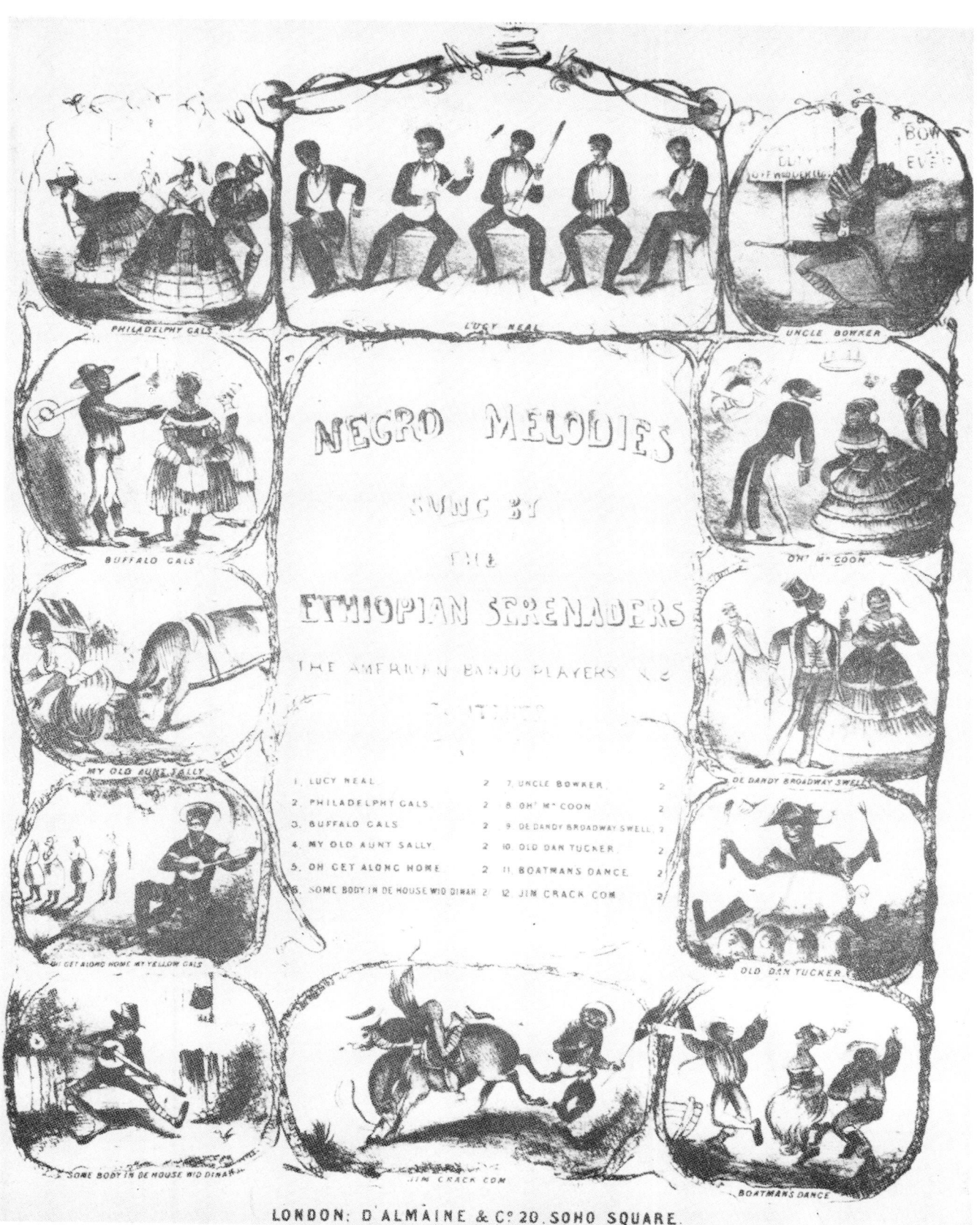

Poster showing Negro minstrels in London in the 1860's. They were extremely popular.

Minstrel Show. White men in Black Face.

236

GLUT OF ETHIOPIANS.

WE have been recently much astonished and bewildered at the enormous glut of Ethiopians, whose black faces are everywhere as plentiful as blackberries. Our imports from Ethiopia are indeed becoming perfectly overwhelming; and as we have nothing to exchange with that country, we are afraid that the drain of bullion may be, in some degree, increased through the sums that may be going out in payment for the numerous parties of serenaders who are continually being sent over to this country.

There are no less than four-and-twenty sons of Ethiopia at this present moment requesting Old Dan Tucker to get out of the way, and lamenting the fate of Lucy Neal, every night, in London, to say nothing of the numerous parties of the children of the sun, or sons of their fathers, who are perambulating the provinces, in the shape of Ethiopian Serenaders. We should be glad if MR. HUME would move for a return of all the Ethiopians at present in this country, whether Lantum, Ohio, or otherwise; as, in the present paucity of provisions, every unnecessary addition to the population is a serious evil.

So universal is the taste for these dingy melodists becoming, that we should not be surprised to find the stars of the Italian Opera reduced to the necessity of competing with the present attraction by adopting the peculiarities of Ethiopian Serenaders; LABLACHE on the bones, and MARIO on the banjo, would be an irresistible novelty. At all events it would be worth while to try the experiment of a revival of *Otello*, in which the Moor, assisted by his Lieutenant and his Ancient, might introduce "Buffalo Gals, come out to night," with the usual accompaniment furnished by the Ethiopians.

English satire on the great number of "Ethopian" minstrels in England. It was the rage in the 1860's and 1870. The performers were white.

were first sung in Emmett's shows. Other internationally famous black-face comedians were the Christy Minstrels, the Ethiopian Serenaders, and the Bryant Minstrels. The black-face minstrel show, as that of Lew Dockstader's, was very popular as late as the 1910's. Other white men who won fame and fortune by blacking their faces and imitating Negroes were Eddie Cantor and Al Jolson.

And, of course, the genuine Negro "blackface" as Williams and Walker rose very high in the amusement world. This tempo of the Negro as seen in the work of W. C. Handy, has invaded and been made welcome not only in the white world but Africa and Asia. Today we see the immense popularity of entertainers as Harry Belafonte, Eartha Kitt and Dorothy Dandridge. At the Brussels World Fair in 1958, the only American, living or dead, who received a higher vote than Louis Armstrong, Negro trumpeter, was Albert Einstein. The vote, as recorded on machines installed there by the United States Commissioner-General's office, gave Einstein 49,631 votes; Armstrong, 45,674, and Lincoln, 42,350 (N. Y. Daily News, Nov. 6, 1958).

(It might be noted in passing that long before the discovery of America, a style of dancing which originated in Africa, was very popular in Western Europe. This was the morris, or Moorish, dance, in which those who took part in it blackened their faces, including even royalty. The morris-dance was for centuries the national dance of England. For sources see "Nature Knows No Color-Line," pp.82, 87. 1952.)

SOME WEALTHY NEGROES OF THE SLAVE ERA

Some who made fortunes in various ways and ranked with the wealthy whites in their respective towns were W. Q. Atwood of Saginaw, Michigan, who made a fortune out of lumber and was known as "the Lumber King"; Stephen Smith of Columbia, South Carolina, made an estimated $500,000 out of lumber and real estate; Thony Lafon, of New Orleans, made nearly a million in real estate deals and left $600,000 to charity; Robert Gordon of Cincinnati, who owned several coal-barges was the leading coal merchant of that city. He made a fortune during one very cold winter in the Civil War. Berry Meechum of St. Louis, Misouri, owned a paddle-wheel steamer on the Mississippi, and Owen Barrett, of Pittsburgh, made $85,000 from the sale of a patent medicine in the 1840's.

John Jones (1816-1879) was one of Chicago's leading citizens. A County Commissioner, he helped make some of the city's earliest laws. Starting as a barber, he grew wealthy and owned valuable property. In his building, one of the best in the city, was founded the city's first public library.

James Forten (1776-1842), a sail manufacturer, was one of the richest Negroes of his time. In the War of 1812, he helped raise 2,500 men for the protection of Philadelphia. He was prominent in the anti-slavery movement and aided Garrison liberally with money for "The Liberator."

Amos Fortune, born in West Africa 1710, and sold into slavery in New England 1730, was one of New Hampshire's most noted early figures, and still is. Knowing nothing but his African language, he learnt English and to read and write.

Thanks to his knowledge of tanning leather, which he had brought with him—ingredients for which he found in the bark of trees in the woods—he accumulated enough to buy his freedom and that of his wife and twenty-five acres at Jaffrey Center, where he built a six-room house with his own hands. At his death, he left his fortune for education. In 1946, the Amos Fortune Forum was founded in his memory in the old meeting-house where he worshipped. Collier's, January 7, 1950, which has a fine article on him, says, "Average attendance has been between 265 and 365 enthusiastic millworkers, farmers, tradesmen, and men and women whose names are famous throughout the country. . . . News of the forum which honors him is spreading." Among its members are Harlow Shapley, Harvard astronomer; Karl Compton, former president of the Massachusetts Institute of Technology; Benjamin K. Emerson, professor of geology at Amherst; Herbert Elliston, editor of the Washington Post, and Pulitzer Prize winner. The house he built is still lived in.

Basile Croquere was the most famous, most dashing swordsman of New Orleans in the 1830's. "His skill with the sword was phenomenal," says Lyle Saxon. He was very handsome and his manners and dress were impeccable. On the streets, crowds followed him. White men sought him out for instructions in spite of the prejudice against his color. He was also an art connoisseur, especially in cameos. (Saxon, L., Fabulous New Orleans, p. 192, 1928.)

In the South there were even Negro educators of white people. The most noted was John Chavis of North Carolina. An unmixed Negro, born in 1763, he kept a private school for sons and daughters of the rich. Among his students

238

Potrait said to be that of John Chavrs.
(See text.)

Above: Home of Amos Fortune, New England pioneer, now a Shrine.
Below: Tombs of Fortune and his wife. (Courtesy Collier's Magazine).

SOME OTHER REMARKABLE INDIVIDUALS OF THE SLAVE ERA

Alice. One of Philadelphia's oldest and best loved citizens. She helped William Penn.

Alice, born in Barbados in 1686, a slave, was one of the most famous figures in early Philadelphia. A friend of William Penn, she knew the city when it was largely woods. She died in 1802, at the age of 116. Many came to her for reminiscences of Penn and other pioneers. She was so highly thought of that in a book of biographical sketches, she is included with such others as Joan of Arc and Empress Catherine I of Russia (Eccentric Biography, or Memoirs of Remarkable Female Characters, Ancient and Modern. 1804).

Lucy Terry of New England is the first known Negro poet, one of America's earliest, and a popular story teller. Her poems on the massacre of the inhabitants of Deerfield, Massachusetts, by Indians, August 25, 1746, of which she was an eyewitness, is said to be the only account extant on that. She was a slave to Ebenezer Wells. She made an eloquent plea to the authorities of Williams College to get her son enrolled there. (Sheldon, G., History of Deerfield, vol. 2, p. 899. 1896.)

London, an African slave to the Maxwells of Georgia, wrote the Four Gospels and several hymns in Arabic. Not knowing English, he had the Bible read to him and wrote the words in Arabic as they sounded to him . . . his manuscripts were exhibited by the Ethnological Society of New York in 1857 as the only known document of its kind. . . .

Thomas Fuller (1710-1790) of Virginia, known as the African Calculator, could figure sums involving billions in his head faster than others could with a pencil. He could give the diameter of the earth in inches despite interruptions. Brissot de Warville of France, who saw him, says, "Asked how many seconds in a year and a half he replied in two minutes, 47,-304,000, counting 365 days to the year. Asked how many seconds would have lived a man

were later several distinguished ones, as U. S. Senator W. P. Mangum and Governor Charles Manly. Chavis was educated privately at Princeton University in an experiment to see whether Negroes could absorb a college education. A veteran of the Revolutionary War, and much beloved, he was noted for his dignity of manner, his purity of diction, simplicity in style and knowledge of the classics. His printed sermons were best sellers. (Dictionary of American Biography, Vol. 4, p. 44. 1897. Smith, C. L., History of Education in North Carolina, pp. 1'8-141. 1888.)

240

Elizabeth Keckley, close intimate of President and Mrs. Lincoln. Wrote a best seller on life in the White House.

aged seventy-four years, seventeen days and 12 hours, he replied in a minute and a half, 2,210,-500,800. In a contest with a white opponent, who had pen and pencil, on how many seconds in seventy years, he won. The opponent had forgotten the leap years. (Nouveau Voyage dans les Etats-Unis, etc. in 1788.)

The Columbian Sentinal, December 29, 1790, recording his death, said, "Thus died Tom, this untaught arithmetician, this untutored scholar. Had his opportunities of improvement been equal to those thousands of his fellow-men, neither the Royal Society of London, the Academy of Science at Paris, nor even Newton, himself, need have been ashamed to acknowledge him a brother in Science." W. F. Poole has given added details about him in "Anti-Slavery Opinions, pp. 2123. 1877.

Julius Melbourn, a writer, who was recommended to Thomas Jefferson, was entertained by him at dinner with Chief Justice Marshall and other dignitaries. Jefferson called on Melbourn several times and gave him the run of his library. Melbourn, who wrote the story of his life, was also received at the White House by President Madison.

Cordovell was the leading tailor and designer of fashions in New Orleans. His fame extended to Paris, France, where his ladies' styles were popular. He retired to Paris in 1850, after making a fortune in New Orleans.

FAMOUS NEGRO WOMAN IN THE WHITE HOUSE

Elizabeth Keckley (1818-1907) was one of the ablest women who ever lived in the White House. At first only an employee, she later became something of a privileged guest. She was the closest friend and confidante of Mrs. Lincoln and gave Lincoln himself much valuable information on the Confederacy. Born a slave, she earned enough to buy her freedom, thanks to her skill at dressmaking. She had once worked for rich families and met Mrs. Lincoln, who became extremely attached to her. Her book, "Behind the Scenes," dealing principally with Mrs. Lincoln, was the literary sensation of 1868. Later, she taught domestic science at Wilberforce University and prepared the Negro exhibit for the Columbian Exposition at Chicago. She was tall, stately, cultured. One writer said of her, "She would have been an outstanding personality at the court of Louis XIV."

The above-mentioned are some of the hundreds of Negroes born in the slave era, who rose in spite of the great handicap of a dark skin.

Gilbert Hunt, blacksmith, hero of the great theatre, Richmond Va., Fire, December 26, 1811. Died 1863, aged 90 and was given a public funeral

Mary, an escaped slave jumping from a window in Washington, D. C. rather than be taken back South. Her **bravery** won her great praise in America and abroad. She preceded in this a Russian woman who did the same in New York in the 1940's rather than be taken back to Russia and received world-wide fame.

AFRICA AND THE WEST TODAY

"We are concerned today with a giant.
So vast is his size that no man can comprehend his dimension.
So much variety is within him that his complexity defies description.
In the past some have said that the giant was asleep.
They saw no movement, detected no signs of wakefulness.
He was not asleep. There was always within him a wakeful, vibrant life.
What was asleep, quite often, was the ability of the observers to detect
  and know his wakefulness.
Now everyone can see that the giant is awake and stirring, preparing to
  claim a place in the world.
Now everyone can see the stirring of the giant
For his name is . . . Africa."

—UNITED NATIONS RADIO BROADCAST, September 20, 1958

Almost a hundred years ago Victor Hugo predicted that in the twentieth century Africa would occupy the center of the world's attention. That prediction is becoming true. Take up almost any large European and American newspaper and periodical and you'll find mention of Africa, its revolts, its struggle for freedom, and its economic possibilities on the front page. Life, Time, Newsweek, have had several features on it. In recent months the New York Times has often had three articles on it daily as well as several editorials. The same is true politically. At the founding of the United Nations there were but three African nations—Egypt, Ethiopia and Liberia. Today there are twenty-three others in it—the latest being Sierra Leone, admitted April 1961. Certainly others as Kenya, Tanganyika, and Mozambique, will follow shortly. White South Africa is not included in the above. These African nations, acting with the Asian ones, have considerable influence in the United Nations and in world affairs. In August, 1958, Foreign Minister Magoub of Sudan, an unmixed black, was spokesman for the United Nations in accepting President Eisenhower's formula for peace in the Near East.

The world's industrial future is closely tied to Africa, especially to that of Europe, which moreover has been so for the past hundred and fifty years. Africa, today, is the world's greatest storehouse of many of the commodities necessary to the West. It leads in some of these, as gold, diamonds, bauxite, and uranium. There is also an abundance of tin, chrome, copper, titanium, molybendum, coal, with large promise of oil. In cattle-rearing it could at least equal the American West. Africa is also the natural home of coffee (which grows wild in some regions), cotton, tobacco, vanilla, peanuts, bananas, palm-nuts, corn, cocoa, tea, copra, cloves,

hardwoods, and many other products. There is even wheat, as in the Ethiopian highlands.

There are also possibilities of limitless mechanical power. Africa's mighty rivers can furnish hydro-electric power, which is estimated to be greater than that of Europe and the two Americas combined. Among these now in use are Owen Falls in Uganda; Katanya in the Belgian Congo; and Kariba on the Zambesi. That of Inga, now being built on the Congo, will have, it is said, ten times the power of the Grand Coulee Dam. There is also the proposed Volta River project in Ghana. These great rivers will also furnish irrigation as the Nile now does. One of Hitler's great dreams in his invasion of Africa was to turn some of the waters of the Niger into the Sahara and make it again fruitful. And there is, of course, Africa's all-the-year-around sunshine. When solar energy supersedes coal and oil as fuel, it is going to prove a very handy asset. And there are millions of willing hands to develop these enormous resources.

Africans have the same potentialities for progress as the European and the white American. And because modern learning and science are new to them they are more eager for them than Western youths. I was particularly struck with that from my contact with them in their own lands and abroad. One incident in the Sudan I shall never forget. A group of students were telling me how starved they were for books and better education when one of them, overcome by his frustration, dropped to the ground and cried like a child.

←≡

Above: Dr. S. L. Manuwa, Chief Medical officer of Nigeria. Below. Dr. Hastings Banda of Nyassaland. As a young man, he walked a thousand miles to find work in the gold mines. With the money earned he went to the United States, and twelve years later was graduated in medicine at the University of Chicago. Took post-graduate course at Edinburgh, Scotland, thence to London, where he had a prosperous white practice for nearly twenty years. In 1958, stirred by the oppression of his people he returned to Nyassaland to work for their freedom and was thrown in jail where he now is.

Some noted African leaders of today. Upper, left to right: Kwame Nkrumah of Ghana; Julius Nyerere of Tanganyika; Jomo Kenyatta of Kenya; and Nnamdi Azikiwe of Nigeria.

Left to right: Marella (King Tom) of East Africa; Ignacio Pinto of Dahomey; Sekou Toure, French Guinea.

I have seen these Africans in the great universities of Europe winning scholarships and prizes. To cite just one: Dr. Manuwa of Nigeria. Starting in a little mission school there he finally reached Edinburgh University, where he was one of the most brilliant students in anatomy that institution ever had. He taught it there for some time. Today he heads the Medical Department of Nigeria, with white physicians under him.

I have seen native Africans, too, in high positions in France—senators, cabinet ministers, heads of departments. Felix Houphouet-Boigny, physician and planter of the Ivory Coast, West Africa, was Minister of State in the first De Gaulle cabinet. In 1946, when France's newly constituted assembly looked around for one of its members to pass on the correct style and grammar of the Constitution of the Fourth French Republic, it selected a native African, Sedar-Senghor, as the one best qualified to do so. He was the only one of the hundreds of deputies who had an "Agrege de l'Universite (equivalent to a Doctor of Philosophy degree). He is also one of France's leading living poets.

Just as Egyptian culture and influence helped change Europe from a wilderness to the mighty civilizations of Grece and Rome, so European know-how is helping to change Africa today. Parts of some African cities, as Brazzaville, Leopoldville, Dakar, Ibadan, Accra, look as modern as any American city. They have broad avenues, baby skyscrapers, airports, fine harbors, steel mills and huge smelters. There are also several fine medical schools, universities, and free libraries. Even as William Penn would be amazed to see now the wilderness once called "Penn's Wood"; or Washington his America, so would Henry M. Stanley to see the land he once called "Darkest Africa."

Europe needs Africa more than ever now. For America it is a huge undeveloped market. The United States, recognizing that, has just set up a Bureau of African Affairs. Trade marches on goodwill, and that is assured best by regarding others, no matter what their so-called race, religion, or point of view, as human beings like one's self.

Africa, as has been shown, has enriched the New World, and particularly the United States, immensely. And what her people and her descendants have so far done for America is small in comparison with what they are capable of doing, provided the true spirit of humanity and cordiality leads in future relations.

246

Some Noted African Leaders Today: Top, left to right: Gamal Abdel Nasser, Egypt; Houphuet-Boigny of Senegal; Gikomyo Kiano of Kenya. Lower, Said Ibn Harub, Sultan of Zanzibar; Gen. Ibrahim Abboud of Sudan; Tom Mboya of Kenya.

Left to right: Obafemi Awolowo of Nigeria; Momolu Dukulu of Liberia; Musa Amalomba of Kenya.

Africans respond readily to friendly whites. Livingstone, Moffat, Dan Crawford and other missionaries spoke eloquently of this. Albert Schweitzer is proving it now. The future peace of the world is going to depend largely on whether decent, democratic Americans are able to curb the racists, who are now giving America such a bad name not only in Asia, Africa, and South America, but in Europe, also. Europeans are finding that reports of color prejudice, especially American ones, are hurting them in their business dealings with the Asians and Africans.

If America is to retain her present world position she will increasingly need Africa and the Africans. Two world wars and a long cold war in which America has been supplying her scores of allies with arms, have depleted her mineral resources.

But for success in this new Africa, the white nations, and the United States in particular, will have to divest themselves of the ingrained be-

Some African Leaders of Today: left to right: Abdullah Khalil of Sudan; Kroba Edusa, Ghana, Abubekr Balewa of Nigeria.

248

Mountbatten Considers Africa The Keypoint in NATO Defense

By HENRY MAULE

London, July 18 (Special).—Earl Mountbatten, uncle of Prince Philip and newly appointed supreme commander of Britain's armed forces, sees Africa as the key land mass in the East-West struggle.

Earl Mountbatten

In his new post, Mountbatten is not only chief adviser to Defense Minister Duncan Sandys but also is likely to have considerable influence on NATO which he, along with French Premier de Gaulle, is eager to reshape.

De Gaulle is in agreement with Mountbatten on Africa's importance to NATO.

★ ★ ★ ★ ★ ★ ★ ★ ★ ★ ★ ★ ★

He believes that any Soviet attack on Europe would not be a frontal one but would be a left hook through Africa and the Middle East.

Stresses Diplomacy

Mountbatten contends this would be the route of a Soviet attack.

But he also asserts that the only way the West can get Africa on its side is by encouraging better relations between independence-minded Africans and whites. ★ ★ ★ ★ ★ ★ ★ ★ ★ ★ ★ ★

Prime Minister Macmillan is said to be awakening to the growing importance of Africa. As an example observers point to the recent visit here of Central African Federation Premier Sir Roy Welensky. Welensky was given one of the plushest red-carpet welcomes on record.

Some sources say they would not be surprised if Macmillan soon flew into Africa on a diplomatic mission, as he did to the Kremlin.

---

lief that there is something inherent in them that makes them superior to human beings of darker skins. Peoples, regardless of their so-called racial composition, rise and fall. The progress of nations is a play of wheels, like the individual on a ferris-wheel. Those who are on top go to the bottom and vice versa. As Omar Khyyam said:

For in and out, above, about below
'Tis nothing but a Magic Shadow-Show
Played in a Box whose Candle is the Sun
Round which we Phantom Figures come
        and go.

Another important consideration. Blacks will always outnumber whites in Africa and the mere armed force of the latter will not always suffice. To the 5,000,000 whites in Africa now there are at least 300,000,000 Africans.

Africa, on her part, needs the white man for his scientific and industrial know-how, and even for his organizational one. In short, successful racism, the exploitation of one people by another, is doomed. That of brotherhood and interdependence is taking its place. There is but one race—the human race.

INDEX

North, its aid to Confederacy, 146; as chief beneficiary of slavery, 141-2; attempts to appease South, 142; profits from slavery in the South, 142; its opposition to Negro soldiers, 158.
Nyerere, J. 245.

Oneal, James, 58.
Otis, James, 42
Ottley, Roi, 77.
O'Reilly, Miles, 169.
Ormond, John, 62.

Painters, Negro, 225-26.
Parker, Theodore, 143.
Parton, James, 37, 39, 191, 230.
Penn, William, 54, 240, 246.
Perry, Adm. M., 119.
Perry, Commodore Oliver, 117.
Peterson, F., 225.
Philipps, Wandell, 198.
Physicians, Negro in Civil War, 223-25; in Colonial times, 224.
Picasso, 209.
Pickett, A. J., 68.
Pike, Zebulon, 84.
Pilgrim Fathers, 29, 30, 33.
Pinto, Ignacio, 246.
Pinckney, Chas., 112.
Pioneers, Negro, in West and Mid-West, 82-90.
Pitman, F. W. 39.
Pitt, William, 81.
Pliny, 9.
Political Parties of 1860, their stand on slavery, 134-35.
Pompey, Negro spy, 110.
Ponce de Leon, 67.
Poor, Salem, 103.
Porter, Kenneth, 84.
Prester, John, 11.
Priestley, N. I., 68.
Prince, Negro pilot of Union Navy, 200.
Prostitutes, white, shipped to Africa and America, 31-32.
Putnam, Carleton, 7.

Quarles, B., 206.

Race Riots, Northern, 147-49; 161-65.
Racial intermixture, 138-39.
Reed, Philip, and Statue of Freedom, 216.
Revere, Paul, 43.
Rhode Is., slavery and slave-trade, 39, 41.
Rice, Daniel, 232-33.
Rillieux, Norb., 228-29.
Roberts, Kenneth, 56, 121.
Roberts, Preston, 153.
Robinson, Dr. Victor, 9.
Rochefoucauld-Liancourt, Duke of, 29, 37, 220.
Rolfe, John, 67.
Russell, J. H., 58, 61.
Russell, Sir Wm. H., 129, 132, 141-2.
Rum and slave-trading, 38, 39-44.
Rush, Dr. Benj., 224.

Saco, Jose A., 29, 46.
Salem, Peter, 103.
Sandburg, Carl, 161-2, 203, 206.
Santomee, Luycas, first Negro physician, 76, 224
Scobell, John, Negro scout, 187-88.
Schweitzer, Albert, 248.
Schuyler, Gen'l, 106.
Schlesinger, A. M., 41.
Schoepf, Johann, 220.
Seavers, Rich. (Big Dick), 120-21.
Senghor, Sedar, 246.
Seward, Wm. Henry, 130.
Sewall, Judge, 62.

Shackleton, R., 79.
Shaler, Nath., 112.
Shapley, Harlow, 238.
Sheldon, G., 240.
Singleton (Pap), Benj., 89.
Slave empire, proposed, 142.
Slave, last living ones, 142; musicians, 230; origin of word, 46; physicians, 222, 224-5; printers, 218; revolts in Civil War, 154; smuggling, 141.
Slave-trade, African, 36; illicit and profits from, 122-23; American captains engaged in, 62-66.
Slavery in Colonial New York, 70-76; in other colonies, 82.
Slaves, African, in Europe, 36; in England, 61-2.
Slaves, European in Africa, 46-52.
Slaves, white in America, 208.
Slaves, value of, in Virginia, 38; in South Carolina, 38.
Stanard, Mary, 58, 69, 221.
Stanley, Henry M., 14, 246.
Stanton, Edwin W., 140.
Stassen, Harold, 81.
Stokes, I. N. Phelps, 71, 77.
Stowe, Harriett B., 201, 226.
Sousa, Matthias, 80.
South, The, Rise of Negrophobia after Civil War, 205.
Smalls, Robt., 195, 199.
Smith, Capt. John, 66.
Smith, Sydney, 34.
Stuart, Gilbert, 225.
Stuyvesant, Peter, 36.

Taussig, F. W., 43.
Taylor, Bayard, 34.
Ten Eyck, Joseph, 224.
Terry, Lucy, 240.
Texas, Negro role in settlement, 90-91.
Thomas, Lowell, 93.
Thorpe, Geo., 29.
Tillman, Benj., 205.
Tillman, John, 192, 197.
Timbuctoo, 11.
Tinker, Edw. L., 2.
Toure, Sekou, 246.
Triangular Trade (Slave), 39.
Trollope, Mrs., 147.
Trumbull, John, 105.
Tubman, Harriett, 188, 194.

Pictures of the Civil War are principally from Harper's Weekly, Frank Leslie's Weekly, and the Illustrated London News of that time.

Material for a follow-up of this work from 1865 to the present has been assembled and will probably appear. The subjects to be treated are:

Labor and Industry—Property Owners. Agriculture.

Business. Banking, Real Estate.

Service in the Armed Forces—Army, Navy, Air Force. Deeds of Valor.

The Fine Arts—Painting, Sculpture, Architecture, Designing.

Music—The Theatre, Motion Pictures. Television. The Dance.

Education—Pioneers in Education. Schools and Colleges.

Scientific Achievements—Medicine, Surgery, Discoveries in the Art of Healing. Engineering, Mathematics, Nuclear Energy.

Inventions.

Aviation.

Literature—Historians, Poets, Novelists, and others. The Negro Press.

Law—Judges, Government Attorneys.

Politics—Senators, Congressmen, Leaders.

Sports—PrizeFighters, Field Sports, Olympic Winners, Basket Ball, Baseball, Jockeys and Others.

Religion.

Civil Rights.

Some Negroes of Unusual Note—Awards, Honors, etc.

Incredible but True Facts. Ridiculous Side of the Race Question.

Miscellaneous Contributions. Ethnic, Psychological, and General *Influence on American Life.*

There will be hundreds of pictures.

254

APPENDIX TO THE 1961 EDITION

AFRICA

AND ITS POTENTIALITIES

His Imperial Majesty, Haile Selassie of Ethiopia, on his visit to London, October 8, 1960.

INDEPENDENT NATIONS

Cameroun. Capital, Yaounde. 166,880 square miles. Population, 3,230,000. Principal products: cocoa, palm kernels, timber, coffee, rubber, bananas, cotton—Ahmadou Ahidjo, President.

Chad, Republic. Capital, Fort Lamy. 496,000 square miles. Population, 2,850,000. Principal products, peanuts, palm nuts and oils, rubber, cocoa, cotton, Francois Tomalbaye, Prime Minister.

Congo, Republic (former French). Capital: Brazzaville. 132,000 square miles. Population: 795,000. Principal products: peanuts, fruits, palm nuts and oil, rubber, cotton, cocoa, lumber. Abbe F. Youlou, President.

Congo, Republic (former Belgian). Capital: Leopoldville. 904,757 square miles. Population 13,559,000 (1958) Africa's richest territory. Abounds in wild animals — elephants, lions, leopards, deer, hippopotamus, apes, birds of many varieties. Great tropical forests with mahogany, ebony, cedar, banana, cocoanuts, cotton, coffee, many varieties of tropical fruits. Very rich in gold, diamonds, silver, copper, iron, zinc, tungsten, radium, and world's greatest supply of uranium, essential ingredient in nuclear energy. Its rivers supply immense water power, chief of which is the Inga water development. It also has the legendary Mountains of the Moon, its chief peak, Margharita, 16,795 feet high. President, Joseph Kasavubu.

Central African Republic. Capital: Bangui. 238,000 square miles. Population: 1,175,000. Principal products, coffee, cocoa, many varieties of tropical fruits. Minerals: gold, diamonds, crude oil, ivory, copper, lead, crude oil, and woods. David Dacko, President.

Dahomey: Capital, Porto Novo. 45,000 square miles. Population 1,720,000. Principal products: coffee, cocoa, peanuts, palm nuts and oils, rubber, sulphur, tin. Hubert Maga, President.

Egypt: Capital, Cairo. 386,198 square miles. Population: 23,365,000. Products: wheat, cotton, rice, grapes, dates, figs, bananas, olives. Minerals: petroleum, gold, iron, copper, granite, alum, sulphur, magnesium. President: Gamal Abdel Nasser.

Ethiopia. Believed to be the world's oldest existing state. Capital: Addis-Ababa. 398,350 square miles. Population 22,000,000. Principal products: wheat, barley, tobacco, sugar, coffee, most tropical fruits, cattle in immense numbers, mules, sheep, goats, horses, wild animals, including abundance of deer, skins, hides. Minerals, gold, platinum, silver, tin, copper, sulphur, coal, iron. Immense water-power. Barateri, waterfall of the Blue Nile is nearly three times as high as Niagara, or 459 feet. Climate: from burning hot to temperate with snow-clad mountains. Haile Selassie, Emperor.

Gabon. Capital, Libreville. 103,000 square miles. Population 411,000. Products the same as Central African Republic of which it was a part under France. Leon M'ba, President.

Ghana. Capital, Accra. Population 6,609,000. Main crop, cocoa (some 275,000 tons annually) also coffee, rubber, and tropical fruits. Rich in minerals, gold, diamonds, silver, copper, manganese (with a monthly production of 75,000 tons) and lumber. Immense water power for furnishing hydro-electricity. Exports, approximately, $500,000,000 annually, with correspondingly high imports. Kwame Nkrumah, President.

Guinea. Capital, Conakry. 96,865 square miles. Population, 3,200,000. Products, corn, rice, palm nuts and oils, bananas, coffee, pineapples, honey, wax. Has world's largest supply of bauxite. Other minerals are gold, diamonds, iron, tin, aluminum in vast quantity. President, Sekou Toure.

Ivory Coast. Capital, Abidjan. 123,000 square miles. Population, 3,088,000. Products same as Central African Republic of which it was a part under France. Felix Houphouet Boigny, President, and former Secretary of State in the first De Gaulle Cabinet in Paris.

Liberia. Capital Monrovia, 43,000 square miles. Population 2,750,000. Chief products: rubber, palm nuts and oils, rice, coffee, cocoa, sugar. Minerals: gold, diamonds, iron (300,000 tons annual production) and lumber. William V. Tubman, President.

Libya. Capital: Tripoli and Benghazi. 679,358 square miles. Population, 1,200,000. Largely desert. Products: olives, figs, carpets, leather and leather goods. Mohammed Idris el Senussi, King.

Malagasy Republic (Madagascar). Capital: Tananarive. 228,000 square miles. Population, 5,174,523. Products: rice, vanilla (of which it is the home), corn, coffee, cloves, tobacco, sugar, cocoa, cabinet woods, tanning bark. Minerals, graphite, mica, nickel, phosphate, gold, uranium. Philibert Tsiranana, President.

Mali Republic. Capital, Bamako. 450,000 square miles. Population 3,708,000. Products: peanuts, peanut oil, rubber, cotton, cocoa, lumber. Formerly part of French Senegal. President, Modibo Keita.

Mauritania Islamic Republic. 15,900 square miles. Population, 624,000. Oil-fields. President, Moktar Ould Daddah. Admitted to United Nations Oct. 25, 1961.

Morocco. Capital: Rabat. 172,104 square miles. Population, 10,780,000. Products: wheat, dates, skins, hides, wool, carpet, ornamented leather goods, woolen and silk wear. Minerals: copper, lead, coal, tin, petroleum and 8,000,000 tons of phosphate annually. Sidi Mohammed ben Youssef, King.

Niger Republic. Capital, Niamey, 494,500 square miles. Population, 2,415,000. Products the same as Central African Republic. Haman Diori, Prime Minister.

Nigeria. Capital: Lagos. 373,250 square miles. Population, 35,000,000. Products: palm oil, cotton lint, cocoa, peanuts, rubber, fish processing, flour, sugar, hides, skins. Minerals: Columbite, tin and asbestos in vast quantity. Abubaker Tafawa Balewa, Premier.

Somalia. Capital: Mogadiscio. 262,000 square miles. Population, 2,600,000. Products: sugar, bananas, maize, gum, many varieties of tropical fruits, hides and live stock. Abdi Rashid Shermarke, President.

Senegal. Capital: Daker. 80,600 square miles. Population, 2,270,000. Products: peanuts, peanut oil, rubber, cotton, cocoa, coffee, lumber. Famed in World War I for its soldiers. Leopold Senghor, noted poet, Prime Minister. Mamadou Dia, President.

Sierra Leone. Capital Freetown. 27,925 square miles. Population 2,750,000. Products: rice, kolanuts, palm kernels and oils and tropical fruits. Rich in diamonds. Also gold, iron, chrome. Colonized by rebellious blacks of Jamaica, West Indies; Negro slaves who had gone over to the British in 1776; blacks freed in England; and white Englishwomen forcibly married to the English blacks in 1787. Sir Milton A. S. Margai, M.D. Prime Minister.

Sudan. Capital, Khartoum. 967,500 square miles. Population, 10,000,000. Immensely rich in natural resources. Copper, gold, iron, gum arabic. Also cotton, nuts, dates, corn, beans, hides, skins, mahogany, ivory, mother of pearl. General Ibrahim Abboud, President and Prime Minister.

Togo. Capital: Lome. 21,893 square miles. Population, 1,100,000. Former German colony.

Products: cocoa, palm nuts and oils, copra, coffee, ground nuts. Sylvanus Olympio, **President.**

Tunisia. Capital: Tunis. 48,313 square miles. Population 3,925,000. Products: wheat, barley, oats, olives, grapes, dates, almonds, oranges, corn, henna, and cork. Minerals: Lead, iron, zinc, phosphate, salt, cement. Habib Bourguiba, President.

Upper Volta. Capital: Ouagadougou. 105,000 square miles. Population, 3,473,000. Products, peanuts, palm nuts and oils, rubber, cotton, cocoa and lumber. Maurice Yameogo, President.

African Lands Expecting Independence in the Near Future

Algeria. 852,000 square miles. Population, 10,265,000. Capital, Algiers. Products: wheat, barley, oats, corn, potatoes, tobacco, olive oil, figs, wines. Minerals: lead, iron, zinc, mercury, copper, and newly-discovered oil-fields. Has extensive manufacturing. French.

Rhodesia - Nyassaland Federation. 486,793 square miles. Population, 7,900,000 of which 220,000 are white. Products: live stock, hides, tobacco, tropical fruits, textiles. Minerals: gold, lead, cobalt, copper, asbestos, rubber. Hydro-electro power. Its Kariba Dam, greatest in the world. Has Victoria Falls, one of the world's greatest natural wonders. British.

Tanganyika. 362,688 square miles. Population, 9,076,000. Products: sisal, coffee, cotton, hides, tropical fruits, beeswax. Minerals: diamonds, ivory, gold, lead. Has small percentage of whites. British.

Ruanda-Urindi. 20,540 square miles. Population, 4,630,000. Products: coffee, live-stock, hides. Has been promised independence by Belgium.

COLONIES

Angola. 481,351 square miles. Population, 4,550,000. Capital, Luanda. Very rich. Products: coffee, corn, sisal, sugar, cotton, cocoanuts, tobacco, rubber. Minerals: diamonds, gold, ivory, malachite, iron. Is connected by rail to colony of Mozambique on the Indian Ocean. Now in revolt against Portugal.

Basutoland: 11,716 square miles. Population, 658,000. Products: wheat, cereals, tropical fruits, live stock, hides. Whites not allowed to own land. British. Under native ruler.

Bechuanaland. 275,000 square miles. Population 397,000. Cattle rearing and dairying. Under native ruler. British.

Kenya. 224,960 square miles. Population, 6,500,000, with whites in the uplands. Products: extensive tea plantations, coffee, cereals, cattle, dairy products, and timber. British. Great agitation against white rule.

Mozambique. 297,731 square miles. Population, 6,234,000. Rich Portuguese colony on the Indian Ocean, connected with Angola on the Atlantic. Capital Lorenzo Marquez. Products: wheat, sugar, cocoanuts, cotton, copra, sisal, beeswax. Minerals: gold, diamonds, uranium, asbestos. Has begun agitation for independence.

South-West Africa. 317,887 square miles. Population, 554,000 of which 69,000 white. Products: Caracul sheep, cattle, butter, tropical fruits, fishing. Minerals: gold, diamonds, lead, zinc, vanadium. Given to Union of South Africa in trusteeship by the League of Nations, the former has now refused to surrender it to the United Nations.

Swaziland. 6,704 miles. Population, 237,041. Products: cotton, tobacco, corn, live stock, dairy products. Minerals: gold, tin, asbestos. Under native chief. British.

Uganda. 93,381 square miles. Population, 6,517,000. Products: extensive coffee plantations, cotton, tea, maize, groundnuts, sisal, sugar, vegetable oils. Minerals: gold, copper, wolfram, lead, also coffee, rubber, and tropical fruits. Rich in tin. Has Lake Victoria Nyanza, second largest fresh-water lake in the world, and source of the White Nile. Under native king. British.

Zanzibar. Island of 93,981 square miles. Population, 304,000. World's largest producer of cloves, copra, cocoanuts. Manufactures leather materials and jewelry.

Other smaller colonies are British Cameroons, 34,081 square miles. Population, 1,591,000; Gambia, 4,005 square miles. Population, 289,-000. British. Portuguese Guinea. 13,948 square miles. Population, 565,000.

UNION OF SOUTH AFRICA

The sole African land under all-white domination is the Union of South Africa, world's greatest gold and diamond country. Of its 13,-368,000 inhabitants only a fourth, or 3,067,000 are white, who are greatly dependent on the labor of the blacks. Their cruelty and policy of apartheid have made mortal enemies of the blacks and they rule only by armed force. The whites have also cut themselves off from the British Commonwealth and have very few friends in the white world. In 1960 they received the condemnation of the United States in particular. Can these few whites survive in the rising sea of black and mixed-blood Africa? During the French Revolution when France gave little support to the slave masters of Haiti the blacks arose, massacred the whites, and finally seized the country. Might not white South Africa meet a similar fate and that before the end of the century?

The United States In Relation to Africa.

President Kennedy:

Until very recently, for most Americans, Africa was Trader Horn, Tarzan, and tom-tom drums. We are only now beginning to discover that Africa unlike our comic strip stereotypes, is a land of rich variety of noble and ancient cultures, some primitive, some highly sophisticated; of vital and gitfed people.

It is a land of enormous natural riches, side by side with stark poverty and cruel disease. And, as events are beginning to reveal, it is a land of immense importance to the world—and to the United States. Some may look at it from the viewpoint of the vital natural resources and strategic materials. Some may be interested in military bases or new allies against Communism. Some may feel a responsibility in Africa because the West thrust itself upon the area and cannot be indifferent to the consequences. Some may have a real concern for Africa and her people. But whatever one's point of view, one fact cannot be denied—the future of Africa will seriously affect, for better or for worse, the future of the United States:

Two Letters To the New York Times:

I am impelled to write to you because of my horror and despair at the news from Alabama. It strikes home to me particularly because I recently returned from an extensive journey through Africa.

Wherever I went the role of our country in shaping the new world there hung in the balance. Whether that balance was to swing in our favor or in that of the Communists depended essentially on whether or not racial intolerance and hatred here at home could be conquered in time—and time was running out.

Again and again in Africa I heard people say, "We want to work with America; we would prefer your leadership to any other. But so long as those of our color are segregated, oppressed, beaten in your country this will not be possible. In the Communist world those barriers to cooperation do not exist."

I am sick and ashamed at what has transpired since. In addition. I am all too certain now that it is too late; we have lost the battle for Africa on the streets of Montgomery.

Our unrelenting prejudice here at home has robbed us of any chance to play a leading part in the development of the new nations of Africa. So long as the manifestations of that prejudice persist we cannot compete with the Communists in that endeavor.

Let us ask ourselves honestly—were we Negroes in Africa today, would we turn for leadership to the United States, where such shameful incidents still occur, or to Russia, where prejudice as to color of skin does not exist? CHARLES LESLIE. Norwich, Vt., May 21, 1961.

Like a cold wind the news from Alabama is blowing through Africa. Our rural and towns people are shivering before this new evidence that even the undisputed achievements of the black man in the West cannot protect him from the stigma of color —even in the United States of America, the land which has claimed to be the champion of anti-colonialism and the rights of man.

Many of my friends in Central Africa are saying, How can we trust the United States of America? Her offers of friendship and help are not really true. She wants us to be friendly to her but is not prepared to prove her friendship to us. Is it not true that in the United States of America men and women of our color have won respect and fame as doctors, lawyers, teachers, business men, scientists, soldiers, airmen, etc.? Did not a black man first stand alone with Commander Peary at the North Pole in 1907? Has not our brothers' blood flowed with the blood of white Americans in the defense of freedom and the rights of man? And yet, in this same country, men and women are suffering because their skin is black. How can the United States of America speak for us in Africa?

Our hearts beat like yours, America. Oh, Alabama, be brief, be quick for once.

GODWIN A. MBIKUSITA LEWANIKA, Member of Parliament for Luangwa. Kitwe, Northern Rhodesia, May 25, 1961.

King of Loanga, West Africa. For his capital see pp. 22-23.

Slaves For Sale. White woman and black man put up for sale in
Moslem market. Drawn from life by G. R. Boulanger and exhibited in the Spring Salon, Paris, 1888.

Oldest house in America—St. Augustine Florida. Built about 1580 by Negro labor.

Negroes in the building of St. Augustine, America's oldest town.

Instrument of torture used by slaveholders.

A TYPICAL NEGRO.

WE publish herewith three portraits, from photographs by M'Pherson and Oliver, of the negro Gordon, who escaped from his master in Mississippi, and came into our lines at Baton Rouge in March last. One of these portraits represents the man as he entered our lines, with clothes torn and covered with mud and dirt from his long race through the swamps and bayous, chased as he had been for days and nights by his master with several neighbors and a pack of blood-hounds; another shows him as he underwent the surgical examination previous to being mustered into the service—his back furrowed and scarred with the traces of a whipping administered on Christmas-day last; and the third represents him in United States uniform, bearing the musket and prepared for duty.

This negro displayed unusual intelligence and energy. In order to foil the scent of the blood-hounds who were chasing him he took from his plantation onions, which he carried in his pockets. After crossing each creek or swamp he rubbed his body freely with these onions, and thus, no doubt, frequently threw the dogs off the scent. At one time in Louisiana he served our troops

as guide, and on one expedition was unfortunately taken prisoner by the rebels, who, infuriated beyond measure, tied him up and beat him, leaving him for dead. He came to life, however, and once more made his escape to our lines.

By way of illustrating the degree of brutality which slavery has developed among the whites in Black River:

The treatment of the slaves, they say, has been growing worse and worse for the last six or seven years.

Flogging with a leather strap on the naked body is common; also, paddling the body with a hand-saw until the skin is a mass of blisters, and then breaking the blisters with the teeth of the saw. They have "very often" seen slaves stretched out upon the ground with hands and feet held down by fellow-slaves, or lashed to stakes driven into the ground for "burning." Handfuls of dry corn-husks are then lighted, and the burning embers are whipped off with a stick so as to fall in showers of live sparks upon the naked back. This is continued until the victim is covered with blisters. If in his writhings of torture the slave gets his hand free to brush off the fire, the burning brand is applied to them.

Another method of punishment, which is inflicted for the higher order of crimes, such as running away, or other refractory conduct, is to dig a hole in the ground large enough for the slave to squat or lie down in. The victim is then stripped naked and placed in the hole, and a covering or grating of green sticks is laid over the opening. Upon this a quick fire is built, and the live embers sifted through upon the naked flesh of the slave, until his body is blistered and swollen almost to bursting. With just enough of life to enable him to crawl, the slave is then allowed to recover from his wounds if he can, or to end his sufferings by death.

"Charley Soo" and "Overton," two hands, were both murdered by these cruel tortures. "Sloo" was whipped to death, dying under the infliction, or soon after punishment. Overton was led naked upon his face and burned to death, slowly described, so that the cords of his legs and the

---

we append the following extract from a letter in the New York Times, recounting what was told by the refugees from Mrs. GILLESPIE's estate on the

---

GORDON AS HE ENTERED OUR LINES.

GORDON UNDER MEDICAL INSPECTION.

GORDON IN HIS UNIFORM AS A U. S. SOLDIER.

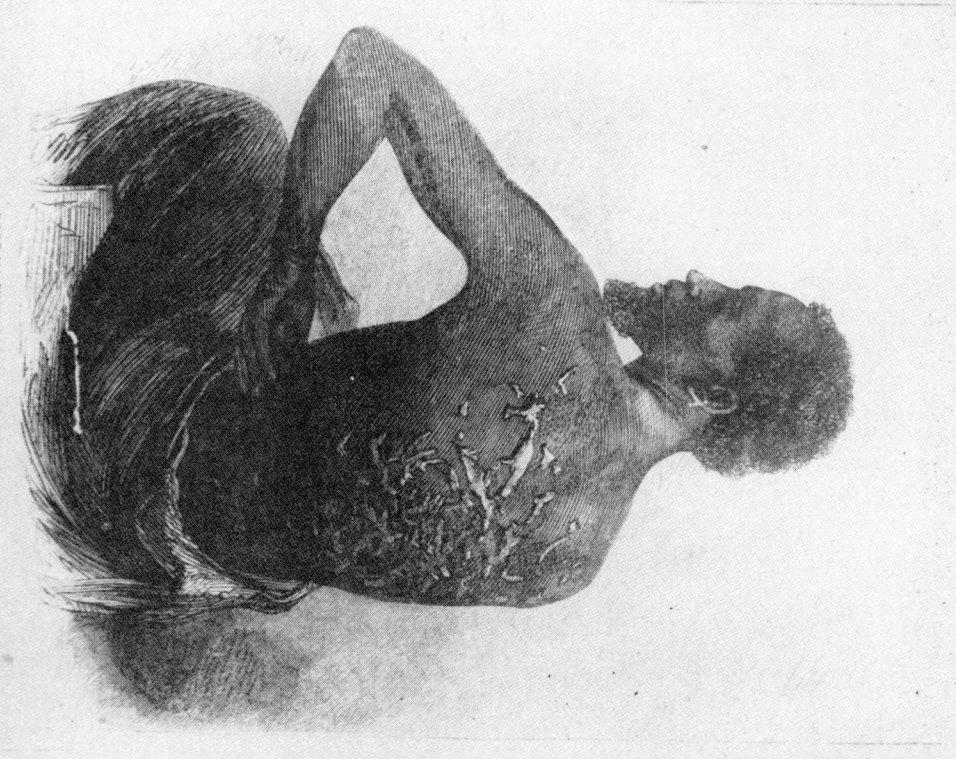

From Harper's Weekly

268

Negro sentinel shooting Burroughs, noted Confederate guerilla and spy.

Teamsters of the Union army.

A scene from Beaufort, S.C. when the master ran away and left his slaves behind. (Harpers Weekly.)

Slaves, dressed in style coming to meet the Union army after their masters had fled.